A Family and Nation under Fire

A Family and Nation under Fire

The Civil War Letters and Journals

of William and Joseph Medill

Edited by Georgiann Baldino

THE KENT STATE UNIVERSITY PRESS KENT, OHIO

Frontis: Major William H. Medill. (Courtesy Colonel
Robert R. McCormick Research Center)

© 2018 by Pearl Editions, LLC
All rights reserved
ISBN 978-1-60635-336-3
Manufactured in the United States of America

Cataloging information for this title is available at the Library of Congress.

22 21 20 19 18   5 4 3 2 1

CONTENTS

Three Generations of the Medill Family   vii

Editor's Note   ix

Acknowledgments   xi

Introduction   1

1 The Call to Action   15

2 Barker's Dragoons, 1861   29

3 The Eighth Illinois Cavalry, 1861   43

4 The Ditch-Digging Army of the Potomac, 1862   55

5 The Eighth Illinois, an Effective Cavalry Regiment, 1863   133

6 The Last Full Measure of Devotion   173

Notes   211

Selected Primary Sources   223

Index   225

THREE GENERATIONS OF THE MEDILL FAMILY

Parents

    William Medill (1792–1865)

    Margaret Corbett Medill (1803–1889)

Siblings

- Joseph H. Medill (1823–1899)
    - Katherine Patrick Medill (Kate), wife (1831–1894)
        - Katherine (Kitty), daughter (1853–1932)
        - Elinor (Nelly), daughter (1855–1933)
        - Josephine (Josie), daughter (1866–1892)
- Jane A. Medill (1825–1847)
- James C. Medill (1828–1864)
    - Hester Bradshaw Medill (Hetta), wife (1832–1907)
- Mary E. Medill (1831–1917)
- Infant Son (1833–1833)
- William H. Medill (1835–1863)
- Ellen (Nellie) Medill (1839–1881)
- Samuel J. Medill (1841–1883)
- Charles W. Medill (1844–1849)

EDITOR'S NOTE

The Medill family, like other Civil War correspondents, had idiosyncrasies. William wrote in haste and did not use consistent paragraphing. He overused capital letters and punctuation, which I changed to be more conventional. He abbreviated military titles, regiments, divisions, and brigades. If the meaning was clear, I left abbreviations as written. William consistently misspelled some commanders' and individuals' names; these were corrected to minimize confusion. If unfamiliar place names could be verified, these were corrected. If they could not be identified, places were left as originally written. In general, my edits are minor and intended to improve readability.

One impediment to readability is that William and other family members signed their names in multiple ways. Another is that family members often had similar names. Major William H. Medill was named after his father, William. In the correspondence, Major Medill is identified as W. H., Will, William, and even Bill. To minimize confusion, I consistently refer to him as William. William's sister-in-law, Katherine Patrick Medill, is referred to as Kate. One of William's sisters was named Ellen but nicknamed Nellie. The nieces in the third generation were Kitty and Nelly. To help readers identify characters, a family tree, including nicknames, is provided as front matter. To clarify letters, appositives such as "father" and "brother in-law" were added to identify individuals. I also added the names of letter writers and letter recipients, included letterhead information, and edited letterhead dates and locations to eliminate writers' variations and make the letters more accessible.

Only a handful of envelopes were saved, but most letters had clear salutations. If salutations or the first pages were missing, familiarity with the family tree or the content of the letter established the recipient. Even after correspondence was combined from all sources, a few gaps existed. Thus, in a couple instances, missing content made it impossible to determine the recipients. I assume full responsibility for any mistakes dating and placing letters that have partial dates or no dates. It is fortunate that the content has been preserved so well for more than 150 years, and I appreciate the generations who served as caretakers of the Medill papers.

GEORGIANN BALDINO
December 21, 2016

ACKNOWLEDGMENTS

I have toured the McCormick Mansion and Cantigny Park in Wheaton, Illinois, many times over the years, always enjoying the five-hundred-acre site, breathtaking gardens, education center, and museums. Cantigny tour guides tell fascinating stories about Col. Robert R. McCormick, his World War I military career, marriages, and professional achievements. A highlight of the thirty-five-room McCormick mansion is Freedom Hall, named to honor freedom of speech and freedom of the press. It houses an extensive collection of books, weaponry, and family portraits. The portrait of Robert McCormick dominates the room, but a fascination for the American Civil War drew me toward the portrait of William Medill, wearing a Union major's uniform. The tour guide, however, couldn't answer all the questions I had about William. To learn more, I attended a lecture about the Medills and read available books about the family.

Maj. William Medill was related to Robert McCormick by marriage—William was his wife's uncle—at first glance a connection that is outside Cantigny's mission. The Colonel Robert R. McCormick Research Center, Military Library, Military Archives, McCormick Archives, and Research Center focus on the U.S. Army 1st Infantry Division from 1917 to the present, providing information to individuals and researchers wanting to know about America's military heritage, and yet William's portrait is displayed in a place of honor. The first reason for this I discovered was his service in the Eighth Regiment Illinois Volunteer Cavalry, the only Illinois cavalry regiment to serve the Army of the Potomac throughout the Civil War. Another contributing factor was his heroism. William suffered a mortal wound in the aftermath of the Battle of Gettysburg. Because of my previous work on Civil War books and articles, I realized William's service was significant.

Diane Gutenkauf, McCormick Museum director, sent me the Research Center's finding aid, outlining their material. Eric Gillespie, director of research at the First Division Museum, made the boxes from the Civil War available in their reading room. Inside I found original Medill family correspondence, typed transcripts, photographs, journals, copies of articles published to commemorate significant Civil War battles, as well as biographical information.

It took two days to photograph documents, dated during the Civil War. The more I read the more intrigued I became. The wartime correspondence fleshed out family portraits, added images of army life, corrected newspaper reports of the era, and explained the ideology that prompted William to endure catastrophic events—a poignant story of a soldier who fought to maintain the Union at great personal cost. It took months to transcribe the documents, but in the end they revealed a remarkable human drama. Modern readers will find it hard to imagine what Civil War soldiers and families were called upon to endure. William's two-year enlistment was one of perseverance and dedication.

A number of original handwritten letters had been removed from the Colonel Robert R. McCormick Research Center archive and replaced with typed transcriptions. Portions of the typed transcripts had been published in a 1943 series of articles for the *Chicago Tribune*. Feature writer John A. Menaugh indicated the articles were "based largely upon and incorporating the recently brought to light letters" that Maj. William H. Medill wrote from the front while serving as a cavalry officer in the Civil War. I used text from Menaugh's articles dated July 11 and August 15, 1943, to supplement what I found in the Colonel Robert R. McCormick Research Center. Two other letters, not included in the McCormick archive, were mentioned in an essay about William Medill in *The Martyrs and Heroes of Illinois in the Great Rebellion: Biographical Sketches,* James Barnet, Ed. (Press of J. Barnet, 1865). Copies of the essay in *The Martyrs and Heroes* and the *Tribune* features had been returned to the family's collection. These outside publications used a small portion of the originals, editing the content to emphasize heroism, downplay controversy, and maintain family privacy. Combining all three sources allowed a more complete picture to emerge. The bulk of the text that follows came from original, handwritten letters. Transcriptions and excerpts, not from the McCormick archive, have been annotated to show the sources.

The documents remain the property of the Colonel Robert R. McCormick Research Center at the First Division Museum at Cantigny, Chicago Tribune Collection. The Medill Family Correspondence is part of the material Robert R. McCormick inherited at his mother's death in 1932. His mother was Katherine (Kitty, 1853–1932), eldest daughter of Joseph Medill and William's niece. Joseph Medill became a driving force behind the *Chicago Tribune* newspaper in the second half of the nineteenth century. Institutional authority was granted to work with these materials. I am grateful to Eric Gillespie, director of research at the First Division Museum, for making these documents available and to Diane Gutenkauf, McCormick Museum director, for making me aware of their existence.

The timeline of William Henry Medill's service in the Eighth Illinois Cavalry was verified using military service files obtained from the National Archives and Records Administration, Washington, D.C. The correspondence is presented in sets, arranged by subject and date. Overviews add social and military background information. One important source of background material became *The History of the Eighth Cavalry Regiment, Illinois Volunteers, during the Great Rebellion* by Abner Hard, MD, published in 1868. Dr. Hard's account came from a digital version the Library of Congress contributed to the Open Library.

I am also grateful to William Underwood, acquiring editor, Kent State University Press, for his guidance and expertise and for engaging first readers whose suggestions improved the final product. First reader Vickie Cleverly Speek deserves special mention for the careful way she read the manuscript and provided astute observations.

Introduction

> Fellow-citizens, we cannot escape history. We of this Congress and this administration, will be remembered in spite of ourselves. No personal significance, or insignificance, can spare one or another of us. The fiery trial through which we pass, will light us down, in honor or dishonor, to the latest generation. We say we are for the Union. The world will not forget that we say this. We know how to save the Union. The world knows we do know how to save it. We—even we here—hold the power, and bear the responsibility. In giving freedom to the slave, we assure freedom to the free—honorable alike in what we give, and what we preserve.
> —Abraham Lincoln, Annual Message to Congress, Concluding Remarks, Washington, D.C., December 1, 1862

After Illinois senator Stephen Douglas failed to win the presidency in 1860, he gave a series of speeches, asking citizens to put party differences aside and rally behind the Lincoln administration. "There are but two sides to the question," Douglas said. "Every man must be on the side of the United States or against it. There can be none but patriots and traitors. Thank God, Illinois is not to be doubted on the question."[1] Douglas was calling for unity—even though Illinois reflected the same highly charged atmospheres that divided northern, border, and southern states.[2]

The state of Illinois was open and changing rapidly from its frontier beginnings. Census figures show the population nearly tripled between 1850 and 1870.[3] An influx of new residents came from Kentucky, Tennessee, Virginia, and other slave states to settle in southern and central Illinois. These upland southerners supported the institution of slavery, limited government, and personal autonomy. Other waves of settlers included immigrants from Europe, settlers from Indiana and Ohio, and Yankees from the Mid-Atlantic and Northeast. These groups of newcomers settled in central and northern Illinois. Yankees and European immigrants brought a progressive outlook that clashed with Southerners. Changing demographics created disagreement in Illinois over the expansion of slavery and the place of blacks in society.

Chicago boomed during the 1850s, its population jumping from 30,000 to 109,000 in just ten years. Rich agricultural lands and growing industries made Illinois a model of a dynamic, enterprising society that rewarded white labor. Fresh arrivals from Europe worked at a variety of skilled trades and menial service. German and Irish alone made up half the city's adult male population. In 1853 Democrats controlled the Illinois general assembly and passed a Black Exclusion Law with strict penalties for any slave or free African Americans who came into the state, as well as anyone who brought in a person of color. By 1855 Chicago's native-born, Protestant middle and upper classes struck back and elected a coalition of antiliquor moral crusaders and anti-immigrant politicians to run the city. As the Illinois population became more cosmopolitan, the center of politics tilted northward and gave rise to a new generation of political leadership. Slavery was becoming the controlling political issue.[4]

In the 1850s hostility to the Fugitive Slave Law grew in Illinois. Geography forced Illinois communities to face the question of returning runaways to bondage. Two slave states bordered Illinois—Missouri and Kentucky—making Illinois a relatively easy escape route for countless fugitives. Most people of Illinois agreed that slave states could protect their rights—but not when they forcibly kidnapped anyone they suspected of being a runaway without a trial or court warrant. After the Fugitive Slave Law went into effect, Illinois "friends of freedom" chartered enough railcars to send every fugitive slave from Chicago into Canada.[5] The Medill family did not support Senator Douglas or the Democratic Party, but they did agree with the way Douglas defined patriots and traitors. Patriots supported the Union—traitors called for secession. The Medill brothers moved from Ohio to Chicago, thriving in its commercial center and helping build its ties throughout the nation.[6]

When Confederates captured Fort Sumter, Illinoisans from all walks of life rushed to defend the Union. In the absence of a centralized recruitment system, Illinois communities raised troops ad hoc. Community-based mobilization met the War Department's initial quota for six Illinois regiments within five days, and thousands of volunteers continued to pour into recruitment camps. Amid fears that Confederates in Missouri might raid southern Illinois, most troops were stationed at Camp Defiance, located at the southernmost tip of Illinois at Cairo. Determined to sacrifice for Abraham Lincoln, the first president elected from Illinois, supporters naively believed that firm demonstrations could quickly defeat secession. Only the more populous states of New York, Pennsylvania, and Ohio sent more troops into battle for the

Thirty-two-year-old Joseph Medill. (Courtesy Colonel Robert R. McCormick Research Center)

Union. Illinois provided 259,000 men in 182 regiments of infantry, cavalry, and artillery, and over 2,200 men to serve the navy. Most Illinois servicemen served in western campaigns;[7] one notable exception was the Eighth Illinois Cavalry's service in the East.

Joseph Medill had become a key player in a new generation of Illinois leadership. Principles he learned from his parents prepared him for prominence. William and Margaret Medill possessed strong moral convictions and courage, which they instilled in their children and grandchildren. William Medill was Scotch-Irish, born in 1792 on a farm near Dram and Coothill, County Monaghan, Ireland, and he was reared as a devout Calvinist to believe that civic life must conform to God's will. He emigrated first to Canada and then Massillon, Ohio.[8] He and Margaret lost three children at early ages. Their eldest daughter died at age twenty-two; the fifth-born son died at birth; their ninth boy died at age five. Four sons and two daughters lived to see the start of the Civil War—Joseph, James, Mary, William, Ellen, and Samuel.[9] In February 1844 a fire had wiped out the family homestead and eldest son Joseph's chance for a college education. His longing to escape the drudgery of farm life survived the flames, as did a sense of duty. To assist his struggling family, he took a position teaching in a rural schoolhouse for twenty-five dollars a month. He also began frequenting newspaper offices, where he learned to set type, work a handpress, and write an occasional article or editorial.[10]

Joseph Medill became fully immersed in the newly formed Republican Party and in his work as a Cleveland newspaper editor until receiving an opportunity to join a Chicago paper in 1854. At this time people called Joseph "the handsomest man in Chicago" and a "good fellow" besides.[11] He was tall and slender with a firm jaw and auburn hair.

As he aged, rheumatism bent his lanky body, creating an old man's posture. When his hearing diminished, he used a black ear trumpet, which further aged him. All his life he wore a vintage costume, even when the frock coat, stiff white shirt, stand-up collar, and narrow black bow tie became outmoded. Summer and winter he wore boots and a black fedora. By the Civil War his appearance made him look older than he was, but he retained his youthful zeal.[12] He was not the kind of person other people told entertaining anecdotes about. He had few friends, but the ones he had were close. Joseph put his whole self into building the *Tribune* and serving the public. His behavior showed steadfast simplicity and austerity.[13] In recognition of a lasting legacy, the Medill School of Journalism at Northwestern University is named in Joseph's honor.

Younger brother William remained on their father's farm until age thirteen when he went to Coshocton, Ohio. There he began learning the printer's trade at the *Coshocton Republican,* which Joseph had purchased. At age sixteen William moved to Cleveland and became foreman of the *Daily Forest City,* a newspaper Joseph founded. In 1857 or 1858 William went to Canton, Ohio, where he founded the *Stark County Republican*. The paper was unsuccessful, so after a few months he moved to Chicago. By this time, Joseph had become editor of the *Chicago Tribune*.[14] Beginning in 1859 William worked as a compositor for the *Tribune*. Good compositors needed to have stamina for standing at a compositor's table fourteen to sixteen hours a day. They also needed comprehensive knowledge of English to correct poorly written copy and still work at the fast pace required for a daily paper.[15] The correspondence William wrote also demonstrated his commitment to hard work.

Two remaining brothers, James and Samuel, also learned the newspaper business at the *Coshocton Republican* from where they worked their way up to increasingly important positions. James Corbett Medill purchased Joseph's interest in the *Cleveland Morning Leader* and became the paper's editor when Joseph moved to Chicago.[16] Samuel John Medill worked various jobs at the *County Republican, Daily Forest City,* and *Northwestern Prairie Farmer* prior to the Civil War. Both Sam and James wanted to serve in the Union army, but illness made it impossible for them to do so. A memorandum among the family papers indicated James was a colonel who raised a volunteer regiment. Genealogy records point out, however, that James died at age thirty-six years in 1864, and no official record of field service can be found. The best explanation is based on the timing of several family letters. Although James raised a regiment of volunteers, which conferred the rank of colonel, before the unit could be equipped, trained, and mustered into the army, James apparently came down with an illness that prevented him from serving.

Sam tried to enlist at age twenty in the Chicago Board of Trade Battery when war broke out, but he was rejected—reportedly because of his young age. Not deterred, in September 1862 Sam mustered into the Eighth Illinois Cavalry, serving at Antietam and South Mountain, but he was discharged that same November due to disability. In a letter dated October 12, 1862, William wrote that rheumatism was a family affliction and explained the extent of Sam's incapacity. Sam returned to Illinois, attended Beloit College, and in the fall of 1864 became a reporter for the *Tribune*, later becoming managing editor, a position he held for eight years.[17]

The career of the eldest brother, Joseph Medill, as editor and proprietor of the *Tribune* and his work for the Republican Party made him an influential figure in American politics and an important early supporter of Abraham Lincoln. With his partner, Dr. Charles Ray, Joseph extended the *Tribune*'s reach until it had national influence. By 1860 they claimed to have elected Abraham Lincoln president, and Lincoln publicly agreed their paper had done more for him than any paper in the northwest. Under Medill's management, the *Tribune* strongly supported Republican goals, which were less about opposing slavery than securing free land for westerners, a railroad to the Pacific paid for by the government, and protective tariffs. Extensive campaign coverage and support for Lincoln boosted Lincoln's presidential nomination. The *Tribune* lashed out against others who called Lincoln a "ferocious John Brown abolitionist" and reprinted Lincoln's promise not to disturb slavery where it existed.[18] Joseph had been a major factor in the creation of the Republican Party and favored protecting the Union—even if it meant going to war.

After Lincoln was elected, Joseph used the pages of the *Tribune* to publicly tell Lincoln how to run the country and the war. Joseph also sent Lincoln barbed advice in private letters. While he continued to support Lincoln, Joseph lobbied for aggressive attacks on the institution of slavery. He felt strongly about the role of a good newspaper in society, arguing that the press must represent truth and goodness in ways that advanced public welfare. Although he rejected unproven news, abhorring rumor and gossip, especially in the form of attacks, his editorials were extremely vocal, even when not founded in fact. He built the *Chicago Tribune* into a powerful force in moral journalism,[19] wielding wide-reaching influence.

The Medill correspondence showed strong bonds between family members. The messages come mainly from William but also include items written by his parents, siblings, in-laws, and political cronies. He wrote in pencil, and his penmanship is remarkably legible. William shared stirring descriptions of army life with his influential brother and other family members. He wrote under duress and trying physical circumstances. His experiences were those of a cavalry officer, responsible for men in battle, and his approach to combat was forceful. "My rule has been to charge the rebels wherever and whenever we have met them," he wrote.

He did much more than describe army life. William voiced strong opinions about the conduct of the war. When outsiders criticized Union generals, he wrote enthusiastic defenses—until those commanders failed to pursue Confederates aggressively. If he saw officers fail to complete their missions, William questioned their will to fight, strategy, and deployment. He contradicted self-laudatory battle reports that Union field officers filed and—like them—criticized or downplayed contributions from units other than his own. Combat exhilarated William Medill, but like other soldiers he struggled to make sense of inefficiency and military defeat.

William's letters also reflected his newspaper training. His accounts mix personal concerns with who, what, where, when, and why. Like other soldiers, William eagerly read any newspaper he could get. However, unlike other soldiers, if newspaper accounts reported details inaccurately, he sent corrections to Joseph. In his letters from the front, William repeatedly referred to war news in the press. For example, he followed coverage in the *New York Times,* and on one occasion asked for a copy of that paper's favorable account of the Eighth Illinois. William also pointed out errors in official military reports, asking Joseph to decide whether it was advisable to make controversial matters public in the *Tribune.* William devised plans of attack, criticized poor generalship, and praised heroism, but like any Civil War soldier his firsthand knowledge of the action was limited and at times inaccurate—notably when he estimated troop strength and casualty counts.

The Medill papers shed light on national, state, and local politics; profiteering; emancipation; and the Lincoln administration. Historians agree with many of their views while some passages contradict prevailing knowledge—but controversies about what really happened during the Civil War continue to this day. William and his brothers were men with strong convictions and uncompromising Union sympathy. They practiced partisan politics, and all agreed that slavery must not be allowed to expand westward. As a Union officer, William never missed an opportunity to deprive slaveholders of their "peculiar property." Other family members also supported emancipation. Even so, like most whites of the era, their statements regarding African Americans and other ethnic groups are dated and offensive. Their attitudes shed light on the larger implications of civil war, the sectional divisions plaguing America, and imperfect human beings struggling to support what they saw as a moral cause.

William's correspondence helped him resolve internal conflicts of duty, political ideology, and social burdens. When William saw shoddy clothing, poor food, profiteering, or wasteful military spending, he worried about the burden placed on taxpayers. He took inept commanders to task and highlighted political infighting among officers. His insights addressed the complex relationship between soldiers and their leaders. He condemned any officer or official who protected secessionist property, described the animosity of Southerners in the path of war, and witnessed the jubilation of freed slaves.

The color portrait of William, which has a place of honor in the McCormick Mansion library, shows he had auburn hair, a slender physique, and a strong resemblance to his brother Joseph. William was a sober young man, as evidenced by a membership certificate in the Sons of Temperance. That the Sons of Temperance values of "Love, Purity, and Fidelity" inspired William is evident in his correspondence and conduct. While serving in Barker's Dragoons, in the Army of the Potomac, he questions conduct unworthy of officers, especially when drunken leaders neglect soldiers' well-being.

Taken as a whole, his correspondence shows William enlisted for two reasons: a strong ideology that supported the Union and opposition to the institution of slavery. Despite these compelling motives, privation and danger became increasingly hard to face. He managed to persevere because family members provided caring support. In addition, William feared that resigning reflected poorly on his manhood and the Medill name. Friends and neighbors at home heard if soldiers shirked, and they praised the ones who fought bravely. As a veteran fighter, William wrote, "What won't man endure to preserve his reputation for courage!" Even though he had honorable reasons to stay, the lack of progress in the war prompted William to write Joseph, asking how it would look to people in Chicago if he resigned and returned home. In June 1862 during Union general McClellan's Peninsula Campaign, poor handling of slaves, hardships, and William's ill health became too much to bear. He wrote, "We will never win a victory until we fight with a purpose and for an object . . . when the rebels push us, we retreat." As a result of General McClellan's failed Peninsula Campaign in August 1862, William submitted a resignation, but his superior officer declined to forward the paperwork. Soon afterward, his younger brother Sam arrived as a new recruit in the Eighth Illinois Cavalry and needed William's help. The following month, after Antietam, William was promoted to major. From then on, though he lost faith in other commanders, he no longer questioned the need to stay, preserve the Union, and end slavery.

The entire family exhibited moral courage. For William, moral courage translated into the physical courage necessary to ride into battle. For Joseph, it meant the emotional courage to let his brother go. They stepped forward as soon as war broke out, but the Medill brothers had no idea how much their courage, capacity for sacrifice, and values would be tested in the coming years.

The government's first call asked Illinois to provide six regiments, but the state assembly authorized ten infantry regiments, one regiment of cavalry, and one battalion of light artillery. Going to war was one thing; being prepared was quite another. Like other states, Illinois was woefully unprepared. The state's military force, for all practical purposes, existed only on paper. It had no available armed, organized militia and suffered from a shortage of arms, accouterments, and uniforms. Despite the deficiencies, men swarmed into service. The first recruits poured out of overcrowded railway cars and assembled on ill-prepared campgrounds in Springfield. They bunked six deep in barn stalls formerly meant to hold one cow. Little or no provision was made to properly feed or clothe them.[20]

William first enlisted for a ninety-day term in Barker's Dragoons. At that time, cavalry units were referred to as *dragoons*. The unit went from Chicago to Springfield and then to Camp Defiance, located at the southernmost tip of Illinois near Cairo. Serving at Camp Defiance provided a rude introduction to army life. The duty consisted of backbreaking labor—clearing land and building Union defenses to protect against Confederate attack from nearby slave states. When Gen. George B. McClellan came to inspect the installation, the situation improved because McClellan chose Barker's Dragoons to serve as his bodyguards. However, when the unit transferred to Virginia, poor treatment from Captain Barker continued. Neglect and uncaring officers caused William, along with most of the troopers, to refuse to reenlist, returning home after their ninety-day enlistment ended.

Even though his first experience left William discouraged, he decided to reenlist under a better commander. The morals, values, and social conventions he learned at home transcended misgivings and connected him to larger beliefs. His civilian family played a vital role in William's continued ability to serve. Their heartfelt concern sustained him. After leaving Barker's Dragoons, William raised a regiment for the Eighth Illinois Cavalry. As part of that unit he served at the Battle of Williamsburg, the Peninsula Campaign, Antietam,

Fredericksburg, Aldie, Gettysburg, and Williamsport. When not engaged in battle, the regiment scouted, performed picket duty, and raided Confederate strongholds.

During the first two years of fighting, Union cavalry suffered by comparison to Confederate cavalry under the leadership of generals like J. E. B. Stuart. One reason for Federals' lackluster performance is the way mounted companies and regiments were sprinkled throughout the army rather than consolidated into a separate division as southern cavalry units were.[21] In addition, early Federal commanders did not make good use of cavalry. Maj. Gen. George B. McClellan resented volunteer cavalry and didn't trust it. He believed it took five years to train volunteer cavalry. Only one Regular cavalry regiment, the Sixth U.S. Cavalry, formed during the Civil War. They mustered in August 1861 and took part in the Peninsula Campaign beginning in March 1862. All other Regular cavalry were experienced mounted troops that had served the U.S. army prior to 1861. They became the Cavalry Reserve Brigade. However, McClellan also deployed Regulars poorly while he commanded the Army of the Potomac.[22] On June 25, 1862, while McClellan pursued the Peninsula Campaign, William described the confusion. In a single day, the Eighth Illinois received a series of conflicting orders:

> Yesterday we were under the command of three brigadiers. In the morning we were under Stoneman when he was ordered to divide his brigade among different commanders and report himself on Gen. McClellan's staff. We were ordered to report to Gen. Martindale. Col. Farnsworth went over there and received orders from him. When he had returned to camp a few minutes, Gen. Martindale sent him word that his brigade had been ordered across the Chickahominy and that Farnsworth should report to Gen. Taylor of the New Jersey Brigade. This order was complied with and no more changes were made till this morning when Col. Farnsworth received word from Taylor that his brigade was ordered across the Chickahominy, and that we were not attached to any brigade but should continue picket duty just as we had been doing for the last week or two. So we stand at present. How many changes there will be made before night I cannot tell, nor don't care.

The only cohesive cavalry unit McClellan utilized were regulars, which served together as a Cavalry Reserve Brigade, but they, too, were generally used poorly.[23]

William suffered through the disappointment of those years and endured long enough to help the situation turn around. At the Battle of Brandy Station on June 9, 1863, the day a Confederate invasion northward was to begin,

Union cavalry commander major general Alfred Pleasonton struck Stuart's men in camp. Despite having the advantage of surprise, the battle ended in a narrow defeat for Pleasonton's forces. Nevertheless, the Battle of Brandy Station, the largest predominantly mounted engagement to take place on the American continent, greatly improved the morale of Union cavalry.[24] William described how Union cavalry came into their own and impeded Stuart's movements. Military service taught him to be more than a passive victim. It gave him opportunities to meet challenges and gain some degree of control. Conservatism, a pragmatic view of death and ethics learned in prewar years, sustained him.

On the first day of fighting at Gettysburg, the absence of Confederate cavalry handicapped Gen. Robert E. Lee. William's letters provide another perspective on Gen. J. E. B. Stuart's movements during Lee's invasion northward. He credited Union troops for delaying Stuart's advance. Stuart undertook an arduous ride, and every time his troopers had to stop for a skirmish or battle, they lost time. Fatigue became a factor, and horses and material were lost. Rather than simply blaming Stuart for a failure to be Lee's eyes and ears, Union cavalry should receive praise for wearing Confederates down.[25] Winning battles was not Stuart's primary task, but keeping diligent Union cavalry away from Lee's infantry became one of his goals.[26] Stuart's progress was also impeded by a frequent need to stop and graze horses. They had no wagons with them at the start of their raid and depended on the countryside to feed both men and horses, while the area they rode through had been decimated by nearly three years of Confederate and Union foraging.[27] William's correspondence brought this facet of warfare to life.

William's letters are those of a vulnerable human being, caught up in events that fully tested his morale. He believed democracy worthy of great sacrifices and expressed a willingness to throw himself into the conflict. His moral vision required him to find ways to better society, and becoming a man of war was his solution. The hard reality of war did not destroy William's commitment to the issues. He embraced the deadly game in order to achieve goals. It was a source of pride that he matured into an effective soldier. Suffering taught him self-reliance, and he found comradeship ennobling, but he worried he would find it hard to leave cold brutality behind when fighting ended. William lacked experience with women and doubted his ability to speak to eligible ladies after a long absence from polite society.

He made some close friends among his fellow officers but distanced himself from the ones who sought recognition at the expense of others. William acted as he believed an officer should, earning respect and trust from the men who served with him. His comrades elected him captain, and his ability to mold men and help them perform well on the field earned him a promotion to major.

The limits of Civil War medicine became painfully clear when reading William's experiences. One example was the ordeal of smallpox vaccination. In the 1860s, doctors vaccinated by cutting the skin of the upper arm with a knife, inserting ground vaccine scab into the cut and pressing the edges together. Not all vaccinations were effective because the vaccine matter might be inert. Immunization itself could be risky. Cutting the skin in unsterile conditions could lead to infection and the introduction of other communicable diseases.[28] Even small cuts could become life-threatening, and one trooper in the Eighth Illinois had to be forced to accept vaccination.

The journal Joseph kept at William's bedside offered a vivid account of what happened in Civil War general hospitals. The Eighth Illinois Cavalry regimental history explained where William was mortally wounded and how he was carried off the battlefield, but the account left what it was like to endure torturous evacuation to the imagination. The large-caliber, soft-lead bullets used in the Civil War created horrific wounds. An army surgeon saw more surgical cases in a couple weeks than he would in a lifetime of private practice. A surgeon set up an area behind battle lines where he could examine wounded men. This area was termed a *regimental hospital,* which is deceptive because the so-called hospital was often just a marked area on the field. The surgeon tried to choose a gully, an area protected by trees or a depression in the field, so that medical personnel and the wounded would not be hit by enemy fire. Minor wounds were dressed, and soldiers returned to battle. Medical personnel used lint, scraped from fabrics, to pack wounds and tore old cloth into strips to use as bandages. Soldiers with severe wounds were evacuated from field hospitals to division hospitals in the rear, and primary operations, such as amputations, were performed under the direction of a corps medical director. As need dictated, buildings were pressed into service—warehouses, churches, private homes, and even barns became hospitals.[29]

Soldiers who were too severely wounded to survive the rigors of an ambulance ride were kept as comfortable as possible and set aside to die. From the front, when patients were stable enough to withstand a second journey, they were evacuated to a system of general hospitals located in large cities. In William's case, he was evacuated to Frederick, Maryland. The most skilled surgeons available, regardless of regimental affiliation, performed secondary and more complex operations in general hospitals.[30]

In this era, before antiseptics and antibiotics, soldiers wounded in the abdomen often died from infection, even if they survived the initial blood loss and shock. The mortality rate for abdominal wounds was 87 percent.[31] The remarks regarding William's condition, found in his military record, placed his wound "one inch above tip of ensiform cartilage," which is the cartilage at the lower end of the sternum. We know from Joseph's journal that a surgeon probed for the bullet, while William was anesthetized, but was unable to locate it. The official remarks regarding William's condition are incredible for what they don't include—attending surgeons had no real treatment options.

Medical treatment remained in the Dark Ages. Doctors used "heroic" methods until a patient's condition changed visibly. Several tortuous methods were used on William. Cupping involved heating small cups and placing them on the skin. As the cup cooled, a vacuum was created inside and the skin drawn up inside the cup to form a raised blister, which was thought to promote better blood flow to the area. In wet cupping, surgeons made small cuts in the skin so the cups also drew blood, thought to reduce the "bad humors" in the body. Mustard plasters were cloths soaked with mustard seed powder, thought to treat inflammatory conditions of the lungs. We don't know the qualifications of the surgeons who treated William. Officials from a regiment's home state appointed physicians for volunteer units; most doctors had no military experience. Some regimental surgeons were not even doctors.[32]

Enlisted men filled many more Civil War nursing positions than women. Commanders detailed soldiers to care for the sick and wounded, but combat officers hated to assign men who would be useful in battle. Instead, they filled nursing positions with men who were sick, recovering from wounds, or unfit for the rigors of the front. Nineteenth-century women cared for sick family members at home, but it was considered improper for them to care for men outside their immediate families. When William was wounded, his sister-in-law offered to travel to Maryland to help care for him, even though she knew it would be more appropriate for William's sister Mary to be his nurse. As it turned out, neither Kate nor Mary could have arrived in time to help. Instead William relied on care from a favorite male nurse and what little comfort Catholic nuns could provide.

Modern medicine could have saved William as well as countless other Civil War soldiers, but doctors of the era did not have antiseptics, antibiotics, X-rays, or pharmaceuticals of reliable strength. Doctors knew that the symptoms of infection, including heat, redness, swelling, and pain could cause a downward spiral, but no one in the medical profession imagined that microscopic germs invaded dirty wounds or were carried from one patient to the next on unsterile instruments or doctors' hands. Inflammation theory was the basis of medical practice, which advocated treating "inflammatory excitement" by relaxation, bleeding, purgatives, and narcotics. Opening any body cavity in an unsterilized hospital could be a death sentence. Internal organs had been studied under the microscope, leaving no doubt about their rich blood vessels and nerve supply. Doctors believed they must counter inflammation by decreasing the amount of blood circulating or by removing accumulated poisons through increasing the patient's sweating, urination, or evacuation of the bowels. Drastic purges did more harm than good. One of the methods used on William was mustard plaster. Doctors believed that causing a reaction elsewhere on the body transferred poisons from the original location. William's attending physician used mustard as a counterirritant to draw blood and toxins away from his inflamed wound.[33]

Dr. Joseph Lister demonstrated in 1865 that using antiseptic carbolic acid spray in operating rooms could prevent infection and save lives. Thereafter, medical improvements came more rapidly. If army doctors had known how to battle infection, many thousands of Civil War soldiers could have survived,[34] William Medill among them. Entries in Joseph's journal recount what happened in the general hospital and make us privy to the scene at William's bedside, where suffering turned to hope and finally to resignation.

The Medill family letters and journals provide fascinating perspectives on army life, military commanders, wasteful government spending, the Lincoln administration, newspaper coverage, partisan politics, and nineteenth-century medicine. These men railed against inept military leaders, watched good men weakened by shortages, witnessed far too many lives wasted, and mourned destruction that defied understanding. Their accounts are part private trauma and part social commentary. The story began with Joseph's aggressive public calls for war but turned into private anxiety and grief as fighting escalated.

CHAPTER ONE

The Call to Action

*If 50,000 men is not enough, call for 100,000, and
if that is not sufficient call for 500,000.*
—Joseph Medill

Joseph to President Lincoln

Office of the *Daily Tribune,* Clark Street, Chicago, Illinois, April 15, 1861
President Lincoln,

There is but one opinion in Chicago—Douglas Dems and Lincoln Reps are a unit, and that is, that Sumter must be retaken, Moultrie retaken, Pinckney retaken, the custom house retaken, and the Stars & Stripes—the National Emblem, must float over the Federal property in Charleston. Chicago will send you a gallant regiment on call, and Illinois fifty more.

England & France met Russia at Sebastipol—localized the war and whipped her there. She has been tame and quiet ever since. Charleston of all spots, is the place to settle our national difficulties. There meet the secessionists and there crush them. If 50,000 men is not enough, call for 100,000, and if that is not sufficient call for 500,000. But crush the head of the rattlesnake. There is where the trouble was hatched. The Tories live there—let them die there. The North West will back you with their last man, dollar and bushel of corn. The authority of the Govt. must be made good. Do your duty; the people are with you.

J. Medill[1]

Joseph made sure that President Lincoln understood how supporters in Illinois viewed the administration's management of the war. Lincoln had given John C. Fremont command of the Department of the West, but on August 30, 1861, Fremont issued a proclamation, placing Missouri under martial law. Fremont decreed that all property of those bearing arms in rebellion would be confiscated—confiscated slaves would be declared free—and he imposed capital punishment on those rebelling against the federal government. Fearing this would push Missouri to join the Confederacy, Lincoln wrote to Fremont, asking him to rescind the proclamation. Fremont refused, and Lincoln looked for a way to remove him from command. Lincoln's solution was to send officials to Missouri to build a case for Fremont's removal based on alleged incompetence.[2] As the following letters show, Joseph supported Fremont and objected to Lincoln's decisions.

Joseph to President Lincoln
Confidential, Chicago, September 16, 1861

President Lincoln,

Your letter to Gen. Fremont has cast a funeral pall over our loyal city. We are stricken with a heavier calamity than the rout at Bull Run. It comes like a mildew, like a frost in June, killing the coming harvest. If there was one thing above another on which the whole people were agreed it was in support of Fremont's noble proclamation. Democrats vied with Republicans in eulogizing it and defending its positions. That proclamation and the pervading belief that you endorsed it had received enlistments and rekindled flagging enthusiasm. Since you have vetoed the *penalties* against the misdeeds of slave-holding rebels, the war will degenerate into duels and assassination. Mr. President, this is a *slaveholders' rebellion.* Slavery is at the bottom of the whole trouble. The revolt was inaugurated to give expansion & greater strength to the system—more territory. More slaves. More special privileges. These are the objects and the dismemberment or subjugation of the Republic [which] is to them a preliminary necessity. Until the Administration sees the contest in the light of this truth, success will be impossible. A slaveholders' rebellion cannot be put down by conducting the war on pro-slavery principles.

When the rebel slaveholder raises his dagger against his country, let one of the penalties be the confiscation and liberation of his slaves. This strikes at the root of the disease and touches the parricide [sic] in his only sensitive spot.

If you had let Fremont and the Northwest alone, Missouri would have been pacified in 30 days. Memphis would be ours before six weeks and New Orleans by Jan 8th. The Great West had taken the job of crushing this unholy rebellion in the Valley of the Mississippi and opening its navigation from the Falls of St. Anthony [Minneapolis, Minnesota] to the Belize. Your own State has nearly 50,000 soldiers in camp today. The heart of our great and noble state is in this work.

The effect of your letter in Kentucky will be to embolden the rebel slaveholders by removing from their eyes the pains and penalties of treason. The halting neutral will be converting into an assassin rebel, and the loyal slaveholder having no selfish motive (the safety of his slaves) for action will relapse into indifference and "neutrality."

And let me say that the reason given for the crushing blow on Fremont will utterly fail to satisfy the people. Since the Executive is obliged to transcend the acts of Congress and the Constitution every day. The higher law of military necessity and national self-preservation furnish you ample justification, and there also Fremont found his authority for his proclamation. The *Union cannot be saved on the basis* of your repudiation of Fremont's proclamation. We waste our blood and treasure in vain. I wish to God! you could pass among the people and touch their pulse and hear their great heart beat, and you would be no longer in the dark in relation to the will and sentiments of those to *whom this nation belongs* and who furnish the men and means to prosecute the war.

Pardon this intrusion, but believe me sincere. My heart is full of anguish. I look into the future with despair if the war is to be conducted on the principles indicated in your letter. I have sent two brothers to the army. Their blood will be shed in vain. Chicago sits today in sackcloth and ashes. Those who were chiefest in securing your nomination for the high post you occupy are shedding bitter tears. Judge Trumbull, who is here, is in agony. Men are here attending the State Fair from all parts of the state and from neighboring states. They are all downcast and in sorrow.

Yours in grief, J. Medill

Even though Joseph had strong disagreements with President Lincoln, the two men continued to regard each other as friends, important allies and sources of information. In addition to the president's friendship, Joseph Medill's connections in Washington included other high-ranking officials. One of these connections was Schuyler Colfax, Republican congressman from Indiana (1855–69). Colfax would go on to become Speaker of the House of Representatives from 1863–1869. Colfax wrote to Joseph to report a meeting he had with President Lincoln, in which he shared a letter Joseph had written. When reading Joseph's letter to Lincoln, Representative Colfax skipped any comparison people were making between the Lincoln administrations and those of Presidents Tyler and Fillmore—because those two administrations had increased sectional divisions between slave and free states.[3]

CONGRESSMAN SCHUYLER COLFAX TO JOSEPH
H.R. [House of Representatives] Washington, June 9, 1862

Friend Medill,

I saw Mr. Lincoln last night & had an hour's talk with him. I told him I had an interesting letter from you, which you authorized me to read to him & asked him if he would like to hear it. He said, "Yes, very much. Medill is a man of brains—a capital friend, and although more radical than myself his views are always well worth considering." I then read it to him, skipping the part where you said people at one time had began to talk of him as Tyler & Fillmore. When you spoke of the fact that [illegible] if he acted so & so, more than Washington, he sighed & replied while I was reading, "I am not looking for reelection. I expect more trouble and difficulty before my present term ends than will be the share of any one man. But I *am* trying to do right."

When I got through, he said, "Tell Medill . . . we can only act where we have power & no slave that works for the U.S. or comes to our lines shall be re-enslaved."

The Colfax letter goes on to cover political concerns, including "Andy Johnson's"[4] telegraph asking Lincoln if he could arrest 70 percent of the "meanest secesh near Nashville." In closing Schuyler Colfax writes that the contents of the letter are not to be reprinted, but he knows Joseph Medill likes to hear President Lincoln's views.

JOSEPH TO PRESIDENT LINCOLN
Office of the *Daily Tribune*, Chicago, October 13, 1862

President Lincoln,

In the name of God and his holy angels! What evil influence is holding our army torpid on the north bank of the Potomac? The summer is passed, and winter approaches and nothing is done. How long will the nation consent to keep a million of idle men in the field? Gen. McClellan deserved to be arrested and cashiered or shot for not pursuing the beaten rebel army the day after the Battle of Antietam. Twenty-six days of superb campaign weather have been since wasted in scandalous idleness and counter profitable reviews. Thousands of soldiers became weary, disgusted and discouraged and *deserted;* it is called "straggling." They have run off to escape *McClellanism* and another winter in tents on the Potomac. That army is rapidly demoralizing and will melt away.

The people are gravely discontented and discouraged. The cost of the war is eating up the substance of the people and mortgaging the property and labor of unborn generations. The elections will go badly against us, I fear, in consequence of the vast preponderance of Republicans in the army—held down by proslavery generals. And public discontent at the do nothing behavior of McClellan, whom you persist in keeping in command. Put Halleck in the field or Hooker or Burnsides—some man who *desires* to beat the rebels.

All patriotic men thank and bless you for issuing the [Preliminary Emancipation] Proclamation, but like faith without works it is dead. The Potomac Army must move. This nation is gone *forever* if the army goes into winter quarters without pursuing and overthrowing the rebels in Virginia, or there may burst forth a revolution in the North. Either men will give up in despair or attempt to break from the coils of the handhold that is strangling the Union and waging war only on the resources of the loyal people. I look upon Geo. McClellan and Carlos Buell[5] as the assassins of the Great Republic. The one has suffocated our endeavors for 12 months in the West and the other for 14 months in the East. They hold exactly the same political views of Major Key, whom you dismissed. He is only an echo of theirs. They are suspiciously popular with the rebels. Their motives suit Jeff Davis to a dot. Buell's present spasm amounts to nothing. He will soon relapse into his former torpidity. These men want a compromise with the rebels, not a subjugation of them. The former is training for your place. Every man of secession sympathies are warmly for him. Is it right that such men should command armies composed mainly of earnest Republicans? The Republican Party is held responsible for the success of the war, while proslavery generals manage it, and a proslavery democracy has thus far dictated the policy on which the war is conducted. Is that right? Gold is 30 percent premium. The Gov't. credit is on the brink of bankruptcy. Hell yawns close by, and McClellan holds a quarter of a million impatient soldiers on the north bank of the Potomac.

Oh, Mr. Lincoln, wake up before all is lost. Drive McClellan to his work or kick him out of the army. The country will sustain you in any act that will give motion to the grand army. Why listen to the reactionary croakings of the hold-back cowardly conservatives? That class never save any cause. You must have Jeff Davis *or he will have you*. One or other has got to be. If he wins, anti-slavery men will be persecuted unto death.

I feel deeply the national peril. And cannot help saying a word to the only man who has the power to avert impending calamity and swift destruction.

Yours desponding, J. Medill

While war enveloped the country, Joseph Medill and Dr. Ray pledged to keep an editor in Washington, and at times they went to Washington themselves to report the news or influence policy decisions. Dr. Charles Ray was present for the "story of his lifetime," the first Union defeat at Bull Run. After he learned the full extent of the disaster, Ray published a full report that began: "The battle is lost. The enemy have a substantial victory. The result, so unexpected, dangerous and mortifying. . . . The well-appointed and magnificent army that is now coming back broken and disorganized into the entrenchments on the opposite side of the river, ought never to have been beaten."[6]

Traveling during the Civil War was arduous and fraught with delays because the Union army commandeered rail lines to transport men and supplies. The rigors of traveling must have been particularly hard for Joseph, who suffered from rheumatism and inflammation of the spine.

When Joseph was in Chicago, he left the job of field correspondent to younger men. The *Tribune* claimed to have twenty-seven editor/correspondents covering the war. These reporters were an unpredictable group.[7] In this era, newspapers were not impartial, instead printing partisan articles and editorials. Subscribers bought papers that printed political viewpoints they favored. Chicago had two other major daily papers, and to compete the *Tribune* had to attract an audience by appealing to men of action.[8]

While Joseph and Katherine traveled, their daughters spent time with their grandparents. The following letter from Joseph's father displayed the tender feelings Joseph's daughters have for their parents. The older child, Kitty, was age seven, and the younger, Nelly, only five. Grandfather William listened carefully to his granddaughters, gave them undivided attention, and encouraged them in their studies.

WILLIAM MEDILL (FATHER) TO HIS SON, JOSEPH
Canton, February 2, 1860

Dear Joseph:

We are all well. The children while I am writing are playing and taking great exercise. Kitty is quite recovered of her cold. Last evening she was highly excited while telling her grandma some old story about her companions in Chicago and frequently used the common phrase, you know. Nelly was listening with grave attention but suddenly exclaimed, Kitty Medill, Grandma can't know what you are talking about before you tell her what it is. Kitty paid no attention but kept on with her story, and again said, you know. "This," now said Nelly, "you are at your 'you know' again when I told you Grandma could not understand you." We all raised a laugh at Kitty's expense, and Grandma had to interfere in preventing Kitty from slapping her.

I often tell them I think the one that learns fastest will get the best presents from you when you come back. It always has a good effect upon Nelly but not always on Kitty. They are both learning fast but before three months Nelly will be ahead.

We have another cold streak of weather at present. The mercury at zero. The *Farmers Advocate* is all the paper we get from Chicago and all we expect until you return.

James Saxon has got into an expensive lawsuit and has made an assignment to Ben Lighter. If it goes against him, it is said it will break him up. He was administrator to a will and acted fraudulently, so the stories go.

We learn there is no speaker elected in congress yet. I fear the Republicans will not hold out.

Kitty sent a hundred kisses and Nelly a thousand to Ma Ma. The balance of us send our love unto you both.

Wm. Medill

P.S. When I was done writing Nelly said I forgot to send kisses to Pa Pa. "How many will you send?" Tell him I send him forty hundred, and Kitty said she would send him sixty hundred.

W. M.

His brother, William, also kept Joseph informed about politics in Chicago and a likely candidate for Chicago postmaster. Postmasters at the largest post offices were appointed by the U.S. president and usually received the job as a political reward. William's letter also detailed how Anthony C. Hesing, a prominent German American who held the elective office of sheriff,[9] had to break up a fight at a political meeting.

In addition, William alerted Joseph to activities of peace Democrats like Cyrus McCormick. Cyrus McCormick was born in Rock County, Virginia, and remained loyal to the Confederacy during the Civil War. McCormick was not the first to build a mechanical reaper, but he prospered in the vast markets of the emerging American Midwest. Ironically, Cyrus McCormick's grandson, Col. Robert McCormick, became president of the Tribune Company in 1911. Robert McCormick and his cousin Joe Patterson became joint editors and publishers of the *Chicago Tribune* in 1914. As editor and publisher, Robert McCormick transformed the *Tribune* from a metropolitan newspaper to a transnational media enterprise, building on the legacy of the Medill brothers.

In 1860 while Joseph was in Washington, D.C., he criticized concessionists, a position advocated by Illinois congressman William Kellogg. At the National Hotel, Congressman Kellogg attacked Joseph, landing blows to Joseph's head and face. Because of Joseph's rheumatism, the attack could have been much more serious than it turned out to be. In the letter, William condoned retaliation.

At this point, William was working as a *Tribune* compositor, but his correspondence showed a grasp of the news business that goes beyond typesetting. He offered story ideas his brother might use, and it becomes possible to imagine several newspaper stories with strong headlines.

SHERIFF BREAKS UP POLITICAL BRAWL
PATRONAGE SCANDAL SURROUNDS CHICAGO POSTMASTER
CONGRESSMAN KELLOGG ASSAULTS TRIBUNE EDITOR

At the time the letter was written, the Republican Party had not yet nominated Lincoln for U.S. president, but Mr. Lincoln had eloquently explained his plan to leave slavery alone where it existed and prevent its spread. "Wrong as we think slavery is, we can yet afford to let it alone where it is, because that much is due to the necessity arising from its actual presence in the nation; but can we, while our votes will prevent it, allow it to spread into the National Territories, and to overrun us here in these Free States? If our sense of duty forbids this, then let us stand by our duty, fearlessly and effectively."[10] Lincoln's statement inspired William, who expressed hope that Lincoln remained true to this campaign platform.

WILLIAM TO JOSEPH

Chicago, February 24, 1860

Dear Brother:

I have commenced several letters to you, but something has always intervened to prevent my finishing them. I hope to succeed better this time.

Kate and Sammy I suppose gave you all the local news up to the time they left here. Since then, we have had rather exciting times politically—especially since the attempt by some scoundrels to drag down the Republican flag from its proud position to the level of the cravens who worship nigger-owners. Several public meetings have been held by the different parties for the purpose of giving public expression of opinion on the existing difficulties. Two meetings were held to denounce the course of the *Tribune,* or really but one as the last one was an adjournment through necessity of the first. At the first meeting, the non-concessionists took possession of the organization and by force kept it. I never saw quite so much excitement on any like occasion. Quite a number were knocked down and a great many good coats were badly torn. Everybody "traveled on his muscle" for a little while dragging his coat for some prank packer to tread on. I got a slight touch on the back of the head, but got satisfaction by hitting two or three others in return. But we finally adjourned the meeting by getting Sheriff Hessing [Hesing] to turn off the lights and order them all out of the room.

The second meeting was a very tame affair. No interruption was attempted, and after half a dozen wishy-washy speeches, they read a series of foolish resolutions, which were *really* voted down, but the President declared them carried. On the day of this last meeting the news came of the fracas between you and Kellogg, so when his name was mentioned there was the biggest kind of hiss all over the house and cries of "brute."

On the Tuesday evening following, the real Republicans held a meeting the proceedings of which you have seen. After the meeting adjourned most of the crowd and a band came around to our office and gave us a serenade. Three rousing cheers were given for you and three groans for Kellogg. This last meeting was twice as large as either of the anti-*Tribune* meetings and was entirely harmonious.

A good deal of feeling is manifested in regard to Mr. Kellogg's assault on you. As far as I have been able to learn, but one impression prevails and that is that he is cowardly, and that if you had *shot* him it would be no more than he deserved. Were I in your situation I think he would get a dose of something, a club if I didn't want to kill him. Were you hurt much?

But few stopped their papers on account of the course it has taken and a great many more have subscribed. Business seems to be good, and everything seems to go along just as though South Carolina had never left the Union. Lincoln's speeches are well liked among all classes, except the McCormick clique. I hope he [Lincoln] will stick to what he has said.

There is a good deal of talk about who are to get the offices in this city. A good many are working for Charley Wilson for Postmaster, and some think on account of his having Seward's influence, that he will get it. You may depend upon it, he is working hard enough to make an impression on a stone. What do you think of it? Wouldn't it be an awful shame to give such a dirty drunken "rat" such an office? There is not as much feeling in regard to the Custom House.

Sammy returned from Canton [Ohio] a week ago, looking and feeling much better after his visit. He says that Mother's wrist will never be entirely well. The Dr. must have been a stupid wretch, not to set it better. I sent them $10 last Saturday again. How are they getting along? Did you see Mary or Ellen?

I learned that little Nelly was sick with the scarlet fever. Is it true? How does Kate like Washington this winter? But I am asking you too many questions. I have not heard from Jim for two or three weeks. When he last wrote me, he was a little better. By a late member of the *Transcript* I notice that he made quite a speech at Peoria at a public meeting of the Republicans and offered some resolutions, which were unanimously adopted. I also see by the paper that he is having a bout with the Peoria *Union* Raney's paper.

Please give my regards to Kate and Sam's also.

Yours, etc. Wm. H. Medill

WILLIAM MEDILL (FATHER) TO HIS SON, JOSEPH

Canton, Ohio, March 16, 1860

Dear Joseph:

I recd. a letter from you about the time that Kate and the children left here for New Philadelphia. You thought at that time you would stop another month in Washington. Wm. was here at the time Kate arrived and went with her as far as Alliance. Wm. was a good deal dissipated when he came here, but the change of food and air, and exercise in the open air has quite revived him to his former state of health. Mother has found jobs for him about the lot such as planting shade trees in front of the house and repairing the fence and making it chicken proof.

During the past week we have had during two days very cold weather for the season with a light fall of snow, but now it is tapering off with heavy white frosts at night and at present showering of rain.

In your letter you wished to know whether the tenant in the Alliance house was paying the rent regularly or not. Within a few days I got a letter from A. L. Janes, Esq., stating that the shoemaker had left the house about the first of this month, and he had no opportunity of renting as yet and that he (Janes) was going out to [the] State of Ind. and would be gone for two or three weeks. (Unfortunate speculation that house.) Mother has been making managements on the expectation of the rent and now all has fell through.

I hope another change is about taking place in my system for the better. I am very helpless at present [from rheumatism,] but not getting worse during the last ten days, and my appetite is better. I hope as the season advances my disease will abate. I want more of the fresh air about me. Oh, how I long to be able once more to saw wood. Write and let us know where you expect to be.

We have not had a letter from Kate since she went to Fus Co, nor I don't think Wm. or Ellen has written to her during that time. Wm. is talking about going down to New Phila. some of these days. Mother feels very lonesome since the children left and talks a great deal about them. The mail is near going east. I must close.

From your affectionate parent, Wm. Medill

Joseph was devoted to his wife and hated to be separated from her, as a letter from Washington showed. He also shared his frustrations with Kate, naming powerful political players and describing their actions. William Kellogg, a congressman from Illinois, was appointed to the Committee of Thirty-Three of the U.S. House of Representatives and tasked with drafting a proposal aimed at averting a civil war. Longtime Lincoln friend and supporter Norman Judd did not receive a cabinet post but was named minister to Prussia. William J. Bross was a Chicago politician and publisher whose paper merged with the *Tribune* in 1858. Bross was another Lincoln supporter, and he helped raise the Twenty-Ninth Regiment, United States Colored Infantry.[11]

Joseph to Kate
Washington, D.C., January 18, 1861, 11 p.m.

My Darling Wife,

On going down into the office to mail a letter I found yours of no date but postmarked Wednesday.

Yes, I will be joyful to meet once more. Our absence begins to seem to me like a little eternity. But one week from tonight, no preventing providence, we will be hastening towards each others' arms by double railroad speed. I propose to leave here on Thursday evening so as to be in Pittsburg on Friday where I may stay over one train to see the girls. I shall surely be in Canton (Ohio) on Saturday if living. Whether before you arrive or after is not certain, but I expect to be waiting for you at the depot. I feel almost like taking a vow that while life lasts we shall never part again for a week. But then I recollect that man is not superior to his accidents. But I earnestly pray that our future partings may be of short duration and far between. Really we have not realized how deeply we have loved each other until deprived a short time of each other's society. This I suppose is the true test of affection.

I have no gossip that would interest you. The only notable personal item during the week has been the purchase of a pair of $8—mind you *eight dollar*—boots, which pinch my corns like thunder. I gave away to a nigger the 2-year old pair and am sorry for it. . . .

Wm. Kellogg started home in a hurry to Springfield to help beat Judd for a place in the Cabinet. He is talking *compromise*. He [Kellogg] is a cowardly Republican and wants to back down. I quarreled with him.

I'll write you on Sunday that will be the last letter which would reach you. See Bross about that family from Pittsburg. Bring $100 in gold with you. Oh, how very long the next 180 hours will be. Roll on ye wings of time & hasten a blissful moment of meeting my precious wife.

Husband

William tried to keep Joseph informed about family concerns, business at the paper, as well as political strife in Illinois. "Long John" Wentworth was considered to be Chicago's first strong mayor in spite of limitations of the office at the time. Known as independent and honest, Wentworth attempted to clean up vice. Mayor Wentworth stood six feet six, weighed around 300 pounds, and was a master of dirty politics. He published the *Chicago Democrat* newspaper until 1861. Critics charged he published more about himself than the city. He served two terms as mayor,[12] using mayoral powers to reduce the police force and impose a midnight curfew. Outraged voters prompted the state of Illinois to become active in Chicago's police force. February 15, 1861, the state established a Board of Police Commissioners for the city of Chicago. On March 21, 1861, Mayor Wentworth summoned the entire police force to his office and fired them, leaving the city without police protection from 2:00 A.M. until 10:00 A.M. the next morning when the new police board rehired most of the fired officers and a considerable number of new men.[13]

WILLIAM TO JOSEPH,
AT THE WASHINGTON HOTEL, WASHINGTON, D.C.

Chicago, February 28, 1861

Dear Brother:

I received your letter of the 20th on Tuesday, but as I had written on Sunday you already have about all the information I have.

Yesterday I received a letter from Hetta, by which I learn that Jim is getting better. She says he is stronger and has less rheumatism than at any time since he has been taken sick. She thinks that if he keeps on improving as rapidly as he has been lately, he will be well by the end of the summer.

I observe that he was a delegate to the Congressional Convention of Kellogg's District and made a speech.

The reason Sam didn't go to Pittsburg to see Ellen and Mary was owing to the fact that he told the conductor that he was only going to Canton, and so he punched his ticket so as to spoil it going any farther from Canton.

In regard to sending money, I only missed once owing to having lent some money, but I will not fail again you may depend.

The feeling here is almost unanimously against any compromising. Only a few old Tories who are interested in southern trade are willing to sacrifice principle and honor for the sake of keeping three or four beggarly southern states. Keep up the fire. Your letters are well liked, everybody commending them for their boldness and straightforwardness. In the country, they are all the go. They are read first and taken as gospel.

Business is pretty good, but we are having some monetary troubles. Under the new banking law, however, it is hoped it will blow over.

You have, no doubt, seen our new charter and police law. It is kicking up a great fuss. John Wentworth says he will resign when the time for which he was elected expires near the first of March. His threats don't create as much feeling as he anticipated. Without command of the police he can't act the tyrant and that is his whole design in being mayor. The election under the new charter takes place in April. The Police Commissioners take possession of things on Monday next, then look out for him. C. P. Bradley will probably be Captain of the Police—anything to worry Long John.

I am glad to hear that Kate and Nelly are better. Give Kate my best regards. Yours, etc. W. H. Medill

P.S. I hear from good authority that Long John intends stopping [publication of] the *Democrat* soon. I am inclined to believe it.

CHAPTER TWO

Barker's Dragoons, 1861

*You have no idea of the amount of discontent among
the men in camp at the ill treatment and neglect
received at the hands of the officers in control.*
—*William Medill*

When news of the capture of Fort Sumter reached Chicago, William responded by joining the Barker Dragoons on April 18, 1861. The *Chicago Tribune* followed the activities of Captain Barker's Dragoons closely, mentioning the unit almost daily, beginning in late April and continuing through the summer of 1861. They were one of the first Chicago units called to serve, and one might expect a Chicago newspaper to focus on them, but the coverage went well beyond that. First, the recruits went to Camp Yates near Springfield, Illinois, named for Richard Yates, Illinois governor elected in November 1860. Soon thereafter the unit transferred to Camp Defiance in Cairo, at the southernmost tip of Illinois, which is farther south than Richmond, Virginia. The Dragoons performed manual labor in Cairo for six weeks. The *Tribune's* coverage meant that the early history of the Chicago Dragoons was preserved.

Here is a sample of the level of detail of the *Tribune's* reporting, dated Monday, April 22, 1861, before the new unit departed for Springfield:

CAPT. BARKER'S DRAGOONS

We looked in at Capt. C. W. Barker's drill room on Saturday. He has a splendid body of men 140 strong. At their armory on Saturday evening they held a meeting when T. B. Carter, in behalf of the Chicago Bible Society, presented Capt. Barker with a beautifully bound Bible, and to each of the corps a testament. The Second Presbyterian Church, Rev. Dr. Patterson, have given the company a choicely selected Religious Library of 200 volumes. This morning the company are to attend church at Rev. Mr. Cox's Church, the Wabash Avenue Methodist Episcopal.

At the meeting on Saturday evening, Geo. W. Gage, Esq. made a brief and excellent speech on behalf of the War Committee, and the intention of that Committee to take care of the families of the soldiers who go [to] the war.[1]

William to James
Camp Yates [Springfield, Illinois], May 4, 1861

Bro James—

I wrote you a short note this morning, which I sent by Mr. Medill and promised to write more in detail this afternoon, which I shall now endeavor to comply with.

The Legislature adjourned yesterday noon after passing all the bills before it. Among others they passed a cavalry bill, which you no doubt have read. It provides that the men shall raise their own horses and in addition to their regular pay, they shall receive $8.00 per month for the use of the horses. Now sir, I never knew a nicer little piece of spending than this bill.

We were all taken aback at first, as but few had the means to buy a horse. But what was our astonishment when forward comes Meyers, Ogden & Hoffman and offer to furnish us all the horses we want, only charging the extra $8.00 allowed for doing so. The bill also provided that if the horses are killed or maimed in any way, so as to make them afterward useless, the State is to pay for them the original price—$110.00. Do you see what a nice little speculation is here made? Suppose they only get the contract on the two Chicago co's, which will number about 260 men, and it will cost them about $29,000, and on this they will receive nearly $1,500 interest per month, or at the rate of $18,000 per year!—nearly the principal. When the bill was introduced, it was pretended that in compelling the men to pay for their horses it was to make them *careful* of them. What do you think of this? My impression is that a little airing of this matter would do no harm, but I would not say that Meyers, Hoffman and Ogden were interested in the matter. I understand today that they have taken the contract to supply some other companies on the same terms. Another thing. A horse fit for service cannot be bought for $110.00. They put the price down to the lowest possible price in order to make as much as possible out of the speculation. I have not heard of a bigger d—d swindle than this for a long time. Just think what the State loses on these horses. Remember, too, that the State also furnishes the forage for the horses.

This is but a specimen of the way in which things are carried on. Whether it is best at this time to pitch into these matters, you are best able to decide.

It is my opinion that but few see through the matter. I don't think White [a correspondent for the *Tribune*] does, for I was talking to him on the subject the evening he left here.

You have no idea of the amount of discontent among the men in camp at the ill treatment and neglect received at the hands of the officers in control. Last evening three companies of the Chicago boys came up from the south and were marched into camp. They were two companies from the Big Muddy, Capt. Hayden and _____ and Capt. Harding's command from Cairo. Now these men are treated most shamefully. I hardly know how to tell you their wrongs. After doing all the dirty work at those two points, opening camp, cleaning up the surroundings and suffering all the privations that were put upon them, with scanty clothing and some of them sick, and just as they got things to rights, a regiment is sent down from here. They are superseded and sent to Springfield. This, of course, made them mad, but the worst was to come. They had never been mustered into the service by a competent officer, and now they are informed that it is exceedingly doubtful whether they can be accepted at all! Hayden's Zouaves may possibly get in to the ten regiment arrangement, but I don't think Harding's men will. After throwing up situations at home, going away down to that nasty rat hole Cairo, living like hogs, wearing out their clothes and almost their health, working like niggers in preparing the place for defense, and just when everything begins to move along a little like living, they are coolly sent to Camp Yates and dismissed with no remuneration but a month's pay $11.00. Most of the men have spent three times that amount buying things and preparing to go. Now all this matter, the whole of this d—d bungling, comes from the fool at the head of affairs.

Something ought to be done. Would it not be well for one of you *Tribune* men to come down here and see Gov. Yates and tell him that these complaints have been made and insist on his appointing a new staff? He is not ignorant of the matter, for he has been spoken to on the subject by members of both branches of the Legislature, and the complaints and threatenings of rebellion in the camp are getting louder and louder every day. How will it look in some of the secession papers that discontent exists in the ranks of our troops. Will it not inspire them with new courage?

Something must be done soon to save a general stampede among the men, and you can be sure that when a company goes home now in this humor, when another call comes for men, the State will find more difficulty in enlisting. I could fill a dozen sheets of paper with these complaints, but I have confined myself to only the Chicago boys.

As regards our company, the capt. says we are all to go, but I understand the law differently. He says it accepts all the men now in camp from Chicago into the regiment, while I contend that the section designating the number of men to a company makes it necessary to divide ours, and in doing so half of us must go home. The Bill says the two Chicago co's now in camp—the Dragoons and Washington Light Cavalry—shall constitute a part of the regiment. If our co. is divided then there are three co's in Camp Yates, and whichever half elects new officers will be excluded. Don't you think this is the meaning of the bill? I should not wonder if half of us should be sent back one of these fine mornings.

Guess I'll stop now. Tell Kate I'll write to her tomorrow.

Yours, W. H. Medill

The following letter from William to his sister-in-law, written while the Dragoons were stationed in Cairo, Illinois, sheds light on the circumstances surrounding their early service, as well as William's unfavorable assessment of Captain Barker's leadership.

William to his sister-in-law, Kate
Headquarters, Chicago Dragoons, Cairo, May 23, 1861

Dear Sister,

I received your letter yesterday and if it continues to rain for an hour or two I'll try and answer it. We left Springfield a week ago on Tuesday and after a tiresome ride in a crowded car over a dusty road of about 16 hours we arrived at the headquarters of the Western Division of the grand army, which is to descend upon the southerners like the Assyrians of old, and I must say I never was more disappointed in my life than at the town and the whole aspect of these surroundings. You have no idea of the dirty, dilapidated appearance of Cairo. It is about ten feet below the level of both rivers[2] and is protected by an embankment resembling a canal towpath, all around it a distance of some fifteen or twenty miles. It is called a levee, and this is what our company came to guard. Should it be broken the whole town and army could be drowned out. It is my candid opinion that the secessionists could knock it down in an hour or two with some heavy cannon, properly placed. Or if they could make a sudden attack with a couple of thousand men from Missouri up the Mississippi about five miles, they could cut a trench through and let the water in, now at high water. The force here is mostly located down at the point across the Ohio River, and as the Mississippi is narrow for a good way up, the crossing could be effected in a few minutes. For the purpose of these defenses, we want the heavy guns. Nothing but six pounders are in use at present. They are hardly sufficient to stop a boat in the middle of the river.

Well, the first night we were quartered in the wharf boat, which was very pleasant. But the next day we were sent up the Mississippi about 3 miles to Camp Smith, where we were located. We had some hard work to do. The ground was covered with all kinds of stuff—large cottonwood trees, underbrush, rubbish and poison ivy. I had not worked as hard for twelve years as I did clearing it away. The sun shone down very hot, and we Northerners suffered understandably from its effects. But just when we got it nicely cleared up and our tents pitched, orders came for us to move down the levee about halfway between Camp Smith and Camp Defiance. Some loud swearing was indulged in by some of the men, which all felt as though they were shamefully treated by someone. Since then we have been engaged in clearing up another piece of ground. Yesterday we pitched our tents and put up a stable for our horses. I feel almost used up from the effect of the heat and the labor. We had so much to do and all had to work. It will take two or three weeks to get all things to rights, as we have to grade the street in front of our tents and clear up two or three acres for a parade ground. I have no fancy for any such work. I didn't enlist for a farmer. My hands are all blistered and my face is getting badly sunburnt. But aside from this my appetite and health never was better. I can eat anything—except beef. I guess I weigh more than I ever did. I suppose I'll get over the effects of the hard work.

But then we have all a great many complaints to make. I have thought so much about it that I am almost ashamed to make them. In the first place we have been stinted ever since we have been here in provisions, and even what we do get are of the poorest kind. The meat is bad, the potatoes are little, and a great many are rotten. The bread is generally stale and some of the sugar and coffee is of the very cheapest quality and not enough to go around. While we were in Springfield the victuals were dealt out with a lavish hand; half the time we were supplied with double rations, but now when we have hard work to do we are stinted. This is pretty hard. I understand that the citizens of Chicago sent a quantity of good things to our company, and we have never seen anything of them. Our officers live well and can entertain their friends with the luxuries of the season while the men are put upon the poorest and shortest allowances. Something is awry. It is not a difficult matter to procure good provisions and any amount of them in Illinois. One man can buy enough bread and meat in Chicago to supply an army of 10,000. Just as I wrote to Mr. Medill, the officers are either unfit for their positions or they are stealing. Almost every copy of the Chicago papers one sees ever since the war broke out contains statements of the large quantities of clothing made up and sent to the volunteers from Chicago. Now our company did not receive a thing until last Saturday when we got a couple of woolen shirts, two pairs of socks, a pair of boots and a pair of blue overalls. We have seen nothing of our uniforms. I had to buy a pair of pantaloons the other day, as the pair I wore when I left Chicago became all worn out. Most every man in the company is in the same, or worse, condition. We are not an exception. Other companies are in the same condition. We supposed our uniforms were ready before we left Springfield, but what was our astonishment the other day to be informed by Mr. Tittsworth that he had been to the state officers about the matter, but they would not give him an order; so we had to each become individually responsible by signing an order for a month's pay to Mr. T. for them. What think you of that?

Then we have other things to complain of, but the most humiliating is the treatment received by our Capt. He has become a perfect tyrant and begins to show his nature. At home, he is a rather low fellow, and his only recommendation was a knowledge of cavalry tactics and bravery, but as a citizen, he was an associate of pretty hard people. Until we left Springfield we saw but little of him, and when he was in camp he acted very well for the reason that the men were not sworn in, and he dared not abuse them. But as soon as we were sworn in and we left Springfield, he commenced by appointing all the sergeants and corporals from the most disreputable members, with one or two exceptions. These men act in the capacity of overseers to the men when on guard or when working. It is not pleasant to be domineered over by a person one would not speak to in Chicago. But to cap the climax, last Saturday General Prentiss sent us to Capt. Barker to pick out the best and most trustworthy man in the company to act as a sort of special aide-de-camp, and who do you suppose was sent? I blush to think of it, and I have always been ashamed and astonished to think the person was a member of the company. Jerome Foster! He is one of the most disreputable characters in Chicago. He has been in the Bridewell [a prison for petty offenders] many times and ought to be in the Penitentiary now. Your husband can tell you about him. While we are digging up stumps and sweating in the sun Mr. Foster has a waiter and rooms at the St. Charles [a hotel in Cairo.] And this is the last appointment of Capt. Chas. W. Barker. Last night at roll call, Capt B. was in a towering passion because some of the men had not worked hard enough to suit him. He ripped and swore, and threatened to put anyone he caught loafing on guard [duty] for 48 hours, without relief. He has not said anything cross to me because I have said nothing to him. When I want a favor, I wait till he goes downtown, and then go to Lieut. Osband.³ But then it is humiliating to see the men he appoints to command you. I grin and bear, knowing that there is an end to all things human. I shouldn't wonder to see a general disbanding of the company when he attempts to swear us in for three years, which I understand will be attempted one of these days. I thought I would take the oath, but since I see the disposition of the Capt. and know that all the respectable members will leave, I have some hesitation. My patriotism is pretty strong but not sufficient for that.

Our horses were given to us last Sunday. I got a beautiful little mare, but she shows some symptoms of lameness. The ferrier [sic] says she has corns. I am not certain they were produced by *tight shoes* or not, but I know she has very *small feet*. If I remain this summer, I think I can make a perfect little pet out of her.

You say I have not acknowledged the receipt of the blanket and pillow or the money Mr. Medill was good enough to send to Mr. Hatch to let me have. I acknowledged them three different times. Once from Springfield, just as we were leaving town and twice from here. And I will now do so again. They are just what I want. I have had several opportunities of testing both. One night last week I was on guard all night, and it rained during the whole time. In the morning I was as dry and as comfortable as though I had been in my tent. The pillow is the envy of the company. I thank you from my heart for your kindness and will try to deserve them.

Although the weather is much more disagreeable, the location less pleasant and the work harder, I think I would prefer remaining here to returning to Springfield. We are in the midst of excitement. Every day or two some steamer is reported coming with secessionists on board. We all get ready. Clean our sabres, load our pistols and carbines and prepare, but thus far we have been disappointed. This morning we learned from General Prentiss that we would have a fight in less than ten days. We have been notified to drill three times a day and to double the guards at night. Whether we are to go to the secessionists or they are coming to us, we privates are not informed. All the boys are in high glee over it. If some of them get wounded during this infernal hot weather, they will wish they had stayed at home. As for myself I care but little one way or the other. I don't want to go home without a fight, and I suppose we are . . . well prepared for battle. . . .

There comes the call to get out our horses, and I will have to adjourn this till later in the afternoon.

5½ p.m.

I have just finished a good long drill and got my horse cleaned. My hand is rather nervous, which makes writing somewhat difficult.

About twice a day, the artillery company on the levee fire across the bow of some steamer. This always creates an excitement. As a general thing three or four companies of infantry are called to arms and rush down to the landing in double quick time. They take possession of her and overhand her cargo and take off everything contraband of war, and this consists of nearly everything carried as freight. I think it is a poor policy to permit any steamers to go south, as Jeff Davis does not permit any of them to return north. In a short time they will all be south so, when we come to make a descent on them, will be short of vessels to transport men. No more should be permitted to go below this point.

I have often heard of Cairo mosquitoes, but I never saw any of them till I came here. They are as large as two such grow in Chicago, and when they bite, it leaves a mark for three or four days. Several of our men got badly poisoned with ivy—one so much as to have to be removed to the hospital for a few days. Two or three others have been sick. The water is very disagreeable to a person not accustomed to it. It is almost thick with mud. However, I am getting to like it. I have not felt the least evil effects from its use.

I learn there is a box downtown for me. Probably it is the one you spoke of sending. If it is, I thank you for it in advance of knowing its actual contents. If it is not, I suppose it is from some of the boys in the office, as I learn they intend sending me some things.

I don't need a woolen blanket. Our company were well supplied with that description when we left Springfield. I would like a little apple butter if you have not sent the packet already. I see but few dainties. I find a greater lack from butter than anything else. I can live on bread and butter but poor bread without butter don't go down very well. The people around here make but little and charge such shameful prices as to make it robbery to use it. We can buy milk at 10 cents per quart. . . . The weather being warm the year round they [locals] live in the meanest hovels, made of round logs and chinked up with chips and mud. Ordinarily I would not live in this place for a good sum of money.

Do you know whether Mrs. Ann Chase's sister, Mrs. Edson lives? She used to live here. If she does now, I will call on her. I have not spoken to a woman since leaving Chicago. Should I remain for three years, I suppose I'd be afraid of them.

On Sunday last we had preaching in Camp Smith by Rev. Mr. Dickinson. His sermon was very interesting. Well, I must close as we have roll call in a few minutes. I suppose I have made numerous mistakes, and repetitions, and consequently it will be tiresome to read so much and find so little to interest.

You will have to follow the numbers of my paging[4] as I made some mistakes and I wrote in such a hurry.

Tell the children I'll send them a picture some of these days when I get my uniform. Respects to all friends.

Your affectionate brother,
W. H. Medill

WILLIAM TO JOSEPH
Camp Barker near Cairo, Illinois, June 9, 1861

Dear Joseph,

We will have to decide within a few days as to whether we will take the three years' oath or not. I suppose those who do not will be sent home at once without waiting for the three month's enlistment.

My going home or remaining here depends to a great measure upon what you think of it. I have many objections to the officers and internal arrangements of the camp, and should I take the oath for three years, I should try and get transferred to some other company. I don't want to return to Chicago if people would think I returned home through any cowardice and would rather choke down private feelings and humiliation and remain in the army.

My objections are these and every one of them are substantial. Drunken Captain, lieutenants and orderly; tyrannical sergeants and corporals; lazy disagreeable, incompetent commissary and very poor horses. These objections do not exist with me alone. Today when the question was asked the company, in order to discover how many will take the oath, more than half the company refused; and they were the best men in it, too. I refused to give a decision. Capt. Barker returns to Chicago tonight to enlist enough men to fill up the ranks.

Now then, I go or stay at your answer. Personally I cannot well afford to go at present. I must soon look out for a living for the future, but if you think the country needs me more than I do myself I'll stay.

Please answer by return mail. I am quite well. Regards to all.

Yours in haste
W. H. Medill

Before it became necessary to decide about a three-year enlistment, Gen. George McClellan visited Cairo to inspect the troops and fortifications. Barker's Chicago Dragoons impressed McClellan and he made them his bodyguards, ordering them to join him at Clarksburg, Virginia. For the next two months, the Chicago Dragoons were actively engaged in contests, including a brisk skirmish at Philippi;[5] fights at Buckhannon and Rich Mountain; and a battle near Beverly, in which the Confederates lost two hundred killed and wounded, two hundred prisoners, several pieces of artillery, and all their baggage. In this battle the Chicago Dragoons dismounted and fought as sharpshooters with revolving carbines, and William distinguished himself.

When the order to charge was given, William was among the foremost of his company to open the attack on the enemy. The fighting was done Indian fashion—every trooper took shelter behind a tree or log and dodged forward from one hiding place to another. In this encounter William became engaged with a Georgian lieutenant. Each took cover behind a small tree separated by a distance of about sixty yards. The rebel fired first but missed. William raised his carbine and fired, hitting the sapling behind the rebel; William then sprang forward, calling on the rebel to surrender or he would let daylight through him.

The officer threw down his gun and handed his sword to William, who marched him to the rear. William took the lieutenant's sword as a trophy, and it is now one of the artifacts preserved in the Robert R. McCormick Museum collection. After the battle of Beverly, the Chicago Dragoons joined the pursuit and helped defeat the enemy at Carrick's Ford, where the rebel General Garnett was killed and twelve hundred prisoners taken.

William expressed disappointment when Union forces did not pursue Confederates further. He indicated their force was 12,500 strong with five batteries of flying artillery, and the enemy was demoralized. He thought McClellan ought to pursue Confederates to Stalinton and continue a forced march toward Richmond, which William felt they could capture and hold with help from the navy. He optimistically thought they could achieve all of this in a week, marching across a state full of provisions on good roads that were easy to travel. He wrote, "Now is the time to strike vigorously at the secessionists. If I commanded this army, the pursuit would certainly be made. I like our General, but I think he is too cautious. He lacks boldness and enterprise."[6]

William to Joseph
Clarksburg, Virginia, June 27, 1861

Bro. Joseph,

From Parkersburg we were removed to this place, which is 84 miles from there and 22 miles from Grafton. This is the nearest point to the enemy, which is some 12 miles off, near Philippa. We are right in amongst what is known as the Blue Ridge Mountains. The town is beautifully located in the hills, and I should think contains 1,000 or 1,500 inhabitants. There are some

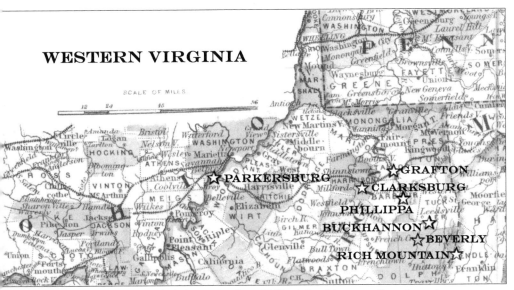

Action at Parkersburg, Clarksburg, Grafton, Philippi, Buckhannon, Beverly, and Rich Mountain, which at the time were part of western Virginia. (Library of Congress Geography and Map Division; adapted from Fisher's *A Chronological History of the Civil War in America*)

10 or 12 regiments of infantry, two cos. of artillery and our cavalry. Most of the infantry are from Ohio, and the remainder are from Indiana. In the 19th Ohio regiment is one company from Canton, commanded by Capt. Manderson, and the regiment is commanded by Col. Beatty, Sheriff of Stark Co. I know most of the boys. One of the artillery cos. is from Michigan, and the other is one United States co. lately quartered in Nebraska. They are splendid cos. In fact all the troops are good men and very anxious to proceed against the Chivalry, who are preparing, we learn, to attack us. Yesterday two regiments of Indiana troops were sent five miles on the Philippa road to guard a town, which was threatened. Two guards, belonging to one of the Ohio regiments, were shot night before last, and three secessionists were taken prisoner on suspicion of having perpetrated the deed. We sleep on our arms every night in preparation for an attack, our camp being in a somewhat exposed position. Gen. McClellan is at Grafton, and it is understood that as soon as he gets some men together he will attack Gen. Wise, who is encamped at a place called Tottersfield, I think.

Word has just arrived that the tenth Indiana regiment has been cut off from the front of the army by the secessionists at a bridge, eight miles from this place towards Philippa, and that five regiments from here, with artillery and our company are about to march upon them immediately. I am not certain that such is really the case. But I hope we will see some of them secessionists soon. Our sabers have become rusty often enough by water; it is time they were rusted by blood.

Now for a little personal matter. Since we left Cairo, our captain has treated us like a set of dogs. When we received the news in Cairo that we were coming here to fight, a test was made to find how many would enlist for three years, and all but three or four stepped out and cheered at the idea of having a chance. As we moved so suddenly the quartermaster did not have time to prepare our rations, so he gave Capt. Barker the money to purchase provisions for 110 men for eight days, three meals per day. How many meals do you suppose we received out of that money? *One* in Cincinnati and *five* in Parkersburg!—instead of *twenty four*. From Cairo to Cincinnati we did not get anything but what the people of Indiana gave us except a little dried beef. Some of us took the precaution to carry a few crackers in our haversacks. From Cincinnati to Parkersburg we received one meal, and after a 28-hour fast we got a miserable supper in Parkersburg about 11 o'clock on Saturday night after a walk for it of a mile and a half over bad roads.

Since we left Parkersburg we have been living on short allowances. But, as if to add insult to injury, when the ground was selected for our encampment, which is in an orchard, after pitching the Capt's tent, he ordered the tents for the men to be pitched in a line right over a ditch used as a drain, so that the center of our tents is this ditch, leaving a couple of feet only on either side to sleep. When we came to get all our things in—saddles, arms, clothing, etc. it didn't leave room to sleep without getting into the ditch. Since we have been in camp, two days, it has rained nearly all the time, as a consequence nearly all the men have been wet through their clothing and no chance to dry them. When Capt. Barker was told that the men could not sleep in such a place, he said he "did not care a d—m for the men," that *he* wanted the tents pitched there. He has kept us shut up in the camp, not allowing anyone to go outside the guard. Other troops have been seen to leave camp for an hour each day.

Other things are done in the same way. Men who have stood by the Capt. through thick and thin, evil as well as good, prepared to go for three years even if they were kept after the war was over, looked mad, but said nothing, hoping for the day of deliverance, which at last came. Capt. Garity of the U.S. Army came into camp to muster us in for three years. We were drawn up in two ranks, and after stating the object of his visit, he took the muster roll and called off the names, desiring those who were willing to go for the three years to step in front four paces. He first called the commissioned officers and sergeants, and they all stepped out. Next came the four corporals and then the privates. *Not a corporal and but eleven privates came forward!* Of course, there was no company to swear. Capt. Barker looked blank, and Capt. Switzer got on his horse and rode off. Barker gave us twenty minutes to hold a meeting and make out a statement of our grievances, and he would try to remedy them. We met, talked the matters over and passed a resolution that if our officers knew so little about the wants of their men as not to know the cause of their disaffection, then we did not wish to serve under them. Nothing more was wanting. Capt. Barker has not said anything since as to what he intends doing. The company is very anxious to go for war, and if we have a good, competent officer, we would have no hesitancy about going. If we do not reorganize, we will return to Chicago when the three months are up, which will be about the 20th of July. If we do, we will publish a statement of the causes of our returning. Since yesterday, three of the privates and two of the sergeants have refused to go.

P.S. We are ordered to hold ourselves ready to march at 7½ this evening to the relief of the Indiana troops. Two or three regiments will go along. If I have a chance, I'll write the effect. Our boys are in the highest glee over the chance. I would hate to get shot in the first fight, but I gladly run the chance for the purpose of getting a shot at some secessionist.

I have no idea where we will be located, so as to receive a letter or paper. I hope you did not send anything to Grafton, or I may never see that place, nor have a chance to receive a letter from there. I presume we will receive no pay till we return to Illinois. We are unsure of it, and the State should have given the boys some. Prentiss promised the boys their pay at home. They begin to lose confidence in everybody. No uniforms, no pay for victuals and mean officers tend to create discontent in many volunteers. I think the people of Chicago can find no fault with us for returning when they hear our cause. We are willing to go again under proper officers, or stay where we are if we can be furnished with arms. Capt. Barker will, no doubt, return to Illinois and recruit enough to fill up the co. He can get them at Cairo among the dissatisfied troops there. Consequently we will lose our arms.

You can use the facts in this letter as you think best. All can be substantiated and a great many other things which I have not detailed.

Give my love to Kate and the children. I have seen a Chicago paper and one from Cairo. Have you a correspondent here? You should as this will be as important a retelling of the army as any other.

Yours, etc. W. H. Medill

The enlistment agreement signed by each man in the Dragoons required only three month's service. When most men chose not to reenlist, they were sent home from Virginia, William Medill among them. After their commitment ended in July 1861, the soldiers of the unit wrote the following message:

To the Chicago Public:

That the Chicago Dragoons are now in this city, and not with Gen. McClellan, is the fault of but one person, and he is their Captain—Charles W. Barker.

The company left Chicago with almost implicit confidence in their Captain. They have gradually lost that confidence, and today the undersigned are those who refuse to serve under him any longer. We have been under his command three months and ten days, in the field and in camp. We ought to know the man. We pronounce him incompetent as an officer, and habitually dissipated.

We bear no malice against Capt. Barker. The majority of us will again enlist, but not under him. If others wish to do so we have no objections to make. . . .

There was a time when eighty odd men declared with wild cheers their willingness to go for three years. But, as they came to know the man better, to feel his indifference to their welfare, expressed, on one occasion when our line of tents was by his orders, pitched in a wet ditch, and he declared that he did not "care a damn for the men"; to endure his abusive language, and to know that he was not preparing them for encounters in which their lives and the glory of the nation were at stake—a change came over the spirit of their dreams [and] they determined to serve no longer under him.

The troopers cited examples of Captain Barker's shortcomings as an officer, alleging that he was insensitive and uncaring, a liar and a thief. Sixty-four Dragoons (58 percent) signed the accusing letter. Sixteen Dragoons (15 percent) signed a rebuttal letter. Thirty (27 percent) abstained. Only 21 of the 110 three-month Chicago Dragoons (19 percent) decided to stay with Captain Barker. Even so, by August 17, 1861, the company's rolls had once again been filled and officers elected.[7]

On August 10, the Chicago Dragoons had served a month over their time, returned home, and were mustered out of service. After a fortnight's rest and recreation, William Medill decided to reenter the service.[8]

CHAPTER THREE

The Eighth Illinois Cavalry, 1861

> We are progressing rapidly with our drilling,
> and the men begin to look like soldiers.
> —*William Medill*

Chicago Tribune, July 25, 1861, report on the Union defeat at Bull Run: "We have before us, then, a serious struggle, which demands all the strength of mind and body of the nation. Flippant talk in the streets of cities about the superiority of the North, and abusive editorials against secession leaders, or misrepresentations of the rebel strength by newspapers, must be abandoned.... Let us now take it for granted that we have a stern, obstinate struggle to pass through, that impatience of the operations of our generals, incendiary stimulus to our armies, self-flattering praises of our own valor, and depreciation of the enemy can never bear us through with success, and that the nation must now go on to the future impressed with the vast import of the events around them, and with a resolution henceforth to be calm and sagacious, as well as brave and patriotic—to be practical, as well as enthusiastic, in the conduct of hostilities."[1]

The shocking Union defeat at Bull Run was only the opening salvo. When President Lincoln called for five hundred thousand soldiers in July 1861, owners of the *Chicago Press and Tribune* recruited a company for the Eighth Illinois Cavalry. Joseph recruited twelve volunteers from the paper's staff the first day.[2]

Men leaving Barker's Dragoons mustered out on August 20, 1861, and on August 24, William Medill applied to Gen. J. F. Farnsworth at St. Charles, Illinois, for permission to recruit a company for the Eighth Cavalry, which was in the process of formation. Receiving permission, he recruited the "Fremont Dragoons" to the maximum in less than two weeks, and it became Company G, Eighth Illinois Cavalry. He was unanimously elected captain of the company.[3]

Colonel John F. Farnsworth to William

Chicago, August 26, 1861

Mr. W. H. Medill, Dear Sir,

Your application and also a letter from A. W. Adams, Esq. upon the same subject is received.

I will accept your company provided they are good men & ready to be mustered into service within two weeks from this date.

I have all the orders for horses, clothing, camp equipage, uniforms, arms, etc. etc.—& they will be ready as fast as any companies are ready to go into camp. Our especial desire, that only good reliable men may be enlisted.

Truly yours, Colonel J. F. Farnsworth

In the next letter, Andrew Patrick petitioned Joseph for political favors. Other men in Andrew's circle had profited from supplying horses to the army, and Andrew hoped to make money the same way. To do that, he prevailed on Joseph to provide him with an introduction to powerful Washington officials. No subsequent correspondence in the archive indicated that Joseph speculated or helped his brother-in-law supply horses during the Civil War. In fact, William weighed in on the other side of this issue, writing a letter scornful of profiteers.

Andrew opens his correspondence with family news, shrewdly letting Joseph know how well he took care of William as he passed through Ohio. We know from a letter William wrote November 2, 1861, the woman named Anne mentioned in the opening line was Kate and Andrew's sister and that Anne traveled with William from Illinois to Ohio.

Andrew J. Patrick to his brother-in-law, Joseph

New Philadelphia, Ohio, October 16, 1861

Dear Medill,

Anne's arrival last Wednesday evening was entirely unexpected. I had made my arrangements to start on Friday morning, but was thwarted in consequences of her arrival with "Will." The "Captain" remained here until Friday afternoon when I took him in my buggy to Massillon. As military men are always favorites with the ladies, he had a glorious time while in town. Anne had Lieut. James and a caudle of young ladies to tea for his benefit. Moffett says "Will" showed off decidedly to the best advantage. He appeared, or rather made those present believe, he knows more about military affairs than James who had been at West Point for five years. It is evident he possesses much more tact when off than either you or I or in our younger days. But to be candid, "Will" has much refined since his removal to Chicago. I was so much pleased with him that I made him a proposition and if I remain here, I believe he will become a resident of our town when the war is over.

In the last letter I recd. from you, I believe you stated that all *friendly* correspondence with you had ceased, not that you thought less of your old acquaintances, but that the stark realities of life—hardships—request your attention. The same remark I can apply to myself. So I take up my pen to offer you a line on the question of dollars and cents, in which we may both be benefited. But to the point. Lair Sargent and [illegible] Stuart are anxious to get a contract for one or two thousand horses for the government. They offered to make me a partner if I would go to Washington or in any way connect them to a contract. They proposed to give me one-third of the profits, and if the speculation should prove a failure, I was to lose nothing. They to furnish all the money, and I am to face no trouble whatever in bringing in or billing the horses. I told them I could write to you and, if you would assist me by entry to Chase[4] or any other influence you could bring to bear, I would then divide equally with you the one-third of the profits to which I would be entitled. This is the kind of speculation that would suit you and me—either of us would not have to advance a farthing. We would have no trouble in buying the horses, and yet if money would be lost, they do not ask us to bear any part of the loss.

Sargent proposes that you submit a bid in his name for 1,000 horses at $118 or $120 each—the horses to be delivered in Washington, Cincinnati or St. Louis. They think they can buy them here on an average of . . . $85 each and the other $15, making $100, will pay all expenses of buying and livery to the place where the horses are to be delivered. You see they would then clear $18 on each horse or $18,000 on the one thousand head. We would be entitled to $6,000 or $3,000 a piece on the profits.

O'Hara of Columbus cleared $20,000 on one thousand head and through Chase's influence he has got another contract for one thousand to be delivered in Cincinnati.

Think of this matter. We use nothing and gain everything.

They would be willing to deliver the horses in Chicago if you could get a contract to have them delivered at that point. Say nothing about this to any person—then we cannot succeed. Sargent and Stuart do not want it known that they attempted and failed. Write to me immediately on this subject and let me hear what you think on the subject. If we could get one contract, it would be the stepping stone to another.

A few weeks ago Sargent went to Washington and failed. Everything he says goes by favor, and he is too modest to contend with sharpers [swindlers].

The Union ticket was decided in this county by 400% majority. We had a splendid canvas, but toward the close of the campaign the humbug kept shady. Even on the day of the election not a single leader took the elect. as the peace. The soldiers called them secessionists, and thereby felt rather fearful in supporting the Union ticket. Some of the "unseparables" refused to vote. They declared it was a union of the "silver gray" Whigs and Douglas[5] men to crush out the anti-slavery element.

. . . When I was in Massillon, Mr. Pease . . . declared I was utterly too conservative for a good Republican. I am frequently charged with being an "old foggy." . . . The fiercest trouble results thru whether or not we were correct. But now that we are into this fight, we should indulge in no recrimination. The whole power of the government should be included to crush the rebellion. After it is over we can talk over what party or faction is to blame.

In next week's *Advocate,* not this week, you will find a song "For the Gallant Volunteers" written by Father. I think it contains the soul of the party. Show it to Kate.

My love to Kate and her two children. My careful heart waits to see her good-natured face.

Yours truly, Andrew Patrick

In her letter Mary Medill indicated she helped the war effort by working for the Soldiers' Aid Society, a women's organization that collected private donations and held "fairs" to provide clothing, medical supplies, and food to soldiers in the field.

Mary Medill to Joseph

October 16, 1861

Dear Brother,

The cars containing the cavalry regiment passed thro' here last night about 11 o.c. We saw Will a few minutes at the depot; he told us that he had not seen you or Sam, that the train left there shortly after he arrived, giving him no time to see anyone. It was not really necessary that he should have returned to meet the regiment, but receiving no dispatch to that effect, he was uneasy & tho't best to go. Beside that, he had some money in gold, which did not seem genuine. When he first came, it had spots over it & around the edge, like quicksilver. He tho't that it was from carrying it with some silver change in his pocket, but the next day there was no gold visible & it could not be distinguished from any silver coin. He said it was from a Chicago bank, & he wished to have it changed, but I think he had no time to attend to it. I forgot to ask him. Mother says the piece you sent her had spots on it, too, but she paid it out the next day. Have you any of it, it is spurious. Do you think he can pass it where he is going? I should like to know.

I sent a couple of little parcels by Will to Sam & your little ones. He said he left them in the office. Did you get them?

All are well, except my head. Mother is having a cistern made, with which she is much occupied. She is more reconciled about Will since seeing him.

My note, which you lost, was of no consequence. It is just as well that it so happened.

I find some employment now in being connected with a Soldiers' Aid Society, which has just been organized. It does not require much money to constitute membership, so I can contribute labor.

Love to you all, Yours affly. Mary

Before reporting to the Eastern Front, William traveled through Ohio and recounted his visit to his sister-in-law, Kate, providing her with reassuring family details.

When it came time for the Eighth Illinois regiment to choose field officers, William was offered the rank of major but declined it, preferring to be in direct command of his friends who had joined the company.[6]

WILLIAM TO KATE

Eighth Illinois, Camp Illinois, Washington, D.C., November 2, 1861

Sister Kate:

I have been waiting for a rainy day when I could have time to write you a letter. The looked for event has arrived; and, sitting in my tent, with a puddle of water between my feet, and the wind flapping the edges, and the rain beating against the canvass sides, I commence. Quite a storm of wind and rain opened upon us last night about nine o'clock, which has kept up from that time till now nine in the morning. We had been changing our tents during the day and some were not very securely pitched. The effect was to upset a large number and send the poor fellows chasing after their things through the rain and darkness. My tent did not fall, but the rain beat in through the door, and as much as a dozen pails full of water accumulated on one side. Strange it did not disturb me on my cot. I was tired, and slept soundly all night. Our camp is located on the place occupied by some infantry regiment, and the ground has been dug over, which makes it very soft and unpleasant during wet weather. But we have been fixing up and have it greatly improved since our arrival. A few more pleasant days and we would have had things pleasantly arranged. I suppose, however, we need not anticipate any change for some time.

But to commence at the beginning. I reached Massillon, in company with your sister, safe and sound, and proceeded with her to New Philadelphia; found your relations all well; mine ditto, had a good time all things considered; saw the regiment encamped near the town; took dinner with Andrew and tea with Mrs. Moffett; according to promise previous to leaving Chicago, she had Ellen there; also Leroy, Mrs. McFarlan and Miss Coventry; had a good supper and spent a very pleasant evening; found Andrew had to postpone the hour of departure till after dinner the next day. Visited around in the morning, took dinner with Abe, and at one o'clock on Friday Andrew and I started for Massillon, and I reached Canton in the evening of the same day. I believe this is the summing of my visit to New Philadelphia in the way of action. I made the discovery—and just as I supposed—that Miss Jones is engaged and will be married before a great while. I promised not to tell who the person is, but can assure you that he is a good fellow, and she thinks he will make a good husband. My impression of her was about correct, and you need give yourself no thought of our ever fancying each other. I don't know what Mrs. Moffett thinks, but I know what I think.

I found our folks all well in Canton. Father was improving and could sit up the greater part of the day. He has recovered his memory and reads and converses as readily as he did years ago. I was very much astonished to find such an improvement. His strength is not so much improved as his mind, but his pains are not so great. Mother is as healthy and vigorous as ever, and feels well. Mary was looking quite well; but thought she would not remain very long in Canton. Little Annie is growing very fast, and becoming invaluable to Mother. She learns rapidly, and unless Kitty and Nelly hurry up with their studies she will leave them far behind. I remained at home until Monday morning, and hearing nothing from Lieut. Forsyth, I started for Chicago. At Crestline I met the last of the horses and Lieut. Hynes; he said he thought the men would not leave St. Charles till Tuesday and I had plenty of time to go on to Chicago. I proceeded, and reached the city about three-quarters of an hour before the train containing the men started. I ran up to the office but did not see Mr. Medill. When the train started, I got on and went with the men. We reached this city on Friday, thus giving me a good long trip on the cars. It is much more tiresome traveling with troops than as a passenger—accommodations are not so good, and the cars travel slower. As regards the arrival here, and the location of the camp, you can gather a very good idea from a letter published in the *Tribune,* the other day, written by one of the members of this regiment.

When the weather is at all fit, we drill the men six hours per day, and have two hours of an officer's drill. This about fills up all our time. From six till nine at night we read "army tactics" and recite in the morning. During bad weather we read and write. We are progressing rapidly with our drilling, and the men begin to look like soldiers. Our saddles and overcoats have not arrived yet. Drilling the men is done mostly on foot. The officers have mounted drills.

I have been getting things into shipshape. The Lieutenants and myself purchased a nice little sheet-iron stove, and pots, pans, etc. and have our own mess. I have a first rate servant, who does the cooking, and Lieut. Forsyth's boy takes care of the tents, blacks our boots, etc. It is much more satisfactory acting as Captain than as private. We draw rations from the Quartermaster and make our expenses as light as possible. I am in hopes to save over $100 per month of my wages.

My horse stands it very well, but this stormy weather is severe on him. I keep him well blanketed. I would not part with him for a good advance on what I paid.

I have seen but little of Washington since coming. Can't say I like it. Take out the public buildings and the city don't amount to much. McClellan is very strict about soldiers and of leaving camp. Everyone in the cavalry must have a pass from Gen. Stoneman, from the col. down to a private unless they have the patrols take them up. This is a good regulation.[7]

The Eighth Illinois cavalry remained in the Washington vicinity several weeks. On October 21, 1861, soldiers of the regiment heard the cannons that accompanied the battle of Ball's Bluff but thought it was harmless artillery practice. When an epidemic of smallpox broke out, the entire regiment, from the colonel down, had to undergo the ordeal of vaccination. It was necessary to threaten one of the men with physical restraints before he would allow the doctor to scrape his arm.[8]

The regiment spent the winter of 1861 in Alexandria as part of the garrison. The men quarreled with U.S. Army Gen. William Redding Montgomery, federal military governor of Alexandria and rebel sympathizer, who took sides with the secesh inhabitants, removed the American flag from houses owned by rebels, drove off editors of Union newspapers, and spent hours denouncing abolitionists as being the cause of the war. Montgomery succeeded in getting the regiment removed from comfortable quarters and sent to camp on a low, wet piece of ground some distance beyond Alexandria, where the men were exposed to rain, snow, and knee-deep mud. Two-hundred-forty men came down with fevers; thirty-five brave boys died.[9]

William's letter of December 1861 mentioned his acquaintance with Horace White. At the outbreak of the Civil War, the *Chicago Tribune* made White a Washington correspondent, which also permitted him to hold the important post of clerk of the Senate Committee on Military Affairs, giving him a remarkable insight into the conduct of the war.[10]

William to Kate

Camp Illinois, December 1, 1861

Sister Kate:

I have attempted two or three times to answer your very acceptable letter, but as often have had to abandon it for another time. My duties seem to increase day by day. Until within a few days I could have a portion of the forenoon to myself by sending the sergeants with the company in squads to drill. But now we are compelled to have our company drills in the morning and get ready for regimental drill in the afternoon. By this arrangement all the day is taken up. Five evenings of the week are occupied in schools. This leaves but two evenings a week—and one of them being Sunday we are expected to attend church in our "Big Tent."

Well I was real glad to hear from you, and I would have you write often whether I write or not. It seems such a luxury to receive a good "newsy" letter from home. Your husband writes frequent enough, but he don't appear to have time to tell the news. Could I get the *Tribune* regularly it would partly answer the place of a letter; but I only received a copy about once in two weeks. It is only an irritation to receive it. Every piece of interesting news seems to lack a commencement, and I am certain I never see the conclusion of anything. I have tried every way in my power to get it. I suspected our Post Master of not doing his duty; so I got a pass and called on the Washington P. M. He said everything for our regiment was sent up by our regimental P. M. He was very impudent and would not give me much satisfaction. I asked him to send one of his clerks to examine the pile of papers lying in the office. This he refused positively to do. Since then I have not given myself any uneasiness on the matter but would very much like to receive it. Today I received a package, sent by Sammy, I guess, of four papers of the 18th, and two papers by the regular course, one of the 13th and the other the 7th of November. All these reached me by the same mail.

We are still in camp in the same place; but don't be astonished when I inform you that we are now ordered across the River into "Secessia." Immediately on the arrival of Gen. Sumner from California he detached us from Gen. Palmer's brigade of cavalry and attached us to his division, which is beyond

Alexandria on the most exposed part of the whole line. Thus are hurried right into active service, without as much preparation. I don't exactly understand why this course when there are two regiments of regulars lying along side of us nicely stowed away in winter quarters. We have not had any arms till now. On Saturday our pistols were brought up, and our sabers will be furnished within a week. We will be sent across within ten days, so I understand. This looks like York. Within a week more than 30 regiments have crossed the Potomac, which have been occupying camps near us. There seems to be a continuous stream going down 14th Street. Yesterday the 69th (Col. Carcaran's old regiment) struck their tents and marched across. It is a good body of men.

I suppose we have picket duty to perform. Our men are very willing to go but think Government should have provided us with arms sooner, in order that we have had some practice in their use.

We have had several visits from Chicago people lately. They all spoke well of our appearance. We have all our saddles and make a fine show on horseback. I have received the credit of not only having the best drilled company but the best squadron in the regiment. This morning at our regimental inspection the colonel complimented me for my squadron. You must know that I am senior captain and have two companies under my command—Captain Cleveland's and my own. The second captain has nothing to do when we are formed in regiment. I tell you I felt pleased, for some of our captains are always bragging about how well they keep their companies, and these same ones got together a week or two ago and purchased a sword and presented it to the colonel. I have no doubt the praise was awarded by the advice of Colonel Gamble. I am bound to keep ahead.

On Thanksgiving day we had a grand feast of oysters—that is, the men did. I went downtown and took dinner with the Sturges [sic] Rifles. [Illinois Sturgis Rifles was a separate company organized at Chicago and ordered to West Virginia to serve as bodyguards to General McClellan.] I sent you one of their bills of fare. So you will see I had my Thanksgiving as well as tho I had been in Chicago. The Sturges boys have a good time of it. Little to do and plenty to eat.

I received a letter from Sammy a few days since. He wrote me a very good letter. Today I received one from Nelly. She was well.

Congress meets tomorrow. A great many members are known here. I went down to see Horace White today but was unable to find him. Since returning to camp, however, I learned that, he is boarding with Judge Chipman on 7th street. If I can, I will go down tomorrow again and see him. I hope Congress will wade right into the negro business and abolish the institution.

We have not been paid yet. Some of us begin to feel the bottom of our purses. It is understood that we will get it on Thursday. This is a shame. Plenty of money, thousands of idle clerks and needy soldiers. When a soldier neglects his duty and is behind in performance, his Govt. makes a terrible fuss about it and threatens to take his life, but in fulfilling its contracts it is always late. We dare not even say a word in complaint for fear of courts martial. It's all one-sided when a man enlists.

Give my best regards to all your friends in New Philadelphia when you write; all those in Chicago. Love to Kitty and Nelly, and thank Nelly for her thoughtfulness in remembering me in her prayers.

Your Brother
Will H. M.

William to Joseph
Granwill, December 2, 1861; Camp California,
December 26, 1861, near Washington

[No salutation was written]

I received yours of the 25th this evening and hasten to answer. I acknowledged the receipt of the articles you sent me by express some days since and would have returned the other bridle at once but for two reasons, first, I have had no facilities for sending. The express office is in Washington, and we seldom have an opportunity of visiting that city. C B Waite [Battalion Quartermaster] has been negotiating with Messrs T and S for a saddle and equipments, and knowing that I had a bridle, requested me to keep it till he received a letter from them, and if he purchased, he would take the bridle, which would save at least the charges by express. Had I known Captain Cleveland was going to return to Chicago I should have sent it with him, but I did not know he had gone for two days afterwards. I will try and start it on Monday.

Now in regard to the money. I tried to explain why I had not sent it. We received pay for 1 month and 14 days, but were not paid for one month and six days after it was due. Our money pay amounts to $70 for captains, but there are extras, such as the pay for servant, rations, forage and commuted for, making up the whole amount to $150 per month. We draw nothing from the quartermasters department but take the whole in money. Then we have to turn round and pay for our rations for ourselves and servant, our forage, in cash. Thus the quartermaster buys certain articles from the government quartermaster, paying for it himself in cash, then we buy from our regimental quartermaster, and pay him in cash for these articles. On payday we have our rations commuted, that is govt. allows a certain amount for a ration in money—16 cents—and pays us that much for it in money.

Now the only articles we can buy from the Qr. M. Dept. are bacon, flour, sugar, coffee, tea and rice. Govt. don't keep potatoes, fresh meat, for sale to officers on the Potomac and when there is a scarcity of provisions, which is of frequent occurrence, we can't even buy what I above enumerated. Now I pretend to say that I live as cheaply as any officer in this regiment but I can't do much more than make my rations pay for what I want for myself and servant, at 16 cents per ration, or 84 cents per day at the rates I have to pay. You must remember that when I received my pay for one mo. and 14 days I had gone one month and six days in advance of my pay, that is, we only got pay for one month and 14 days while we had paid for our board for two months and 20 days. You speak of others having sent money home and of Lieut. Hynes among them. He did, but he is out of money now and tried to borrow $20 from me today to pay his board till next payday. He sent $125 home, he said he was sorry he had sent so much by 50.

Captain Cleveland you must remember had no expenses in raising a company and was not in camp by a month as I was and yet he received the same amount of pay I did. When he came here he had some $200. Previous to payday he had precious little left. I heard him refuse to lend $10 to Lieut. Forsyth. When he was paid, he sent all he had brought with him home. But he told me he didn't believe he could save a cent.

Lieut. Forsyth sent no money home and he tells me that he hasn't over $20 left. I forgot to mention that Hynes had not bought any arms, and if we should be ordered forward tomorrow he would be in a fix if he should fail to borrow. He manages to borrow from some of the men who are not on duty each day to drill.

The horses were not charged to the officers till after the payrolls were made out either, so you will see none of those, who sent money home have spent as little as I have by a long shot. I think I have explained where the money goes. Now I will inform you that I have not only paid my way since being here but have over $100 in my pocket. I must have another horse. My "Charley" can't stand it. Too much work for one horse living on short allowances and exposed to the weather. I expect to have to pay most of the price down. I might have taken a horse from my string but I would not pay $110 for one of them. So I preferred sending by some reliable person to Illinois, who was buying and get one.

As I told you in my last letter, I will send you over $200 next payday. I can send you the amount of my horse—$115, if you think I had better run the risk of being ordered out and have a sick horse, and probably not go, thereby endangering my commission now. I have been riding a horse of a sick man for two days, my horse having a very severe cold.

I am sorry things have turned out as they have, but I acted as I thought best under the circumstances.

We are all very well except bad colds. Weather very cold. Company is unpleasant therefore. We expect a fight soon. Things look serious. Regards to all. Hoping to hear from you soon, I remain,

W. H. Medill

CHAPTER FOUR

The Ditch-Digging Army of the Potomac, 1862

*Two such armies as these cause a great sacrifice to the
owners of land through which they pass.*
—*William Medill*

WILLIAM TO JAMES
Camp California,[1] Virginia, January 1, 1862

Bro. James:

I have commenced several letters to you but never had time to finish any of them, much to my regrets. However, I don't know that you would have experienced any great benefit from a perusal of any of them, farther than a satisfaction at knowing where I was and what I had been doing. Today being New Year's, and we have orders from Headquarters forbidding us to drill, I will endeavor to drop you a line, promising that I am not in the precise humor to write a good letter—being quite sleepy, having been on as "Officer of the Day" yesterday and was up nearly all last night.

Well, as you are no doubt aware, this regiment is now on the sacred soil of "Old Virginny." I will not detail our changes after leaving Camp Kane, in [St. Charles,] Illinois.

For three or four weeks we are encamped behind Washington until we received our arms when we were marched over here; which is about 10 miles from Washington and three from Alexandria. Our location is between and to the West of Forts Ellsworth and Lyon and back of Alexandria on what is known as the Little River Turnpike.

Clouds Mills are a few hundred yards beyond us on the same road. If you have a map of this army you can easily find us by first finding Fairfax Seminary. We are just South of that building at the juncture of the roads leading past the Seminary and to Mason's Hill—we are about three miles from our picket on Edson's Hill. This is a miserable, God forsaken country. It is Virginia all over. The earth is cropped out, until it is as poor as the Old Welty farm in Pike. The old hilltops can be seen for miles with their red tops. But it is not as broken a country as I expected to find. Western Virginia is ten times as bad. The aspect is about the same as through Pike Township. Previous to this war, there was a large portion of its surface covered with scrub pine, oak, etc. but now it is all cut down. Both armies have in turn had a hand in clearing up the timber, the rebels use it for wood, and we use it for wood and also cut it down to prevent the villains from concealing themselves in it. One can have some conception of the condition in which Europe must be in passing through here. Two such armies as these cause a great sacrifice to the owners of land through which they pass. I have often thought it strange and tyrannical for the European nations to force people by law to desist cutting timber unless by special permit. If this army goes through the rest of the South in the same manner it has through here, the same protection will be necessary in this country. The great majority of this land was owned by secessionists, and as such it is treated. Our men, at least, presume it did and so confiscate it. Outhouses, sheds, barns, houses, churches and school houses, are all appropriated in an alike manner. The men are not to be blamed for doing so either. They are not in comfortable quarters, but are kept in their tents without stoves, unless they choose to buy them with their own funds. This they have done to a large extent. Every mess in this regiment has a stove.

 I have no means of estimating the strength of this army but judge from what I have seen that it must number near 300,000. I have seen 30,000 out and only from one division. The division to which we are attached contains 27,000 under Gen. Sumner. We are near the left wing, next to Gen. Heintzelman's Division.

 We have not had any very active duties to perform as yet, but I would not be surprised to have a call soon. We are under orders to hold ourselves in readiness to move any hour. Preparations have been going on of late which portend a movement in some direction, and I am inclined to the opinion that it will be forward. We were reviewed and inspected yesterday and were instructed in regard to picket signals. These things are generally the forerunner of a fight. This is the first time this has taken place on the Potomac. We are all in high spirits over the prospects of a fight. It seems to be the impression that we can wipe out the disgrace of Bull's Run and teach these gentlemen that northern mud hills are better men than they are. At least we will do our best.

This regiment is said by all persons to be a little ahead of any similar one on the Potomac, not even excepting the celebrated 5th Regulars. Gen. French said yesterday that we were the best regiment he had ever seen, and he is Major of the 5th Regulars and what is more he said my company was the best one in the regiment. This was a very decided compliment. Well, I have worked hard to make it what it is and feel a pride in my company. Lieut. Col. Gamble frequently compliments my men on their good appearance. He, too, was in the Regular Service. Our men are a splendid body, and I don't wonder they attract so much attention. Our horses are by far superior to any in the service. We have them all assorted so that each squadron ride the same color of horses. My squadron have the dark bays. A squadron is composed of two companies, the captain on the right having command of both. When we are out as a regiment or battalion, we always turn out in squadrons, so that I really have charge of two companies. Capt. Cleveland is my 2nd Captain.

The men are all well and enjoy themselves first rate. Of course camp life agrees with me. I am heavier by ten pounds than when I returned from my three months' campaign. Yet, I don't like this life and would not stay a minute after it is over for a nice thing.

So it appears that we are not to have a fight with England after all unless she pitches in for want of cotton. It is cussed provoking to think that we are not in a position to take satisfaction out of the old hulk for past insults. If she will wait till we have put down this insurrection, I think we will be in a condition to accommodate her and France and Spain and any others she may choose to get to help her. But for the present, we are not ready to fight her. Lyman Trumbull[2] was up to see us a short time since, and he said that the feeling in the Senate and House was in favor of going to war with England just as soon as we end our present troubles. Must build some more ships, fortify our harbors and move our armies towards Canada. Then, sir, I would notify the British Minister to travel home and pitch in. I would teach the treacherous old beast that we, too, could play at the game of war. It has always been a pet idea with me to have a turn at England, and it seems too bad to be unable to accommodate her now when she is so willing.

Alexandria is a dirty old city containing more negroes than whites. Uncle Sam has taken possession of it and keeps the population loyal. He has one regiment in the city to act as police, while in rear of the place is Fort Ellsworth with 50 big rifled cannon pointing down on her ready to destroy every house on the first symptom of uneasiness. In front is the U. S. Steamer Pensacola with her tier of black muzzles pointing into her face. By these means Alexandria is made to appear like a Union town.

Chalmers Ingersoll is very well and wishes to be remembered to you and Hetta. He is a Sergeant. Walker Cassidy, Sherman Pray, etc. ask to be remembered. Can't you send me an occasional copy of the *Transcript?* I want to see what you have to say. I don't get much reading matter besides the cavalry tactics and army regulations, which are rather dry at times. My address is Company G, 8th Ill. Cavalry, Alexandria, Va.

Give my regards to Hetta, and remember me to all my acquaintances in Peoria. When you have time write to me.

Yours, etc. W. H. Medill

P. S. Are having the most delightful weather I ever saw. I am writing in my tent in my shirt sleeves and without a fire. Thus far we have not seen any snow and but little ice.

A letter William wrote in February 1862 still showed his support for Gen. George McClellan. By August 1862 William's opinion of McClellan's generalship and slow progress deteriorated to contempt.

William to an unknown family member

Tuesday evening, February 18, 1862

[No salutation]

I was compelled to discontinue my letter on Sunday evening and have not had time to resume it till now.

Well, we are all rejoicing over the glorious victories of our soldiers. We Illinoisans are especially jubilant over the results of our friends from our own state.[3] We are even envied by the troops from other states and many are the cheers given for the Suckers.[4] In my last [letter] I spoke of Gen. McClellan and those opposed to his policy. I have all along felt confidence in him, feeling that whenever he got things ready there would be a crashing among the bones of Secessia. I knew that there would be rapid work, short work and sure work. He has outgeneraled the rebels in Dixie and his enemies at home. The course he has pursued has raised him higher in my estimation than ever, evincing a determination and reliance upon his own judgment, which betokened greatness. No abuse, coaxing, threatening, bantering or political huckstering could swerve him in his course. The result we have before us.

Any man can see that with any change from the program adopted we never could have succeeded without great, great risk and a terrible loss of life. Gen. McClellan adds to his greatness as a general that most noble quality of human nature, an aversion to a wanton destruction of life. What's the saving of five hundred millions of dollars to the saving of one hundred thousand lives? I presume this army might advance on Manassas and in a desperate conflict lasting probably a week, killing on both sides near 100,000 men, we could drive them out and gratify some dissatisfied people at home and in Congress.[5] I set the loss of life high on the principle that the rebel fortifications are no better than ours, but I have every reason to believe that they are much superior, owing to the fact that we do not anticipate an attack and they do. Who would gain the glory of this victory? A few generals and, of course, Gen. McClellan would stand at the head. How does it stand? He has taken them in the rear and on both sides, leaving their grand army and impregnable batteries at Centreville, Bull Run, Manassas, on the Potomac and at Norfolk and thrown an army equal in numbers here behind them, cutting off their supplies and reinforcements, and by way of practice for this army fought three or four battles in about as many days, beating them each time and taking some 20,000 prisoners and an immense amount of supplies. All this has been done by his orders and in his own good, quiet way, while his enemies were quarreling over foolish stuff in Congress, and casting odium [widespread hatred or disgust] upon him at home even attempting to prove him to be disloyal toward the government.

WILLIAM TO KATE

1862

[The salutation and first page are missing.]

[We returned] to Alexandria. Old Montgomery[6] was hopping mad when he heard we were back, but he could do nothing. The next day, we turned out to receive *our* general [Major General Edwin V. Sumner] in splendid style. I never saw the men looking so well. Everyone felt good to see him, and he was delighted with their appearance. After reviewing the regiment he went to the company quarters and made a rigid inspection. The consequence was that he called on Montgomery and told him that the regiment was one of the best he had ever seen, and moreover that he had failed to see the slightest symptoms of insubordination. This was an awful rebuke; he further told Montgomery that the regiment should remain in Alexandria until such time as the army made a move. Thus we beat Gen. Montgomery and still remain a terror to traitors. Night before last one of our captains captured a secession mail carrier and his mail, which was on its way to Dixie via the Potomac in a little boat. It contained late northern papers, several letters and a map of our lines and camps, and several letters written in cipher. I supposed this line has been a regular one. . . .

No argument can convince me that Gen. Geo B. McClellan is not conducting this war in the only way which can effectually crush out the rebellion and teach the rebels and their leaders that they are inferior to the North.

But I must stop. The men of this regiment are fast getting well, and a few more weeks in our present quarters will place us on our feet again. I have taken day board with an old lady in the city and I have great fun with her. She is about half secesh; she speaks of the southern troops as "our men." I tell her great stories about what we intend doing with the prisoners we catch. She feels dreadfully about the poor fellows caught at Ft. Donelson. When I first went there to board, she was a little afraid, but I told her she need have no fears on my account. This town is full of secessionists. If there was a good man in command, millions of property could be taken.

I don't know of any other news, except a change, which has taken place in my company; Lieut. Forsyth has been promoted to the captain of Company A and Lieut. Hynes promoted to the 1st lieutenancy of my company. I consider it somewhat of an honor to have to furnish a captain for the colonel's home company.

Oh, I suppose you learned by a letter I wrote your husband that my horse died. It was a bad loss to me. I have another one, which I bought a little while previous to the death of my other one.

Give my regards to all my friends and my love to the children,
Your Brother, Will.

JAMES TO JOSEPH

Peoria, Illinois, February 19, 1862

Bro. Josep:

I am much obliged for the perusal of Bill's letter. Pity it is that five regiments was not sent into Kentucky.

My lecture at Ottawa was very well received, but the audience was small in consequence of the bitter cold, and of a St. Valentine's Day party at Judge Caton's.[7] About 200 invitations were issued. I received many congratulations.

Tomorrow night I shall lecture at Monmouth. The audience will be large. The preparations have been well made. A committee has charge of the matter. I am to receive $10 to cover expenses. This will be the first money received. At Lacon [Illinois] and Ottawa I footed my own bills and drummed up my own audience. Hereafter I shall let a committee perform all this labor. It is more satisfactory, insures a better house and pays better.

It is hardly worthwhile to build any hopes on the *Transcript* [*Daily Transcript,* Peoria, Illinois]. Under its present management it will never be a paying concern. I worked for it as hard and as faithfully as if it had been my own. But there is an utter lack of all system and judgment in its affairs. My extra labor was in vain. One day it is conducted by caprice and the next mulish obstinacy. I keep Emery square on two points—slavery and the Chicago *Journal*. On other matters he runs loose.

Herewith I send you an article for the *Tribune*. When I return from Monmouth, I shall send two or three more. I think the editorials of the paper possess abundant vigor but lack deliberation. This "puff" for Bennett was admirably written. I liked the style and temper.

Yours very truly, James C. Medill

WILLIAM TO JOSEPH
Alexandria, Virginia, March 19, 1862

Brother Joseph:

I returned to this place last evening shaking with the fever and ague [malaria] from Manassas where I left my company on Saturday.

I rode all day in a drenching rain, getting myself wet through, and my boots full of water, and at night I encamped under a tree and took a severe cold, rode all the next day in my wet clothes, and the next night at 11 o'clock we were called up to go out on the lines to relieve the regulars and while crossing Bull Run got my feet wet, which produced the ague. Otherwise I am in excellent health and spirits. I think I have the medicine to stop it and, if so, will return for duty tomorrow or the day following.

Well we have taken Manassas! Strange isn't it? For a year nearly Manassas has stood as an eyesore, a terror, a stumbling block in the way of the Union, no one daring to approach it, fearing that it might be an earthquake in waiting to swallow up the person foolhardy enough to venture near its yawning mouth. Every day since the Battle of Bull Run—I am almost ashamed to call it by that name—we have been apprised from different sources of some new defense, or some terrible engine of destruction, or a new mine under the earth filled with powder, etc. each sufficient to destroy an army, which had been placed at Manassas. We, the soldiers of the Army of the Potomac, had about come to the belief that we were all doomed to be killed. We felt like a man under sentence of death and had four or five months in which to prepare—the difference being that we were dying martyrs for our country.

Time rolled on until Monday, March 10th, 1862, when we were all ordered to prepare for an instant march. Everything had been packed for days before, wills made, changed and sent. Pictures taken, love letters written, boxes labeled and directions to those remaining given what to do with private effects should their owners get knocked on the head.

Well, we drew a long breath and *marched* and *marched* and *marched!* every hour expecting to hear the roar of the beginning battle. Still no warlike sound of danger could we hear. Monday evening we encamped about halfway between Alexandria and Manassas, near a former rebel breastwork. We all looked at it in wonderment and thought it a very *weak* contrivance of the enemy to lull us into the belief that they had no stronger positions. We were not to be fooled in that way. We knew better. Didn't we have in our pockets little extracts from Richmond papers in which its terrible strength for defense was spoken of as a maelstrom to engulf the approaching Yankee? Of course, we had. We could almost from these extracts make a diagram of the place, at least to suit our fancy.

Tuesday morning came after having spent a miserable night in trying to find the shady side of a tree (in which endeavor I failed and nearly froze with a clear, cold air and the sun shining brightly.) We got off about 11 o'clock a.m. and marched until 4 p.m. to where we formed a most beautiful camping ground. This brought us up to within 8 miles of Manassas. The division all settled down like a brood of chickens under the protecting wings of the most lovely forest of pines I ever saw and commenced eating hard bread and cackling about the dangers of tomorrow.

About dark a messenger appeared who reported that he heard it reported that Manassas was evacuated! More likely, Washington was evacuated. No such stuff would go down. The thing was so absurd that we were ashamed to talk about it.

That night we slept first-rate, dreaming all kinds of dreams, mingling up pleasant recollections of the past with awful scenes in the future. The morning found us up and dressed and ready for a march. We all expected an early start, so as to reach the enemy as soon as possible. Seven o'clock came, and no move; 8, 9, 10 and nothing to denote an advance. Wonder if we are not waiting to hear the engagement on the right wing. Probably we are only "reserve troops" after all. While these reflections are passing through our brains—we have been too long in the service to ask any questions—Lieut. Hynes, now Provost Marshal on Gen. Sumner's Staff, rides up to where we are and announces that "Manassas was evacuated on Sunday or Monday!" and that Gen. McClellan had already been there and was making his headquarters where Beauregard formerly had his. This was too much. Although it made a very brilliant power of imagination, yet this surpassed even my capacity. We looked blank at each other, then closely scrutinized Hynes's face to see if we could not detect a smile or something denoting a big story. But we could not. He swore it was true that Gen. Sumner had just gone over to meet McClellan at Centreville and, what was more, the rebels had run off in a *panic!*

Action at Orange & Alexandria R.R., Centreville and Manassas. (Library of Congress Geography and Map Division; adapted from Nicholson's *Map of Eastern Virginia*)

In less time than it takes to tell this to you, every man in the regiment knew it. All sorts of reasons for the retreat were given, but strange as it may seem there was a look of sad disappointment, a sort of "d—n the luck," expression on the countenance of every man especially among the boys of the 8th Ill. Cavalry. The men are disposed to find fault with the authorities for sending the regiment away from the West.

Well, the remainder of our march to "Union Mills Ford" [a defensive position for Manassas Junction] was accomplished without any particulars worthy of note except the very bad condition of the roads over which we passed. In fact, all the way from Alexandria out the roads were bad, but this last seemed to eclipse all the past. At Union Mills we came upon the rebel works of defense. We came from the woods, which is nearly all of this nasty little pine, right out upon an open field from which, stretching away off in every direction could be seen earthworks. The country is not level, nor yet are there any very high hills, but there were breastworks to be seen in every direction. To the right on the top of a point, there was a small earthwork on which they had a number of Quaker guns mounted [fake artillery made out of wood.] By the way, I observe the Philadelphia *Enquirer* denies that there were any wooden guns mounted in any of the rebel works on the authority of Cols. E. H. Wright and J. J. Astor. There were none at Manassas, but there were some dozen or twenty of these dummy guns on the top of the hill. I mention, as I can testify, as well as nearly every officer in our regiment!

To the left could be seen the hills protecting Manassas and forming the banks of Bull's Run and Cub Run.[8] We encamped there for the night. Next day I got permission to ride over to Manassas and down to the battlefield. Well, I never was more astonished or disappointed in my life. From the stone bridge to Manassas, I judge, is about 4 or 5 miles, and in that whole distance there was not a ditch or work that I could not ride over without any trouble. Why, sir, I passed all through western Virginia and from Washington to Manassas in eastern Virginia and I have not in all that time seen a piece of country natural or better calculated for a fair fight than thereabouts. Instead of the terrible rifle pits, forts, ditches, traps, hidden recesses, concentrated batteries, etc. told of by the cowards who ran on the 21st of last July and disgraced America, I found a very pretty open country, covered over with numerous substantial log huts vacated by the fleeing rebels on the 9th and 10th of March 1862.

The strongest protection they ever had was the natural banks of the Bull Run, which is a stream about the size of the Sandy in Ohio. We could have flanked them on any side and whipped their whole force, allowing them to have had 170,000 in three hours, and they could not have helped themselves.

Three thousand men on the top of Rich Mountain[9] in West, Va. were stronger than 20,000 at Bull Run or Manassas. You need place no confidence in what lying reporters say about its impregnability. Their object is to defend *somebody* for not advancing and retain permission to ride round with Charles Barker near the staff. I talked with some of them and know what I say. Manassas could have been taken any time during the past six months had the leaders been as capable of leading as the enlisted men to follow.

This is the end of Manassas.[10] It will stand as one of the biggest humbugs on record. Future travelers will point it out as the place where the rebels frightened 227 regiments of Union troops for six months with half the number. As for the battle of Bull Run it is impossible to find any person willing to admit that he was in it; whereas previous to our advance the heroes of that panic were as plenty as blackberries.

As usual there are large numbers of *Union* people to be found living in the country surrounding. I find on inquiry, however, that they are nearly all of recent arrival, having moved to Manassas from farther south for the purpose of speculating on the secession soldiers. Our men do not show them many favors. Whenever I meet one of these professed to be of the Union faith, I ask him to enlist and help put the traitors out of Virginia. I haven't got a recruit yet. Whenever they refuse I accuse them of being secessionists or cowards, and if they have any forage I seize it. I have commandeered about 1,000 bushels of oats in this manner since the advance.

The weather has been very unfavorable for marching or camping out. It has rained every other day regularly and sometimes twice. To be fully knee-deep in the mud is a luxury few can boast of. These hardships are beginning to show their effects upon our horses. We can count their ribs without the use of a telescope; also, on the men's clothing. Our *dress parades* are more frequently *mud parades.*

Here in Alexandria I find everything hurry and bustle of moving regiments. Not less than 60,000 or 70,000 troops have been sent down the Potomac since last Monday.[11] Fleet after fleet of steamers have gone down, loaded to the guards. One Tuesday twenty-six steamers, each carrying a regiment, moved down. Wednesday as many more started and today I don't know how many have gone. There are some thirty batteries of light artillery here waiting transportation. I am in great hopes we will go along, although I understand that our regiment has been ordered to Centreville to await further orders.

I don't know of any very interesting local news, except that C.W. Waite was arrested by Old Gen. Montgomery, compelled to quit the *Chronicle* and leave the City of Alexandria because he told the truth on the old devil. The remaining editor is a poor stick, and as soon as Waite was out of the paper, published a retraction and abused Waite like a pickpocket. If you exchange with the paper, I ask you as a favor to cut it off.

Well, this letter has consumed a part of two or three days in writing it. I will return to my company for duty in the morning, and I want it to answer for a family letter. I haven't time to write out in the field. You can let Kate and Sammy read it, and if you choose to waste a stamp, send it to Mary at home. I have got so far behind with my letters that I have not hopes of catching up. By the way, however, I think both you and Kate owe me a letter. I receive the *Tribune* much more regularly of late than I did before. Continue to send to Alexandria till I notify you to the contrary.

Tell Sam that I have bought another horse, and that he need not look any farther. I had to pay a big price, however.

We have not been paid yet. April 1st is the time set.

I have got over my ague now and am ready for work again. How I do wish we were in the West, where there is some fighting. Our lives appear too precious here in the East. I fear this regiment never will get a sight at a rebel army. I should be ashamed to return home without having been in battle. Give my best and kindest regards to all.

Yours, etc. etc. W. H. Medill

The spring campaign opened early in March with a sudden and unexpected Confederate evacuation of Manassas. Union cavalrymen were ordered to pursue the retreating rebels to the Rappahannock. Illinois troopers had the advance, and William Medill (then a senior captain) commanded the leading squadron. At Bealton's Station he came upon a battalion of rebel cavalry, drawn up on a hillside to receive him. William promptly brought his front into line and ordered his squadron to charge. Away they dashed on a gallop, and when within 100 yards, delivered a well-directed fire from their carbines. The rebels broke and fled and then commenced an exciting horse race for several miles. The rebels scattered, and William ordered his men to disperse as skirmishers, after them. The pursuit was continued to the Rappahannock, where most of the rebels escaped across a bridge, which they burned after crossing it. The rebel loss was two killed, twenty wounded, and twelve taken prisoners. After this affair, the Illinois cavalry returned to Alexandria. The following extract is from William's correspondence, April 19, 1862.[12] Portions repeat what William wrote to Joseph the preceding month, using different details.

We have actually taken Manassas without firing a shot. Astonishing is it not? For nine months it has stood as a menace and as a stumbling block in the pathway of the army. It was looked upon by many as an earthquake standing ready to swallow up all who might venture too near its yawning mouth. We have been assured by spies, by deserters, by Richmond and New York newspapers, that the country all about Manassas was naturally as impregnable as Gibraltar—that it had been converted into one tremendous fortification; the hillsides being honey-combed with rifle pits and covered with masked batteries. On March 10th, we started for the famous stronghold. I will not relate the feelings and talk of the soldiers, except that each considered himself a martyr about to be sacrificed for the sake of his country.

The first day's march brought our regiment within eight miles of the world-renowned stronghold. Tomorrow, the great battle would begin! The evening was spent cracking jokes. One said, our march reminded him of the fable in Aesop, of the tracks that all led into the sick lion's den—none leading out, and that he expected no tracks of this army would ever lead towards Alexandria. Next morning "boots and saddles" sounded, and forward we started, spread out like a fan as skirmishers, every minute expecting to run against a masked battery or be blown up by a hidden torpedo or mine. At nine, a halt was ordered. My Lieut., Hynes, who is acting Provost Marshal on Gen. Sumner's staff, galloped up to our regiment and cried out, "Manassas was evacuated two days ago, and the rebel army has skedaddled across the Rappahannock!" Incredulity was on every man's face, but the messenger declared it was true, and that Gen. McClellan was then occupying Beauregard's headquarters, that the rebels had run off in a panic, that their works of defense were all shams, that Gen. Sumner said that they had not numbered 60,000 men. That we all felt sheepish you may well imagine. Here was an army of almost a quarter of a million held at bay by this handful. For the first time, we began to lose confidence in our commander. All that Lieut. Hynes told us proved true. When we came upon the rebel lines, there was nothing to be seen but an open country, dotted over with little, trifling earthworks. The ditches and breastworks were poor apologies. I leaped my horse over all the obstructions met with ease.

On the top of a point of ground, where we first came upon the plains of Manassas, was an earthwork, on which the rebels had planted a number of wooden guns. By the way, I observe that some of the New York and Philadelphia papers deny that any wooden cannon were mounted in any of the forts, but I know better. There were a dozen or more in this one fort, as nearly every officer of my regiment can testify, for we handled them.

All the stories you have read about the wonderful strength of Manassas are bosh. I have seen several battlefields, but never beheld a piece of country in Virginia so favorable for a fair, stand-up, give-and-take fight. The strongest protection the rebels had was the natural banks of Bull Run, a small stream a few yards in width. We could have flanked them on either wing, and crushed them like an eggshell. Manassas will go down in history as the biggest humbug on record. Any time during the past four months it might have been taken, if our leaders had been as willing to show the way—as the soldiers were of following.

Armies devoured men on a scale never known before. *Tribune* readers shuddered when the paper had to print a supplement to list all the Illinois casualties suffered at Shiloh.[13] From his faraway position in the East, William decried the losses and commented on the Battle of Shiloh and Pittsburg Landing, which occurred April 6–7, 1862. After fighting ended, General Grant sent Brig. Gen. William T. Sherman with two brigades and Brig. Gen. Thomas J. Wood with his division to pursue Confederates. Col. Nathan Bedford Forrest commanded the Confederate rearguard, and his aggressive tactics at Fallen Timbers caused Union troops to fall back to Pittsburg Landing. Maj. Gen.

Henry Halleck then relieved Grant of field command, assumed control himself, and approached the next battleground at Corinth, Mississippi, with extreme caution.[14]

William also expressed strong opinions about tactics at Rich Mountain. On July 11, 1861, a Federal column had surprised a Confederate outpost. Badly outnumbered, Confederates eventually gave way, and Union General Rosecrans's troops took possession of the field.[15]

One of the engagements William participated in stopped too short, in his opinion. From September 12 to 15, 1861, Robert E. Lee attacked Brig. Gen. Joseph Reynolds's entrenchments on the summit of Cheat Mountain and in the Tygart Valley. The Confederate attacks were uncoordinated, and the Federal defense was stubborn. Lee called off the attack and withdrew to Valley Head on September 17. In October, Lee renewed operations against Laurel Mountain, but the operation was called off because of poor communication and lack of supplies. Lee was recalled to Richmond on October 30, 1861, after achieving little in western Virginia.[16] William despaired over a continued lack of progress, writing, "So you can go on through the whole catalog, and after each victory we have either remained on the ground or fallen back and given the rebels time to fortify some new position." From his point of view, Federal commanders squandered advantages.

WILLIAM TO JOSEPH
Old Quarters, Alexandria, Virginia, April 15, 1862

Bro. Joseph:

We (the regiment) returned from Warrenton Junction beyond Manassas on Saturday last for the purpose [of] going down the Potomac. Our division has been shipped more than two weeks, and I suppose they are at Yorktown. On my return I found your very welcome favor of the 3rd inst. and also several copies of the *Tribune,* which had accumulated during our absence.

The day following my last letter to you I rejoined the regiment at Manassas. Soon thereafter Gen. Sumner was ordered to move his army corps on towards the Rappahannock and drive the rebels across that river. In compliance therewith the different divisions were set in motion. The roads were in dreadful condition, and it was impossible for the infantry and wagons to make more than 10 or 15 miles per day. The first day out from Manassas we didn't see any rebels, nor the second until just at night when we had halted to go into camp. We discovered half a dozen of their mounted scouts on a hill a couple of miles beyond us. We were now within 12 miles of the Rappahannock at Warrenton Junction. Sumner's orders were to drive the rebels across the river and, if possible, compel them to destroy the bridges. In the morning Gen. Howard was ordered forward with his brigade, two batteries of artillery and our regiment of cavalry, light (that is, with two days' rations in haversack and one blanket.) By light we were on the move, all elated with the prospects of a day's sport. After we had proceed[ed] about 5 miles to a place called Bealton's, we came upon their pickets. My squadron was ordered forward to drive them in. This was our first experience in the business, and I felt a little curious to see how my men would act. Well, we galloped across the hill and through a strip of timber when we suddenly came upon a whole battalion of their cavalry drawn up (apparently to receive us) on the side of a hill. I at once brought the squadron front into line and rode towards them. When within about two hundred yards, and we were yet in the woods, they commenced beating a retreat. I ordered our men to discharge their carbines after them and make a charge. I tell you, the boys went at it with a will, but they were too fleet footed, and as we had a very bad ditch to cross before reaching the open ground, they made their escape. We chased them for about three miles when they commenced scattering over the country. I ordered my men to disperse as skirmishers and pursue them. The boys entered into the sport about as they would in a fox hunt. From this place to the river there was considerable skirmishing. We captured twelve prisoners in all, from whom we learned that we wounded about 20 and two mortally. The rebels crossed the river and burned the bridge just as was desired. Our artillery came up to the bank and fired shell into their works, driving them helter-skelter across the fields. We withdrew a mile or so back from the river and encamped for the night.

The rebels had about 8,000 near the opposite bank and a battery of artillery. The cavalry were the celebrated Black Horse and Prince William cavalry and Stuart's noted Georgia regiment. It was a battalion of this regiment my squadron chased. They are armed about as well as we are, so that the victory—had they stood their ground—would have been with the best men. Our horses are far superior to theirs.

The next day we returned to Warrenton Junction, and it was while returning that our men were captured. A rear guard was thrown out and these men were a portion of said guard. They became careless, and strayed from the road to a house about halfway between Rappahannock and the Junction where they ordered dinner, and while eating a party of the Prince William cavalry came upon them and snapped them up. There were four privates and one sergeant major and one adjutant taken at this place. A few miles from there a surgeon of one of the Irish regiments took one of the men belonging to a col. of our regiment and went to a house to purchase some butter, etc. and remained too long when the same party of rebels who captured the others dropped onto them, and this was the extent of the captures. I don't know the names of the privates, three of them belonged to Company H Capt. Hooker [Rufus M. Hooker] to Co. K Capt. Farnsworth [Elon J. Farnsworth] and to Co. C. Capt. Clark [Alpheus Clark] The adjutant was Horatio Lumbard, a brother of Frank and Jule of Chicago, and the sergeant major was Ed. M. Raworth, formerly of the Chicago Dragoons. These two officers had but recently joined the regiment from Chicago, and I presume had no realizing sense that we were in an enemy's country. They are responsible for the capture of the men under their charge and should be held accountable for the blunder. Gen. Sumner says their names shall be stricken from the rolls, and their pay stopped on account of it.

The health of the regiment is not so good as it was owing to the break out of measles among the men and severe colds brought on by the exposure we experienced at the Junction. For three days previous to leaving the Junction we were short of rations. Five crackers per man constituted the fare. We had but little forage for the horses and were compelled to swim a villainous creek to procure some wheat straw to keep the poor animals from starving. Our camp was on a low flat piece of ground and during those three days and nights it either rained, snowed or hailed incessantly until we were in mud up to our knees and slept on the wet ground at night. We had no covering except a rubber blanket and a woolen blanket. I never saw such a time and hope never to experience it again. Lt. Col Gamble says he never saw such severe weather during all the time he was in the regular army. To add to the misery, most of the men were nearly barefoot. The government contract boots are about as good as pasteboard. However, the boys stood it with little grumbling. We were finally relieved by the arrival of two New England regiments and McDowell's army. We had a good deal of trouble in returning, owing to the high water but finally got through.

We are quartered in our former quarters and feeding up our jaded horses and preparing for another move. All sorts of rumors are current among the men in regard to our destination. The latest is that Col. Farnsworth has been appointed Provost Marshal of Washington City, and that the regiment is to report there for patrol duty. Of course, I place no credit in this statement. Such a regiment as ours will never be put into police service of Washington. The river there is full of transport, and a large amount of artillery and baggage wagons are being shipped. Franklin's Division is waiting for shipment. Probably the appearance of the *Merrimack* has caused a suspension of transports down the river.

We are a little in doubts as to which side won the late battle at Pittsburg, Tenn. It was a bad fight, and our loss was terrible. Why didn't Grant pursue Beauregard and follow the victory by taking Corinth? There seems to be the worst kind of blundering in every battle our army has fought, commencing with Rich Mountain in western Va. when we could have driven the rebels beyond Staunton and joined McDowell in the battle of Manassas last July. We stopped short at Cheat Mountain and our army has been fighting there ever since. (So you can go on through the whole catalog, and after each victory we have either remained on the ground or fallen back and given the rebels time to fortify some new position.) I have got past the notion that bad roads are any hindrance to an army. If four horses cannot draw a cannon, six or eight can. It is cheaper for the government to buy a few thousand horses than to support a hundred thousand men for two months in waiting for good roads. Take for instance the Army of the Potomac. Two thousand extra horses would have been able to drag all the guns the most extravagant artillerist could have devised to take Manassas at any time since our regiment has been on the Potomac. How much the difference between the cost of the horses, supposing them of no account after the war, and what this army eat up during that time? But the men carrying on the war are regulars and will never have to pay any taxes.[17] I have but little fears but that we will whip them out, but what will we do with our debt? I am a young man, and I must say I have no fancy for paying taxes all my life.

Chaplain Matlack answered your inquiries in regard to the deaths in the regiment. I am not a major and don't expect to be until one of the present incumbents is killed or resigned, and I may do one or the other as soon as a major. If a vacancy should occur, I am certain of the position without opposition.

We have not been paid yet for January and February, and it is doubtful when we will be. Probably not until after the next payday which will be the first of next month. I don't know whether I will have any money to send to you this payday or not, owing to the purchase of that extra horse. I will send the $25 at any rate. Next time I will pay Geo. Armstrong. I consider myself out of debt now and two good horses ahead, if I had all my pay.

In regard to the Constitution, I cannot say much.[18] I suppose our regiment will vote against it pretty unanimously, although we have not talked or thought much about politics since being in the service. I consider it very wrong for the soldiers to vote, for their ballots will not be cast in accordance with their judgments, the men having no chance of reading or study[ing] the issue. If any of my men choose to vote for its adoption, I haven't the meanness to say aught against it. An officer stands in a delicate position towards his men. Were

I so disposed I could prevent any man in my command from voting who was in favor of its adoption, but the act would be the worst kind of tyranny.

I am in hopes of getting home by the 4th of July. I don't see how the rebels are going to hold out much longer.

The weather is very pleasant and warm at present, and I suppose it will continue on so.

Give my love to Kate and the children and tell Nelly to hurry and learn to write me that letter, as I am very anxious to hear from her direct. How's Kitty progressing? She will soon be able to write, won't she?

I am very busy making up my quarterly returns and must go at it again.

Yours, etc. W. H. Medill

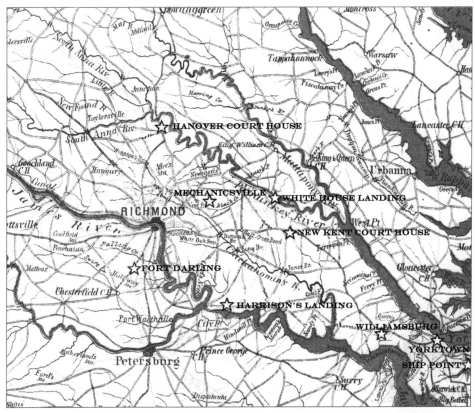

Action at Hanover Court House, Mechanicsville, New Kent Court House, White House Landing, Ft. Darling, Harrison's Landing, Williamsburg, Yorktown, and Ship Point. (Library of Congress Geography and Map Division; adapted from Nicholson's *Map of Eastern Virginia*)

I suppose if you direct to Alexandria the papers will be forwarded wherever I may go. W. H. M.

WILLIAM TO JOSEPH

Williamsburg, Virginia, May 7, 1862

Dear Brother—

I have commenced three or four letters to you, but have in each instance failed to finish. I must be very brief this time.

Our regiment was moved to Ship Point near Yorktown a short time after my last letter to you. We remained in camp there until last Sunday when it became known that the rebels had evacuated their position when we were ordered up in haste. We traveled all day and reached the rebels at this point. The regular cavalry were in advance. Not being exactly certain of the position of the rebels, they ran up upon their batteries, and one or two companies got badly used. Barker's company took another road when it suddenly found itself surrounded and before getting out had three or four killed and wounded. We were not in either of these fights on account of having taken a wrong road, which took us out of the way. The regulars lost some sixty killed and wounded. Night coming on and we not being supported by infantry or artillery fell back a mile or two for these forces to come up. All night they kept coming and all next day no cessation in the stream. Gen. Sumner opened the ball. All day firing was kept up. About four o'clock our right and left having got them flanked, the attack was made. The rout was sudden and complete. Their whole line gave way. Cavalry had no chance in the battle, but we have been running them down ever since. We have captured about 1,000 prisoners since the battle. I am not certain how many were killed in the fight, but think it must reach near 300 and of wounded about 500 or 800. We found nearly every house in this town filled with their wounded. As usual western men did the principal part of the fighting. Wisconsin men on the right and Michigan men on the left made the charges and won the day. Both were badly used up.

Well, where next? Their army here was fully 100,000 and yet they did not stand much of a fight. They are very much afraid of McClellan. I never saw better fortifications than they had at Yorktown and here. At the former it was a chain of works, while here it was a succession of square earthworks. An army of 5,000 ought to have held them against 200,000. I must close as the mail is leaving.

I left my trunk in Alexandria, Va. with Mrs. Martha King, No. 44 King Street, where if any accident happens to me, you can get it. I have hear no news since Saturday last. You need not send me the *Tribune* any longer as I will not be able to get it till it is too old. Letters can be directed to Ft. Monroe to be forwarded to me in care of Sumner's Army Corps.

I will write you whenever I have a chance. Kate's letter was received. Love to her and children and regards to all.

In haste, Yours, etc. W. H. Medill

WILLIAM TO KATE
New Kent Court House, Virginia, Sunday, May 11, 1862

Dear Sister Kate:

I commenced a letter to you from Williamsburg the other day but just when I had it commenced the bugle sounded "to horse," and we had to start. We are just informed that a mail will be sent from our regiment at 10 o'clock this morning; and I will try and take time enough to write you a short letter.

When I ended my three months experience, I thought I had seen about all the hardships of a soldier's life, but I now see that like married life it was but the "honey-moon" to the future. I also thought an officer had an uninterrupted pleasant time but I now discover that his position is worse than that of the men. He is not furnished rations nor nothing and is compelled to pick up both just as circumstances will permit, and is never permitted to even hint at being tired at his way of living. Ever since the commencement of the movement of this army in March this regiment has had a hard time of it. While on the Rappahannock we were nearly starved and frozen. Here we are nearly starved to death and run to death. For three days and nights we have not taken the saddles off our horses, nor undressed or disarmed ourselves. Last night and the night previous we traveled nearly all night.

Gen. Stoneman was sent forward with three thousand infantry and about the same number of cavalry and two batteries of artillery to fall upon the rear of the retreating rebels for the purpose of harassing them and picking up stragglers. He has been very successful and has kept them in a continued state of alarm. They have not dared to leave a rear guard farther than fifty or a hundred yards behind their main column or else we pick them up. During the past three days we have captured near 800 prisoners and a large number of horses and wagons. It has been the good fortune of this regiment to capture nearly the whole of the fellows who caught our men on the Rappahannock. But since leaving Yorktown we have lost four more by straggling. Their names were Quartermaster Chamberlain and his son, Sergeant Stanley and a private of Co. D. They were out looking for forage near Williamsburg when a party of rebel cavalry settled down on them. Yesterday we made a reconnaissance from here about six miles beyond when suddenly our left battalion came upon a battery and three regiments of infantry and cavalry, when the battery fired upon them with shell, which exploded right in among the horses, wounding three or four but doing no further damage.

The battalion fell back about a hundred yards and formed in line of battle and waited an approach, but the "rebs" failed to show themselves. The right was not molested although we were three miles beyond where the other battalion was met. We advanced on two roads. This will account for the non-molestation of our force. We are informed that the enemy have retreated to Chickahominy Creek, about 15 miles from here where commences their fortifications for the defense of Richmond, this, of course, I don't believe. Their prisoners contradict each other. Some say that all the way from Chickahominy to Richmond the country is defended by earthworks. Others say there is nothing of the kind.

I am just informed that the mail is ready to start and I must close. I haven't written anything that I wanted to. I will try and write another one soon. I have captured a present for you in the shape of a pretty little horse, which I will endeavor to bring home with me. Tell Mr. Medill that Gen. Sumner was the man who won the battle at Williamsburg, but owing to the jealousy of McClellan and other army officers who control newspaper reporters his name has not been mentioned. I know what I am talking about, for I was near him all day. Love to all, Your brother Wm. H. Medill

William to Joseph

In Camp within 23 miles of Richmond, Virginia, May 17, 1862

Bro. Joseph:

We are under marching orders at 12 p.m. today and it is now 9 a.m. In the meantime I will try and write a few lines.

In the first place I want to correct two or three mistakes I find in the *Tribune* of the 8th and 9th insts. First, the "gentleman from Washington" was very badly mistaken in reporting Col. J.F. Farnsworth[19] as being sick in Washington, while his regiment was at Williamsburg, Va. Col. Farnsworth on the contrary has not been unwell but once since the organization of the regiment to this present time and that was when we were on the Rappahannock. The cause of it was, no doubt, owing to the order received to fall back and not cross the river and fight Stuart's Georgia cavalry. The Colonel was exceedingly anxious to test the merits of that somewhat celebrated regiment. Col. F. was present at the embarkation of every man of the regiment at Alexandria and has continued with the men ever since, leading them on all marches and on most every scout of any importance. By way of parenthesis, allow me to say that

Col. F. is the idol of the men and officers for his bravery, coolness, judgment, kindness and military bearing. No regiment of cavalry in the army under McClellan stand higher in the estimation of the generals than this one. We are now attached to Gen. [George] Stoneman's advance brigade, and we are the first to drive in the rebel pickets at every movement. This is looked upon as an especial honor.

The second mistake I notice, is a report that two companies of the 8th Ill. were taken prisoners at Williamsburg. This is false. We were present at the battle and witnessed most of it, but we were not engaged, being placed as support to a battery and a regiment of infantry. On the day previous to the main fighting two companies of the 6th regiment got into an ambush of the rebels and were badly cut up. Our regiment being with them in the brigade, I suppose, got the reporters mixed up. We did not lose a man.

The third thing I want to correct is that to Gen. [Edwin Vose] Sumner is due the victory at Williamsburg. He came up with [Samuel P.] Heintzelman's division on Sunday, and without waiting for the rebels to fortify and strengthen their position attacked them vigorously and on Monday evening drove them from their position, which was as strong as that at Yorktown. I presume the omission of his name from the reports of Gen. McClellan is owning to this divergence from his plan of operations, which appears to be to await for the "rebs" to fortify and then by making stronger works, drive them out. It may be good practice for his engineers but death on the soldiers. Sumner, not being a West Pointer, didn't ascent in this light. When McClellan came up on Monday evening, he was so vexed at what Sumner had done that he ordered the old man to at once return to his division at Yorktown that same night, and in his reports of the battle he puffs two pro-slavery brigade generals for doing simply what Gen. Sumner planned for them to execute. I learn that Gen. S. feels very badly about it, and for his sake take only anti-slavery men in command in this army. The facts should be known. I am not speaking from hearsay but from what I saw. Col. Farnsworth and I rode over the field during the fight for two hours, and so I am able to back up what I state. As regards the newspaper accounts, I presume all the letters from reporters are revised before being sent to headquarters, which will account for their silence.

Another piece of information has just come to light in regard to the regulars. It appears that Major Williams, who has been in command of the Sixth Regular Cavalry in Stoneman's brigade, has been doing a kind of wholesale and retail business for the rebels, in protecting their property and giving them information as to our movements. He is a nephew of the rebel General Lee, and a relation of Col. Lee, who owns the "White House" near this point. He was extremely busy in securing all the property and slaves of the rebel col. during our stay at the White House farm; he issued orders against the soldiers trespassing on the premises or taking any of the chickens and had a guard placed all round the house and gardens. It is known that on Saturday last Col. Lee paid him a visit at the White House farm and on Monday last Lee's overseer was permitted to return to watch after the interests of the place, not withstanding it was known that this man had been in the rebel army as an officer. Gen. Stoneman has a design on giving Williams a long halter as he suspected his loyalty, but not having sufficient testimony to convict him, was obliged to permit him to remain in command. However, on Thursday last the evidence of his guilt came tumbling in, in the shape of an attempt to sacrifice our whole brigade—he made out a full statement of our position, numbers, etc. and by the aid of two orderlies he sent these facts to the enemy. I am not certain how these facts were discovered but suppose Maj. Allen Pinkerton could tell. It was discovered that in placing our picket lines in front of the rebels, he left a mile and a half between our pickets and those of the next brigade with the evident intention of permitting rebels to pass through this opening and cut us off. It was discovered in time to remedy the danger. He is now under arrest, awaiting trial. Major Williams was born in the Dist. of Columbia, which is equivalent to being disloyal.[20]

Well, we are now getting up near the rebel capital, and every one begins to hold his breath in suspense to know what is in store for him; whether there will be another cowardly evacuation, or a terrible and decisive battle in defense of what they profess to hold dear. I incline to the opinion that there will be a fight somewhere between here and Richmond, and that it will be a very desperate one. They have the men and all the chances necessary for such a conflict. If such is the case, look out for an eclipse of all previous engagements.

The weather is very warm, and the roads are tolerably good, but all bridges are burned to retard our progress. There are some magnificent farms on our route, and a great many slaves are still left on them. These are fast taking leave of "old Virginny" and the pleasantness of the gratuitous labors.

Our men are in good health and spirits, hoping that the rebellion will soon be crushed out. We all expect to be home by this 4th of July. Rebellion must soon give way.

I must close as we are nearly ready to start. Many interruptions have prevented me from writing as carefully as I desired. You can use such facts as you consider worth publishing but don't let my name be known.

You can send me the *Tribune* by directing it to Washington to be forwarded to McClellan's headquarters. Letters in the same way. You can make mention of this fact for the benefit of those desiring to write to friends in this regiment.

Love and regards to all your family, Yours W. H. Medill

WILLIAM TO KATE
In Bivouac, 16 miles from Richmond, Virginia (C.S.A.),
Monday, May 19, 1862

Sister Kate:

Having a few minutes to spare, I will take advantage of the time to drop you a line. I wrote Mr. Medill a letter a day or two ago, giving him our location, etc., and telling him we were on the point of marching. Since then we have made another advance towards the sacred city of Richmond, "C.S.A." Our progress is necessarily slow, owing to the number of bridges to build, and the caution necessary in advancing on such an immense army as the Confederates have assembled to oppose us, and our limited knowledge of the country through which we are passing. We find their pickets at every turn in the road, and to drive in a picket post has become such a common occurrence as no longer to be spoken of as an achievement.

Yesterday I was in the advance, and made an extension reconnaissance towards the Chickahominy Creek to within ten or twelve miles of Richmond. I drove them over; but found a battery posted on the opposite bank, ready to give me a warm reception. My orders, however, were not to bring on an engagement but merely to find where they were posted. This accomplished, I returned. The "rebs" have not destroyed the bridge yet but have everything prepared to burn it. Another squadron of our regiment which advanced on another road, captured a negro, who was returning in a buggy from Richmond, where he had been for the purpose of returning an officer to his regiment at the city, who had been on a visit to his aunt, living near where we are encamped. The darkey had left Richmond but two hours previous to his capture and had a pass from Gen. Winder, Provost Marshal of Richmond dated at 3 o'clock, a.m. Sunday, May 18th. He also had papers of the 17th for his mistress, all of which, of course, were confiscated for the public good. The darkey was particularly pleased to find himself in the hands of the Yankees and voluntarily gave full particulars of everything he saw and heard. He says he heard a col. telling the young man whom he carried to Richmond that if McClellan brought up all his army, Richmond would fall without much of a fight; he also says everything is in the wildest confusion in and around the city—soldiers, negroes, women, children, citizens—all in a mass, filling the streets. Nearly all the rich have evacuated their homes and fled farther South, while the poor are wandering about the city, not knowing where to go or what to do. He further asserts that there are no catch works between here and the city, and but few soldiers—not over 10,000 or 12,000—and that the works for the defense of the place are built within one or two miles of the city, which will, in case they attempt to make a stand, compel McClellan to bombard Richmond. This fact has produced a terrible panic among all those who intended to remain. They would much prefer that the city should be given up than to force upon themselves the calamity of a bombardment. The papers speak of the "cowards" and "sneaks" of Richmond, who would prefer the surrender of their national capitol rather than have a few dollars worth of property destroyed. From the tone and spirit, I am led to believe that they are confused to know how to act, although they publish resolutions passed by the legislature calling upon Jeff Davis to defend the city even if the Yankee mercenaries bombard it. Jeff promises to stand by Virginia and never forsake her till the last drop of chivalric blood has been spilled. How generous, how magnanimous in Mr. Davis, to be willing to pour out the blood of the F.F.V. [First Families of Virginia] so universally, but he don't say anything about what he intends to do with his own precious fluid. Probably he intends saving it for the "last ditch."

The papers are full of advertisements of patriotic men desirous of raising guerilla companies, whose mission it shall be to avenge the death of some cutthroat who has been killed by our troops. They all breathe forth the same bloodthirsty desire of sneaking upon men unawares and killing them in an unsuspecting moment. My opinion is that after the fall of Richmond, the whole rebel army will be turned into guerilla bands to prowl through the state, murdering, destroying and robbing. If such is the case, McClellan will have to adopt stringent measures to put a stop to their performances.

This is the condition of affairs as I write. I know not, but rather think that ere this reaches you, you will have heard of the fall of Richmond. I hope to spend next Sunday there.

The country through which we are now passing is a very rich one, and the people evidently did not expect us this way, for we find them all at home. In all the distance from ship point to this place, I have not seen as many families at home as I saw yesterday in a march of one day. They were in terrible trepidation, not knowing what we were going to do. The white men we confused and scared, stammered and promised. The white women were impudent and presumptive, bold and coarse in their avowals of secession, while the negroes were as happy as larks, grinning all over and carrying buckets of water to the gates for us to drink. Our appearance was hailed with delight, as the beginning of the end of their bondage.

I noticed a good many of our men who have been inclined to pro-slaveryism, saying they would be glad to see every negro free. Farms here are of a tremendous size, varying from 1,000 to 40,000 acres; a large amount is not under cultivation, having been worn out ten or twelve years since and turned over to the production of a species of stunted pine, which grows in great abundance in this state.

Slaves are very plenty. I have seen as many as fifty on a single plantation. I am getting accustomed to seeing slaves. We are passing through historical scenes. Washington, Jefferson, Madison and the great men of our early history used to tramp over this state when they were not more than my own age. I

White House, formerly residence of Mrs. Custis Washington, but by May 17, 1862, the residence of Colonel Lee, C.S.A. "White House on the Pamunkey," residence of Gen. W. H. F. Lee and later headquarters of Gen. George B. McClellan at White House Landing, Virginia. Image created in 1862 before the property was damaged. (Library of Congress Prints and Photographs Division)

White House Landing, Virginia, ruins of the White House, burnt during the Federal evacuation. Some of the sites of the Seven Days' Battles (June 25–July 1) were photographed only after the fall of Richmond. (Library of Congress Prints and Photographs Division)

have been in the "White House," where George Washington courted and married Mrs. Custis. The house is a plain one, but the scenery about it is the prettiest I ever saw. The Pamunkey River runs by the door, and the R. R. passed about ¼ of a mile away. All the old landmarks are preserved even the old tree under which Washington's servant stood holding the gent's horse while he was courting the widow.

Romance is written everywhere, and I wonder not that Washington's heart was filled with love while stopping at the White House. Even I would be tempted to make love to a handsome widow if I found one in such a delightful spot. It seems too bad to occupy such a beautiful farm as that one for a camping ground. We found every fence up and the whole farm in the most perfect order. Three days since I was there when I found nearly 100,000 soldiers settled down on the meadows and fields, and there was not a fence to be seen as far as the eye could reach, nor a piece of wheat or clover not eaten up or tramped down by the cavalry or artillery.

We are finding plenty of forage through this country for our horses, which with the grass is improving them very perceptibly. The rebels were far from being in straightened circumstances for food or forage. Every plantation is supplied with abundance of corn and wheat. Last season the planters planted but little else than these two varieties of grain. However, we find considerable tobacco still remaining in the barns. Our men supply themselves in the vast quantities of the weed. In my next letter, I hope to be able to give you the continuation of our trip to Richmond and probably a few jottings in regard to the appearance of that celebrated town, which will afford me great pleasure, I assure you.

And so your sister Anne heard about a friendship letter I wrote Miss Ellen Janes, did she? I cannot see anything wrong in writing such a letter to a good girl, even if she is engaged to be married when it is done at her request. By the way has Ellen and Lou Anderman "made up" yet? Hope they will get married as Ellen is old enough to need a husband if she ever gets one, and the poor thing wants one badly enough, I know.

Give my regards to Mrs. Moffett, Mr. Moffett and all the little Moffetts when you write again. I promised to write Mr. Moffett a letter, but I have never found time to write him such a one as I liked to do. I will try and fulfill my promise if we get Richmond.

I begin to get sick of this life and can wish with a will that the war was over and are all ready to return home. The rough manner of living, the roving life the absence from refinement, causes me to wonder whether I will ever be fit for anything again. I am afraid of the effect on the army of young men.

My paper admonishes me to suspend this letter, and I have no doubt your patience is wearied. By the way, I enclose a ladies collar which I picked on the road in an envelope, directed to Miss Mary Brumber, Dunston Station from Richmond. No writing was on it. You can have it as a relic. I don't suppose it is worth much. Give my love to the children and tell Nelly I am waiting patiently for that letter. Write soon and direct to Washington to be forwarded.

Your Brother, Will H. Medill

WILLIAM TO MARY
Seven Miles from Richmond, Virginia, Friday, May 23, 1862

Dear Sister:

For want of time I have deferred writing to you and this morning I will, while my darkey boy, "Olie," is cooking breakfast, let you and the family know my whereabouts and the condition of my health.

From the heading, you will perceive that I am within seven miles of Richmond, Va. We landed at Shipping Point, near Fortress Monroe a few days before the evacuation of Yorktown, and when that event occurred, all the cavalry were sent in pursuit of the flying rebels. One day's march brought us up to them at Williamsburg, where the next day occurred a very hard fought battle. The rebels occupied a strong position behind entrenchments and a swamp. Having a couple of days the start of us, they had time to rest, while our men marched over a bad road 20 miles and then attacked them. The battle was a stubborn one and nearly 2,500 on a side were killed or wounded. Owing to the location, cavalry could do nothing but look on and support the infantry and artillery. Thus our regiment was drawn up in line of battle and were compelled to be silent spectators of the fight. Towards evening our whole force of infantry and artillery made a combined assault on their line and drove them out, making it a complete rout. In one of the redoubts we found over 200 of their dead and wounded, which a regiment of infantry had surrounded and then shot. Nearly the whole of these dead and wounded rebels were of one South Carolina regiment.

As soon as they began retreating, the cavalry were pushed ahead again and during the next two days we captured about 1,000 of their stragglers. Ever since then we have been in advance of the main body of the army, and scarcely a day passes without a skirmish. I have been engaged in more than twenty and have not had a man killed but three slightly wounded. Some horses however have been killed. I like the business tolerably well, but the weather is becoming most too warm for comfort. During the middle of the day it is intolerably hot. One other great nuisance is the vast number of insects and reptiles to be found. Wood ticks are in great abundance and snakes, lizards, . . . mosquitoes and flies, make sleeping on the ground somewhat unpleasant. They don't annoy me as much as they do many others. My nervous system is almost impregnable to their assaults. These Southern climates have their drawbacks as well as the cold North.

Well, I have no idea of when McClellan intends taking Richmond. He has a big job on his hands if the rebels give him a fight, which we have every reason to believe they will do. Through the aid of balloons can be seen their works in and about the city and all their immense army scattered for miles around that sacred city. Their entrenchments are all around it, not over a mile from the centre of the town. In case of a battle, the city will be destroyed by our shells. This seems to be their desire and design in erecting their works. I hope McClellan will not wait long but attack them at once and end the matter. All kinds of rumors and speculations are current in the army about when we will be able to return home. The report current in camp now is that as soon as the city of Richmond is taken all the volunteer cavalry in this army will be mustered out of the service. If such should be the case, you may calculate on seeing me on or about the 4th of July next. I don't expect it is so. Another report is that Halleck and Beauregard had a terrible battle at Corinth in which the latter was beaten,[21] and his whole army destroyed. This, also, is evidently premature.

This is a good farming country and looks very much like the Tuscarawas Valley [in northeast Ohio]. The people are all secession except the negroes. A large majority of the latter remain on the plantations and appear to think a special mission is their liberation. A great many are running off, and a great many are hiring to the officers of the different regiments passing along.

Well, I must end this. I subscribed for a religious paper printed somewhere in New York State for you, in which you will find a letter or two each week from our Chaplain, Mr. L. C. Matlack, who is one of the editors of the paper. He signs his articles "L.C.M." From this paper you can keep yourself posted. I could not get the picture you spoke of for you and Ellen. If there is an opportunity in Richmond to do so, I'll try and have it taken.

With much love to all the family and regards to all my friends in Canton, I remain your Brother, Will H. Medill

When William wrote the next letter, McClellan's army was close enough to Richmond for Union soldiers to hear church bells ring. However, McClellan hesitated, and the real fighting of his Peninsula Campaign began two weeks later.

WILLIAM TO MARY
In Camp near Mechanicsville, Virginia, Monday, June 2, 1862[22]

My dear Sister:

We are still hovering around Richmond, waiting the progress of events before making a descent upon the place. A great many preparations must be attended to, previous to the expected battle. Our regiment is now enjoying a respite from its incessant labors of the past month, and we are only called upon to do picket duty. This is easy in comparison to scouting. Ever since leaving Yorktown this regiment has been on the advance, chasing round over the country. I flatter myself that I have become a good scout and can ride a horse over or through anything. You have seen pictures of cavalry scouts tearing along over fences and through fields, rough and dirty looking. Imagine me at the head of a squad of men, going at full gallop through wheat fields, corn fields, gardens, pastures, anywhere, without reference to what the owners might think or say, rough in dress, and sunburned, and long beard all over my face—not black beard either—and you have some idea of your hopeful brother. An army on duty is not as pretty as an army out for a Fourth of July celebration. A neat uniform is out of the question here. Brigadier generals may keep themselves neat and tidy, but none under that grade. I thought of sending you my picture when I could have it taken but there is no use. You would not recognize it and you will never see me looking as I do here. My first care on returning to civilization will be to clean up and dress up.

Well, there will most certainly be a great battle fought before we can enter Richmond. All day Saturday and yesterday heavy firing could be heard to our left. We have no particulars farther than a rumor that three of our divisions passed the Chickahominy and were fighting their way towards Richmond. It is also reported in camp that the gunboats have passed Ft. Darling and are nearly up to Richmond and that Gen. Sumner's Division is within a mile or two of that city. I can hardly believe these reporters as they look improbable. There are too many rebels between the Chickahominy and Richmond to allow our army proceeding quite so easily. Of course, all hope it may be so.

I was forcibly struck with the reflection of how different everything was here to what it was at home yesterday. At home, the day being Sunday, was kept as such. People all at rest or attending church. No noise, no disturbance. Everybody enjoying rest. Here only one in ten knew what day of the week [it was]. Duty the same as usual in the morning. About 9 o'clock heavy firing is heard along the lines when the order is passed among the different camps to make ready for a march at a minutes' warning. With no cavalry this order meant to pack up blankets, saddle horses and finish up cooking. As soon as these things are accomplished, the men sit round under the trees and spend the day in speculating as to the result of the fight in progress. Nobody is excited, nobody seems to care whether the regiment is ordered forward or remains where it is. Indifference to danger and the battle is apparent in every countenance. All day we keep our saddles on and probably all night—asks some of the men. About this time an orderly from Gen. Stoneman brings a dispatch for the col. Every man who sees the messenger arrive jumps to his feet and "stands to horse." Pretty soon the orderly sergeant's call is sounded when these officers proceed to regimental headquarters for instructions. The adjutant tells them to have their company commanders march their men on foot to the parade ground to hear orders read. This is executed on the quick time—when all the companies are drawn up in line, the adjutant steps to the front and centre, and cries out "Attention to orders." He then reads a dispatch from Gen. Stoneman to the effect that Gen. McClellan wishes the news to be conveyed to each brigade and regiment that the forces under Gen. Sumner, Heintzelman and Keys have crossed the Chickahominy and have whipped and driven the enemy some four or five miles with great slaughter to their foes and only a small loss on our side, and that it is reported at headquarters that the *Monitor* is within three miles of Richmond and also for the men to take off the saddles and prepare for a night's rest. . . . This confounded war will hang on longer than most people dreamed of it doing.

What's the news at home? I have not heard from you for a long time. Send me an occasional copy of the Canton papers, if you please. Tell me how all my friends are getting along, who are married and who are dead? I have not heard from Chicago for nearly a month, either by letter or paper.

Give my best regards to all my friends, male or female, and especially to Miss Ball.

Love to our Family. Your Brother W. H. Medill

Excuse writing and mistakes—Can't do any better when the heat is 100 in the shade.

W. H. M.

William to Kate
In Camp near Mechanicsville, Virginia, June 17, 1862

Dear Sister:

Yesterday I received your very welcome letter and also the note to you from James. I am very much obliged to you for sending his note, as it is the first I have heard of him since I have been from Chicago last fall.

Well, I have scarcely anything new or interesting to write about. We are still on the banks of the Chickahominy, waiting patiently for an order to pitch in. We are most constantly on picket duty; I am on just half the time, and I must say the duty is becoming pleasant. There is something exciting in watching our enemy where things are most constantly in view. We are on one side of the stream, and the rebel pickets are on the opposite, looking as saucy and defiant as you please. We are about a mile apart, but almost every day the men on either side advance down closer and have quite interesting pleasant chats. Day before yesterday one of my men went across and took a lunch with one of the "rebs," and in return the rebel came along back with him and got some coffee and salt. I did not know of the occurrence until today, or I should have put a stop to it. I am opposed to holding any communication with them except through the medium of arms.

We have had quite a little excitement within a few days. On Saturday last the rebels sent out a couple of regiments of cavalry and a battery of artillery on a scout. Passing some ten miles to our right, they succeeded in getting entirely in the rear of our army and passing down to the Pamunkey River, burnt two vessels and then went over to the railroad and destroyed a bridge and, being perfectly conversant with the roads, they managed to retrace their steps to their lines before our men could catch them. On their way back, however, they pitched into two companies of the 5th Regular Cavalry and gave them a sound thrashing and capturing a number of their wagons. This was a very successful scout on their part.

Determining to retaliate Gen. Stoneman, our brigade general, ordered one battalion of our regiment to proceed to where these fellows were encamped and try and capture some of them or at least let them know that we were awake. Their rendezvous was at a town called Ashland, some twenty miles from our lines. In order to get there early, we started at 12 o'clock night before last and by daylight were within five miles of the town. We avoided the public roads and prominent places, thus dodging all their vedettes. In a thick piece of woods we halted and gave our horses a rest, and at eight o'clock we moved on until we came upon their pickets about two miles from town, and by a very nice maneuver we kept them from running into the town. Here we learned from a contraband that the main body of the rebels had moved from Ashland some ten miles. So we drew up near the suburbs of the place in a piece of woods and took two platoons, under command of two lieutenants, and instructed them to divide their force and charge into town and drive out those remaining. My 1st Lieut. D. J. Hynes had command of the platoon taken from my company. Of course, we were all anxious for the result. About ten minutes after Hynes left, we heard three shots and then an interval of a few minutes and about a dozen more. Of course, we supposed he had run into a large force. A few minutes more and we saw, to our delight, three of our men returning with some prisoners on horseback and shortly after some more and then a wagon and four horses. I then rode up into the town and found Lieut. Hynes had full possession of the place and was capturing a large number of horses and considerable property besides having torn up considerable R.R. track. We captured altogether eight prisoners, one wagon, twenty-six horses, burnt three cars loaded with tents and destroyed quite a lot of R.R. track and telegraph and killed one man. There were about 100 rebels in the town at the time, who managed with the exception of the 8 taken and the one killed to make their escape. The town is a very handsome one, containing about 2,000 inhabitants and having some of the finest residences I ever saw. The people were very much excited and frightened; a great many tried to make their escape. We assured them there was no danger. Having accomplished our object, we returned leisurely to camp, bringing in a good load of corn for our horses. This was a very good retaliation for their exploit and for which we received the thanks of Gen. Stoneman. It is in these sudden dashes that cavalry is particularly useful. We traveled near fifty miles, captured prisoners, horses, wagon and a town and returned before the infantry could have traveled 12 miles. It is this, too, which makes our life endurable and dispels the thought of our disagreeable position. Excitement is what a soldier lives and thrives upon. To make a march and not be fired upon is tedious, but when the sharp crack of the carbine or revolver is heard how pleasant every man's countenance appears. Well, I don't know when we will make an advance on Richmond. Probably tomorrow and probably not for a month.

Since the battle at Fair Oaks, I have been over the battlefield and saw the dreadful evidence of the conflict plainly marked by the long rows of trenches and the scattered implements of death and destruction lying about. A larger number of the dead rebels were still unburied when I was there, although over a week after the battle; the stench was awful. I have never seen a full statement of the loss on both sides, but suppose we lost somewhere about 6,000 in killed and wounded, and the rebels about 12,000.[23] Their loss was the heaviest owing to the fact that they attacked us, and our artillery gave them a terrible raking.

Well, I must come to a close. Since returning from our scout, I have not been very well, but expect to be better tomorrow. Our Dr. says I came very near having the typhoid fever[24] but there is no danger now.

Don't forget to give my love to Uncle and Aunt Maxwell and cousin Mary and all the rest of the family. I will endeavor to write them a letter if I can find time. Remember me to Miss Ball and all my friends. Tell Mother that I think very seriously of resigning when we reach Richmond. I am getting disgusted with the way the war is managed. Love to all and don't forget to write me a long letter.

Yours, W. H. Medill

P.S. I should be much pleased to receive that picture of Nelly. Please send it to me. W. H. M.

WILLIAM TO KATE
In Camp near Mechanicsville, Virginia, June 19, 1862

Sister Kate:

I received your letter the other day, which just came in time, for I was beginning to have the *blues* on account of receiving no letters from my friends. In fact, I had about made up my mind to resign and leave the army in disgust. Nothing seemed to go right with me. To tell the truth I have a serious idea of resigning anyhow. I don't like the management of the war on the nigger question, and the life is the most disagreeable I ever endured. I would rather set type at 30 cents per 1000 than be trudging away my life here, suffering the infernal heat and bad living. I am determined that if the rebels evacuate Richmond and move on to some other place and fortify, and we go through the same operation to tender my resignation.

We are still here, looking at the rebels on the bank opposite, waiting patiently for something to "turn up." Day after day the same duty to perform, an occasional scout to vary the monotony. However, even the latter is becoming monotonous for we have been all over the different roads so often. Three days of the week we are on picket duty along the banks of the terrible and world renowned Chickahominy. At first this employment was pleasant because [it was] exciting, but we know now just what it is, and instead of enlivening we consider it the very meanest description of loafing. Even an occasional raid from the enemy does not add much to the interest of the duty. All we have to do is to drive them back, and then sit down and wait again. However, we had a very pleasant variation on Sunday night and Monday last. Tuesday previous the rebels made a bold dash, with a couple of regiments of cavalry through the picket lines of the regulars, passing round to our rear and cutting up many tricks, such as burning a bridge on the R.R. that leads from the White House to McClellan's headquarters and destroying some vessels on the Pamunkey River, capturing a small train of provision wagons. Before the alarm was given, they had taken a circuit to the right of our lines across the Pamunkey and returned. This was one of the most daring scouts that has been performed by their cavalry.

Gen. Stoneman determined to retaliate on them; so on Sunday evening he sent Col. Farnsworth word to have one battalion of his regiment start at 12 o'clock at night, under command of the lieutenant col. and endeavor to surprise the rebel farce stationed at Ashland and out their force. Accordingly, one Squadron (mine) of the 1st and one squadron (Capt. Hooker's) of the 2nd Battalion were ordered to be ready to march at 12 o'clock at night, fully supplied with ammunition for a rapid march. To omit details of the march, I will suppose, we landed at the suburbs of the town by seven o'clock in the morning without having disturbed the rebel picket, which was done by cutting thro' fields and byroads and avoiding their videttes. At the edge of town we came upon a picket and managed to catch him before he dreamed of who we were. A negro now made his appearance from a little shanty by the roadside and informed us that the main body of the rebels had gone some ten miles farther up, leaving two companies to guard the town. Col. Gamble ordered two platoons from the 1st Squadron, under command of Lieut. Hynes and [First Lt. Daniel D.] Lincoln[25] to make a dash into the place and see what could be seen. In they went on two different roads. Just as the nigger had said, about 100 of their cavalry were there scattered about. The rebs were taken completely by surprise and run off without firing a gun. Hynes captured eight prisoners and killed one who was running off. He also picked up 30 horses and one wagon and team, which had been captured from our folks at Bull Run. Not deeming it safe for so small a force to proceed any farther, we returned to camp, which is 20 miles from Ashland. Gen. Stoneman was very much pleased and in his report to Gen. McClellan said it was one of the best scouts yet made. It was especially gratifying to us on account of there being a rivalry between us and the Sixth Regulars to get to the town first. On our return we took the main road and found the regulars within six miles, proceeding very cautiously for fear of an attack. We told them to go on up, that there was no danger, as we had driven the rebels out and captured all the horses. We also tore up some of the R.R. track and burnt a portion of a bridge on the Richmond and Gordonsville R.R. and burnt two cars on the track, loaded with tents. Our boys are becoming experts at "rail ripping."

P.S. Please ask Mr. Medill if he can find me a copy of the *Daily New York Times* of June 10th at one of the News Depots. It contains a puff of our regiment, which I have never seen. The *Tribune* comes very regular.

W. H. M.

The "puff" piece that William asked to have from the *New York Times* provided the following account:

> The movements on the right wing of the army since the battle of Hanover Court-house and the destruction of the railroad bridge at Ashland, are unimportant. The Eighth Illinois Cavalry have daily scouted the country between that point and the place from whence I write, and although occasionally running across small parties of rebel scouts, have seen no demonstrations that would indicate another flanking movement, such as they attempted last week.

The rise of the river, or swamp, would operate against any movement on their part, as there is now but one crossing place held by them over which they could, in any event, throw troops. There are, perhaps, two brigades of the enemy on the other side of the river, above Mechanicsville, but they have railroad facilities extending far enough to enable them to concentrate a large force there at any moment. The light brigade of Gen. STONEMAN keeps careful watch of their every motion, and should a flanking movement be attempted, they will find our army not unprepared. Too much praise cannot be given to this command of Gen. STONEMAN for the energy displayed, and hardship endured, in the extreme advance of the army.

It has been my good fortune to be thrown in company frequently with the Eighth Illinois Cavalry, under Col. FARNSWORTH, who have accompanied the brigade and been foremost in the perils and dangers of leading the way for the balance of our army. For days they have been compelled to go with horses unsaddled, passing sleepless nights, in rain and storm, on picket, or standing by the heads of their steeds to be ready at the first picket alarm to repel the advance of the enemy. It has been a constant skirmish with them since leaving Williamsburgh [sic], and their duties have been more arduous, (and attended with equal danger,) than have those of that portion of the army who have engaged in the great battles of the Peninsula. W.W.C.[26]

William wrote about negligence he perceived in the regular cavalry unit of Colonel P. St.-G. Cook. Regulars allowed General J. E. B. Stuart to pass through their pickets and lines to the rear of the army, capturing, destroying, burning as he went—and escaping unmolested. According to William, Cook did not start in pursuit for several hours, took a wrong road, and marched slowly. William claimed if his regiment had been put in pursuit of Stuart, they would have given a lively chase, and that Stuart never would have had twelve hours' time to build bridges across the Chickahominy and escape. "Cook exhibited no vigilance or energy, but was never court-martialed, because he was an aristocrat and a regular."[27]

William questioned Gen. George McClellan's hesitation, knowing it would cost lives. William further expected the army to "retire" rather than achieve results. At this point, he doesn't target McClellan as being responsible. As the letter closes, he expresses support, writing "I don't think it right to censure McClellan for the partial defeat on the first day of the Battle of Fair Oaks. He did the very best he could . . . only gave way a little before tremendous odds. Next morning, however, he made short work of it." In this instance, William overstated the number of casualties. On June 1, the second day of fighting when Confederates renewed assaults, Federals brought up reinforcements but made little headway. Both sides claimed victory. Union casualties were 5,739, and Confederate casualties 7,997.[28] Throughout June, as Lee prepared a counteroffensive, McClellan petitioned Washington for more supplies and reinforcements. He claimed to be facing some 200,000 enemy troops, but the maximum strength of Lee's forces was around 92,000.[29] It took two more months, until August 1862, for William to denounce McClellan as a commander.

William to Samuel

Mechanicsville, Virginia, June 22, 1862

Dear Sammy—

About two hours since I received your very welcome letter of the 17th, 1862, for which I am under many obligations. I receive so few letters lately that I prize them when they do come.

We are doing nothing worthy of note except picketing along the banks of the *noble* Chickahominy Creek. Our position is on the right from Mechanicsville up as far as Hanover Court House. No one can have any idea of the doings here. One day we advance, and the next we fall back and dig a trench. The whole surface of the earth seems to be dug over and on every hill may be seen earthworks of every formidable character. Even today I observe Gen. Reynolds is having a new ditch thrown up about one mile back of Mechanicsville from the Chickahominy. What is wanted of this ditch no one knows.

To me it looks like a preparation against defeat. It may be, however, done to keep the men in practice in the science of ditching. It will no doubt make good farmers of the boys, as they will be able to adapt a good system of drainage, not only for the benefit of the land but for their own protection. Hurrah for the ditch digging army of McClellan! I doubt not but we will dig our way clear into Richmond, provided the rebels don't drive us away before that time. If they had as good men as Mc and their present numbers, I guess they could do it without much trouble. They have not less than 150,000, while we cannot raise over 80,000 or 90,000 fighting men. Nearly half the army with which McClellan left Alexandria is now worn away by deaths and sickness and wounded in battle. I am afraid this noble army, if it remains here another month, will have become used up by sickness. Look at our regiment, for instance. We started off with 12 companies of 92 men and 3 officers in each, making an aggregate of 1140. Our report now shows about 730 men fit for duty, and you must bear in mind that we have lost only about a dozen by capture or killed by the enemy. The others have either died, are in the hospitals sick, been discharged through physical infirmities or are at home on sick furlough. I have lost five by death and two by discharge, which reduced me to 84, but through details for extra duty etc. and by sickness, I never can get out more than 60 men for duty, and I have the largest company in the regiment. But we are in good spirits. Few other regiments can show as full ranks as we can. It looks sorrowful to observe some of the regiments, as they march along, looking scarcely large enough for a camp guard. A great many of the men, no doubt, are at home on furloughs, who will now return on account of the late order from the War Department.

I have just learned from Maj. Beveridge, who has come across from headquarters that the belief is current there that the big fight will open tomorrow morning. We are ordered to hold ourselves in readiness to move at a moment's warning. This is encouraging in the highest degree. Notwithstanding the awful heat, I am well to do one good day's fighting. I believe we can break their lines and go into Richmond. From our outside pickets we only have to move about five miles to get into the City. If it does occur, I don't doubt but you will hear the noise in Chicago. Pittsburg Landing and Fair Oaks will be nowhere in comparison to the killing. By the way, Fair Oaks was much the severest battle of the two.[30] The whole of the two day's [sic] fighting didn't last more than six hours. In this time[,] between 15,000 and 20,000 men were killed or wounded. The fight was more of a hand-to-hand fight. The boys demonstrated that they could use the bayonet better than the rebels. If the fight takes place tomorrow, the bayonet will be used to good purpose.

Our regiment as I said before is doing picket duty with an occasional scout. The regulars are on our right, and it was through their lines that Stuart passed when he made his famous reconnaissance in our rear. We knew nothing of it for eight hours after the thing was known by the regulars. I have the most contemptuous opinion of the regulars. They are slower than the Dutch and more conceited than the English. I would have no hesitancy to bet that our regiment can whip them two to one. As an evidence of that Gen. Stuart remarked to an officer, whom we caught at Ashland, that he would rather meet the whole regular force of 4 regiments than the 8th Ill. Cavalry. By the way, I observe that some of the New York papers give the regulars credit for going to Ashland and capturing prisoners, horses, etc. when the truth is the regulars did not go within five miles of the place, while one battalion of our boys went there and made the capture. This is the way these things go. Their officers are always toadying [groveling] around headquarters, and the reporters hear their story and publish it. It is very mean. Besides, there can be no doubt there was criminal carelessness on their part for permitting

Stuart to slip through their lines, and it is said that there is no relationship as close as that of brothers-in-law existing between P. St. G. Cook,[31] who commanded the regulars and Gen. Stuart of the rebels. At least it is known that when the rebels attacked one squadron of the regulars at Old Church, the officer in charge informed Gen. Cook, who was only a mile distant with two regiments of the state of affairs, and that Cook refused to send succor. He didn't even start in pursuit for several hours and then took a wrong road. In my opinion, there was a connivance somewhere. The idea of Stuart going where he did and not to catch him is the very strangest kind of evidence.

I perceive by the *Tribune* of the 18th that the Locofoco Constitution has been adopted.[32] This is as I expected. The Republicans had no business to form a coalition in the election of the members of that convention. I never believed in the Union humbug in party. The Loco's were willing, of course, for then they were certain of a majority. In the southern part of the state they, of course, carried everything while in the northern end the Republicans gave them one half the number. This was all they wanted, and we now have the effect. I swear I am heartsick. We elected Lincoln President. The Democratic Party dissolve[d] the Union, and in order to restore it, we dissolve the Republican Party. This is virtually throwing up the contest. I have about determined to resign if we reach Richmond. I have no object in fighting. If the Union is restored, these villainous rebels will all demand to be readmitted to the seats they once held, and through a split in the Republican Party and such infernal apportionments as in Illinois will give them a sufficient majority to vote themselves in. I hope if they do, they will immediately pass a bill confiscating the property of all Republicans for being the *cause* of the war and for fighting against the Constitutional rights of the South.

So Miss Goodman is married. I had some hope she would wait until I returned. However, I guess I will remain a bachelor. Three married brothers will be enough for the family. I think I will be able to take care of myself when I have finished here, which will be about all, too. I am afraid I am acquiring a habit of indifference that will stick to me through life. This soldiering is only good for that and nothing more. Sometimes for a week we do nothing at all, and while on picket all we do is sit around and see that no one passes a certain point. I will have acquired the habit of doing whatever is ordered that, I suppose if someone was to order me to stand on the street corner till he returned I would remain there for 24 hours waiting to be *relieved*. The same with all the others. Yes, my girling days are over; I'll never marry. Kate wrote to me that you were going to school. How is it? Go if you can. I am going to put in one year after my return, at least, in reading and studying. Wish I had done so years ago.

I forgot to say that our regiment voted unanimously against the Constitution, but I presume the vote will not be counted.

The boys send their best regards. Remember me to all my friends and especially to Joseph's family. Write soon.

Yours, etc. W. H. Medill

William to an Unknown Recipient

June 25, 1862

[No salutation]

Before this reaches you, the long gathering storm cloud will break. We have wasted a month here in inaction. Our army is doing two things: ditch digging and dying. The sickness and mortality in this hot weather in those marshes are terrible. While our army is wasting away, the enemy is rapidly growing stronger by means of a sweeping conscription. We are 40,000 fewer for duty than we were a month ago, and the rebels are 50,000 stronger than they were a few weeks since. I have just heard that Stonewall Jackson, with 30,000 men, has arrived from the Shenandoah Valley and taken position on our right near Hanover Court House. If this be so, a battle may take place at any hour.

I am disgusted at the way this fine army is employed. One part is ditch digging, and another stands guard over the plantations and property of slaveholders, whose sons are in Lee's army, fighting us. Our generals will never put down this slaveholders' rebellion by pursuing a proslavery policy. The chief support of the rebellion is derived from the labor of four millions of slaves, who supply the commissary and quartermasters' departments of the enemy and support the families of the rebel soldiers besides. We must knock away this great pillar of their edifice, else we shall never succeed in putting down the revolt. I am not sanguine of the result of the impending battle; our boys will make a stubborn fight, but McClellan has waited too long. He has neglected his opportunity. Mark my words.[33]

Note that the following portion of the letter appears to be a continuation of the previous letter, but there is no way to be certain.

I presume you are becoming as anxious to see an advance in this army now—as when it was before Manassas at Yorktown and wonder what we are doing. Apparently we are waiting. We are not fortifying as we did in the other cases, but quietly bringing up men and cannon and placing them in position. At present all seem to be up, and yesterday and today there are many mysterious movements of the troops on both sides. Yesterday McClellan moved three new divisions over the Chickahominy, and the rebels broke up all their camps within sight of us and left with the exception of their pickets and apparently with haste. Along their front about where Richmond is, there was an immense fire, which burned nearly all day. This looked as though there was something mysterious going on. This morning Madam Rumor says that gunboats have captured Ft. Darling and are engaged in removing the obstructions from the James River.[34] If this is the case, I expect to hear of another "retire."

The health of the army is very good, all things considered. Our position is anything but healthy, and I wonder there is not more sickness. Our regiment is not attached to any brigade at present. Yesterday we were under the command of three brigadiers. In the morning we were under Stoneman when he was ordered to divide his brigade among different commanders and report himself on Gen. McClellan's staff. We were ordered to report to Gen. Martindale. Col. Farnsworth went over there and received orders from him. When he had returned to camp a few minutes, Gen. Martindale sent him word that his brigade had been ordered across the Chickahominy and that Farnsworth should report to Gen. Taylor of the New Jersey Brigade. This order was complied with and no more changes were made till this morning when Col. Farnsworth received word from Taylor that his brigade was ordered across the Chickahominy, and that we were not attached to any brigade but should continue picket duty just as we had been doing for the last week or two. So we stand at present. How many changes there will be made before night I cannot tell, nor don't care.

We all feel glorious over the victories in the West and especially the taking of Memphis and the destruction of the rebel gunboats. It was about time the Mississippi was cleaned out. I hope the government will not keep G. N. Fitch [Graham N. Fitch, brigadier general, Democratic congressman and senator] long in command, or he will spoil all the good work performed by the boats, by giving the traitors permission to recapture their slaves who run away. This is a bad notion to let them get into their heads. We all hope soon to eclipse all the deeds of the western army. I, however, don't think it right to censure McClellan for the partial defeat on the first day of the Battle of Fair Oaks. He did the very best he could, and instead of getting routed as Grant did at Pittsburg Landing, he only gave way a little before tremendous odds. Next morning, however, he made short work of it, as the 12,000 killed and wounded rebels can testify.

The Chicago and New York *Tribunes* seem to doubt it's being a victory. If it was not one, there never was such a thing. It is wrong, in my opinion, for the newspapers to be all the while trying to create distrust in the soldier's mind as regards the capacity of his commander. Supposing every man in the army, or even one division, thought McClellan an inferior man, and we were brought into a fight tomorrow, what would be the effect? Feeling this distrust would produce fear, and the first charge the enemy made, some bigger coward than the rest would cry out that the whole army was routed and away they would go, and all the others would follow. This is just the result that would be produced and then these papers would attribute the defeat to McClellan's want of generalship when in truth they were the cause. But, I am becoming tiresome and must come to a close.

And so Miss Goodman is married, and they had a grand splurge over it. I suppose Johnny was happy. He is good at putting on airs, at least he kept them up in Canton. Wish I could have been present, as I have never seen anybody married yet and never expect to unless I get up one on my own account. Speaking of my marrying reminds me of that joke about my wedding a lady in Alexandria. Hynes, the scamp, thinks it was real funny. So Miss James is still waiting. Guess I'll have to *open our correspondence again* and when the war is over, I'll marry her.

My opinion is firmly established in regard to Miss Carpenter. Never thought she was above par in good sound sense and don't now. The preacher will not make much out of his bargain, that is, if he is smart.

I enclose a couple of little notes for Nelly and Kitty and must thank you for sending theirs to me. The pony is doing well, and I'll bring it home when I return. Remember me to all your family when you write.

Yours etc. W. H. Medill[35]

On June 26, 1862, the Seven Days Battles began near Richmond with the Battle of Mechanicsville, also known as the Battle of Beaver Dam Creek. Gen. Robert E. Lee attacked George B. McClellan's Army of the Potomac. After both sides suffered heavy losses, McClellan withdrew back toward Washington. McClellan won what he described as a "complete victory" at Mechanicsville but then failed to go on the offensive. Instead, he fell back to Gaines's Mill and fought only to protect his retreat, calling it a "change of base." Defeat at Gaines's Mill left the Army of the Potomac in fairly good shape, but General McClellan had a defeated mental attitude, pulled back to the James River, and continued the retreat.[36]

William to Joseph

Near Harrison's Bar, James River, Virginia, Monday, July 7, 1862

Brother Joseph:

I have had little time for writing for over a week or since our sudden movement from the right to the left flank of the army, partly on account of our extra amount of duty, and partly because all corresponding was forbidden.

William Medill's letters were written in pencil. This one, written July 7, 1862, details the loss of all his personal property at Mechanicsville. (Courtesy Colonel Robert R. McCormick Research Center)

The restriction is now off and at the same time our regiment has been relieved from hard duty, and we are promised a good rest. There can be no movement made for at least a month, even if disposed to do so. We must receive 50,000 or 75,000 reinforcements before we can fight the rebel army opposed to us. Now during this interval I would like to get a short furlough. Besides needing a little rest, I am cleaned entirely out of clothing and company property. My teamster had the misfortune to break his wagon just when the rebels came rushing down from Mechanicsville and, getting frightened, he cut loose from the wagon and cleared out. A few minutes after this occurrence a straggling party of the Pennsylvania Buck Tails passed along where this wagon was, and to prevent the rebels from getting it, they burnt the wagon and contents. By this accident I lost every particle of clothing I had, except an old suit I was wearing, together with all my company books and papers. Lieutenants Hynes & Wing also lost their clothing. I haven't even an extra pair of stockings or a change of handkerchiefs. I would like to buy some. I applied to Gen. McClellan for a leave of absence, but he says the War Department has taken the power to grant leaves out of his hand and reserve the right to grant them itself. I have written to White to apply for me, but knowing his laziness in hot weather, I thought probably you might have some influence with someone in Washington who could procure a short furlough for me.

Although our regiment was actively engaged in all the fights, in the retreat we only lost about 20. Capt. R. M. Hooker of Company H was mortally wounded and left on the field. My company escaped without harm although in imminent danger.

With the exception of a bad diarrhea and an occasional headache, I am well. If I get a furlough, I have some things to tell you, which I don't dare to write about our retreat, etc. Hoping to hear from you soon and giving my regards to all, I remain,

Yours, W. H. Medill

WILLIAM TO JOSEPH
Yorktown, Virginia, August 20, 1862

Brother Joseph:

Suddenly when everyone supposed the army was going to move on Richmond, we have been ordered to retreat back to Yorktown. We have been four days in making the movement. Everything was conducted in an admirable manner. Have heard of but one life lost. The rebels did not know we were leaving until the whole army, except the rear guard was nearly to Yorktown. Our regiment and three other regiments of cavalry and two battalions of flying artillery under command of Gen. Pleasonton formed the rear guard. We held our position near Malvern Hill for two days after the last of the main army left the works at Harrison's Landing. The second night we pulled up stakes, set up "dummy" pickets and moved off twenty miles. We completely fooled them. I presume this is considered a very successful retreat but whether it is in accordance with the "original plan" I am unable to say. To me it is rather humiliating thus to be running out of the Peninsula especially as the rebels boasted that they were going to drive us out in less than six months from the date we landed. I understand we are going to be shipped to Aquia Creek and then join Pope. Whether McClellan will assume complete command of the whole army I know not, but I can assure you this army will be sorry if he does. It has dug enough trenches and guarded enough secession houses to have a rest from such duty for a brief season. If the same policy is to continue, you can set this army down as little better than useless. The men will not fight under such circumstances.

My time and facilities for writing are limited and poor. Consequently excuse the brevity of this note. Will write as soon as we make a halt for a few days. We are to move somewhere this evening—supposed to Fortress Monroe to ship.

I have not heard from the $500 I sent you. If it has not arrived yet, I want you to write to the Assistant Treasurer at New York to have the payment stopped on the draft until he hears from you. Please let me hear from you.

Give my love to your family. My health is somewhat better.

Yours in haste, W. H. Medill

William to Mary
Yorktown, Virginia, August 21, 1862

Dear Sister:

I am utterly disgusted and disheartened. I have tendered my resignation and hope to have it accepted. I have no heart in this war and do not wish to fight any more battles until there is a change. We will never win a victory until we fight with a purpose and for an object. At present we dig trenches and guard secession property and that is the extent of our duty. When the rebels push us, we retreat. From day to day I can see the disposition of the men to fight giving way and a feeling of hopelessness taking the place of former prestige. Men will straggle from the ranks, get taken prisoners in order to be exchanged, hoping thereby to get home. Even sickness is welcomed as it relieves the soldier from performing duties arduous to his sense of what he enlisted to do.

How can an officer enforce discipline and respect from soldiers towards their generals when their generals do not merit any? I have not the will to do it. I have done so thus far and have gotten the ill will of my men for doing it.

On the 13th of the present month this army commenced to retreat from Harrison's Landing, and yesterday the rear guard, composed of our regiment and three more of cavalry and two batteries of artillery, reached this point. We did not leave our position for two days after the main portion of the army had marched. The rebels did not find out that we had retreated until we had been away one day. Of course, to follow was of no use. A few of their cavalry made their appearance when we reached the Chickahominy, but merely to see us taking up our pontoon bridge under the cover of three gun boats. We moved very slowly rather courting an attack. The rebels, however, did not attempt to force us any. McClellan's friends, no doubt, will speak of this as an extraordinary fine piece of strategy and will applaud him as the greatest general living. But I don't desire to be classed among this number. My notion of the matter is that he has made one of the worst campaigns known to history. The biggest fool in all Ireland[37] could not have managed affairs worse than he has. Every movement since he has been in command of the Army of the Potomac has been a blunder. As I said before, I do not wish to serve in this army any more.

Another motive is, that my health is becoming very bad. I can scarcely stand the fatigues of the service. I have never been so reduced in flesh as at present. I only weigh 130 pounds. When I left Alexandria for this place last May, I weighed 162 pounds. I have gradually fallen away until now I am so weak that a day's ride tires me more than a week's ought to. When a man don't feel well, he cannot perform a soldier's duty. My appetite is very poor, and the victuals do not agree with me. I don't want you to say anything to Mother about this matter. My resignation may not be accepted and then she will be uneasy about me.

I don't know where we will go from here, but rather suppose we will go to Aquia Creek, which runs with the Potomac somewhere near the Rappahannock. From there move to the support of Gen. Pope. Of course, Gen. McClellan will assume command and then you will see another inactive campaign of the ditch digging and sickish protecting kind. I hope I am not necessitated to accompany the army.

I have no other news of note to write. We have done nothing worthy of note. Give my love to all our family, and my regards to my friends.

Yours, etc. etc. W. H. Medill

William to Joseph

Yorktown, Virginia, August 24, 1862

Brother Joseph:

We are still at Yorktown and will remain here for a few days yet until government furnishes us with transportation when we will ship for Alexandria. This will make our retreat complete. We shipped from there last April, and now we return the 1st of September without having accomplished anything except to spoil a rich country and kill and discourage a vast number of men. I don't believe the world can show a more profitless campaign than since the 10th day of last March when this army advanced toward Manassas. It has not gained one victory worthy of note. Confidentially, Gen. McClellan is the worst "played out" man in the United States and nowhere so completely as in this army. Here and there a man is found to defend him, and he is a "regular." None but those indebted to him praise him. I don't wonder that those foreign princes left him in disgust although they were still pufferies of intolerable airs.

The main portion of the army is being shipped to Aquia Creek to join Pope. Hay's Corps will probably go to Suffolk. Why we are sent to Alexandria I am unable to tell. Gen. Pope I learn has a large force of cavalry in addition to some six or eight regiments sent him from this army. Our brigade consists of four regiments viz. 1st and 6th Regulars and the 8th Pennsylvania and the 8th Illinois. Gen. Pleasonton is our commander. The men have got the idea that we are going to be sent to Kentucky to fight Morgan. That would be too good luck. There is not a man in the brigade but would give a month's time for the privilege of being sent there. I think we could start Mr. Morgan southward were we landed in Kentucky. Our regiment especially would be delighted with such a move. The men have always been desirous of going west anyhow. They are not at home among these eastern troops, and there is such confounded jealousy of everything western that makes it unpleasant for our boys.

I have no idea how long we will remain in Alexandria. I presume long enough to recount up our horses and men and get things in order again. Our saddles are nearly all worn out, and a large number of our arms are out of order. These will have to be replaced and repaired. A great many of our horses will have to be condemned and fresh ones furnished.

There is also some talk of calling on the Governor to fill the regiment up to the maximum again. We have two officers at home now recruiting, but I don't suppose they will get many men. Speaking of filling the regiment makes me think of the folly of raising new regiments. There was no need of one new regiment. There are enough for colonels, brigadiers and major generals already to do all the fighting that is needed. Besides look at the men who are getting appointments. There is Charley Barker, who was in reality compelled to resign by Gen. McClellan, has gone to New York State and is col. of one of the new regiments raised by that state. There was not a more drunken and incompetent officer in the Army of the Potomac than Charley Barker. And then look at home, there is Capt. Whitney, who was Captain of Co. B of our regiment. About the time Col. Farnsworth went home, Lieut. Col. Gamble compelled him to resign because he was incompetent to command a company, and now I see that Whitney is col. of one of the new regiments and stands for being made a brigadier general. I know several other instances of the same kind.

It is the very worst kind of folly to create new regiments. There are at present some 600 or 700 regiments in existence. Fill these up and put all the surplus men into camps of instruction under drill sergeants and keep them to fill up the regiments in the field. Every new regiment that is organized is an extra cost to the government of 50,000 or 60,000 dollars to no purpose. The old regimental organizations are kept up even if there are more officers than men. In this way [we] will soon have 1200 or 1400 regiments with a couple of hundred fighting men in each. In two week's time men in an old regiment are well drilled, while three months won't drill them in a new organization. Then see the folly of paying bounty. Give them two or three weeks to volunteer and, if the number of men are not forthcoming, draft.

Every cent of tax levied now will be a burden to pay when the war is over. I have made up my mind never to invest my money in taxable property in the United States, for I consider two-thirds of the debt that will be to pay is caused by folly, cheating and extravagance. If the government will hang all the contractors and annul all contracts, then the debt of the government will be about proper. Look at the item of rations for the soldiers. I figured up the other day, and I find that we get very little more than half what is allowed, and yet we have to make requisitions in advance for the full amount. Now where does the extra unissued rations go to? Some villainous quartermaster pockets the proceeds, which in our regiment alone amounts to a fortune in a short time.

We are encamped within a few hundred yards of the spot where Cornwallis surrendered his sword to Washington. There used to be a stone monument enclosed in a neat fence with the facts engraven upon the stone to mark the place, but the rebels carried the stone away with them when they evacuated last May. The fence is partially standing yet although our soldiers are cutting it up for relics. I procured a piece of it this morning and also a leaf from a shrub growing within the railing. I sent you a piece, which you can give Kate to place in her cabinet of curiosities. Standing there what thoughts of the past came up before one's mind. Then there is Yorktown with all its ancient rust sticking to it yet. The old building, in which the council of officers was held to decide about the surrender, is still standing and is used as a hospital. The old earthworks thrown up by the British for their defense are still in a tolerable state of preservation, but how insignificant they are in comparison to the gigantic works of the rebels. These latter are the most formidable I have ever seen, and I have seen nearly all of any consequence in the east. I have been through them from the James River to the York and find them to be apparently impregnable. McClellan's works are rough and temporary in comparison to the rebels'—they will last a century and then be in good condition. Most of the heavy guns are still in position on the works around the town, which looks as though the government intended to hold this position.

The weather is quite cold. Overcoats are in demand. I have seen much warmer weather in November than yesterday and today. It rains, too, nearly every night. Some think the comet[38] has some effect upon the weather. Our mails have not come to hand since we left Harrison's Landing, and as a consequence I have not received a Chicago paper or a letter for over a week, [I] understand the mail is at the fortress. I am somewhat anxious to hear something about the check I sent you.

I intend to send Kate the pony as soon as we reach Alexandria. It is in splendid condition and will be ready for Kate to continue her exercises on after returning from Minnesota. Capt. Cleveland's son is here and is going to Chicago when we reach Alexandria and has agreed to see that the pony gets through. Furloughs are about "played out," so that I have no hope of visiting home until the war ends or I resign, which I think I'll do if McClellan should continue in command of this army. I don't wish to serve under him any longer.

The hour for dress parade has arrived, and I must conclude.

Love to the family, Yours, etc. etc. W. H. Medill

William to Joseph
Darnestown, Maryland, September 7, 1862

Brother Joseph:

Yesterday we received our back mail, which has been flying round from pillar to post ever since we left Harrison's Landing. It brought up all my back *Tribunes* and letters. Two of them were from you and one from Kate. I was

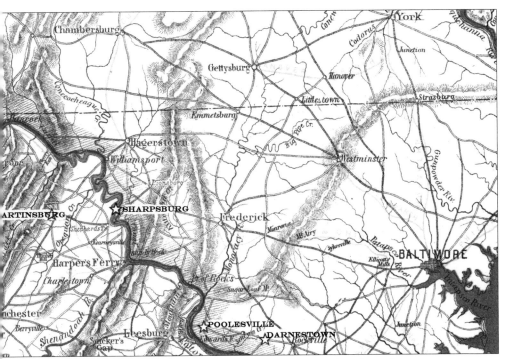

Action at Martinsburg, Sharpsburg Battle of Antietam, Poolesville, and Darnestown. (Library of Congress Geography and Map Division; adapted from Nicholson's *Map of Eastern Virginia*)

very much gratified to know that the $500 had reached you in safety, and I am satisfied with the way in which you invested it. As regards my wishes in regard to the disposition of my effects, my direction is to pay off all debts that may be presented and authenticated against me, which is embraced in what I owe Geo. E. Armstrong, and then give the rest of it to Mother for her use and investment. Government owes me about $400 at present, which in case of accident you can draw and invest the same way. Of course, all the money Mother receives will be used in such a way as to be useful to Mary and Ellen in case of her death.

Besides my money I know of no other property I have to dispose of, except my military "fixins," which consists of one horse (my other one having died the other day,) one cavalry sabre, two cavalry revolvers and two uniforms, which you and Jim can divide to suit yourselves; that is, provided the rebs don't get them if I am killed. This I believe ends my affairs, except one trunk, which is not so valuable.

Well, we have finally got into Maryland and find our friends Jackson and Ewell are a little ahead of us. These gentlemen crossed the Potomac at Edward's Ferry on Thursday night and Friday in large force, and proceeded to Poolesville, a village some seven from here, where they have been holding high revel ever since. I have no idea what our army is doing. Our force here consists of three regiments of cavalry and two batteries under Gen. Pleasonton. Our force is not sufficient to do much against them. Yesterday I went up and drove their pickets into the town, and this morning another force has been sent up to reconnoiter them again. The people here are pretty equally divided between secesh and Union. Jackson is getting quite an addition to his army.

So Sammy has enlisted and is on his way. The col. has returned and is now in command. I was running the machine when he came, both Major Clendenin and Beveridge have been sick ever since the regiment left Yorktown.

In regard to my resignation, I did tender it, but Major Clendenin declined forwarding it as the regiment could not spare me. I was disgusted and sick and wanted out of the army. But since Sammy has seen fit to enlist, I'll try and do as well as I can by him. As soon as Dustin's resignation arrives, I'll be promoted and Lieut. Hynes made capt. of the company. He has promised me to make Sammy a sergeant, and if he is attentive will be in the line of promotion. Under the new cavalry bill there are a number of new offices, and he will stand a good chance.

I sent the pony to Kate by Ezra Cleveland on Thursday last. The trip on the boat and the long ride on the cars I suppose will reduce her somewhat in flesh. However, it is an easy keeper and can be fattened up very easily. Kate and the children will be fond of this I have no doubt. I sent you a letter by him directing you what to pay him.

I am ordered out now to look up some horses that the rebs captured the other day but which escaped from them. I'll try and write you a communication this afternoon for the *Tribune*.

Yours in haste, W. H. Medill

Samuel to Mary
Kirkwood House, Washington, D.C., September 8, 1862

Sister Mary:

We arrived here safely at 12:30 a.m. today. We had to remain in Baltimore from 12 o'clock yesterday till 10 o'clock this morning. It is awful hot here, and we have had to travel about ten miles in order to obtain transportation to our regiment, which is stationed about 15 miles north of Washington on the upper Potomac. In my travels about the city today I have seen the capital buildings, President's House, State, Treasury, War and Navy Departments. Washington don't amount to much—I expected something of a city, but it don't amount to a "row of pins."

I see by the papers that McClellan has assumed chief command of the Army of Virginia and that Pope has been sent to Minnesota to fight Indians. I half wish I had not enlisted.

The hotels here are swarming with "shoulder strap gentry"—why half the people I have seen are officers. I have no doubt two regiments of officers could be formed if necessary.

I will write again as soon as I get to my regiment. Give my love to all. Mr. Kecheson sends regards.

S. J. Medill

The Battle of Antietam (or Sharpsburg) was fought September 17, 1862, in the vicinity of Antietam Creek, flowing in a southerly direction into the Potomac River above Harpers Ferry. General McClellan made the mistake of attacking piecemeal in five separate attacks at different hours. As a result, the battle was a draw. Despite the fact that he received reinforcements the next day, McClellan allowed Lee to remove his army across the Potomac. The Union force might have severed the Confederate line of retreat by the way of Boteler's Ford but failed to do so.

In the first part of the Battle of Antietam, the Eighth Illinois cavalry regiment, under Medill's command, remained in reserve. When ordered to the front, they supported two batteries near the center of the Union line. In this position the regiment came under enemy infantry and artillery fire and suffered a number of casualties. During the day neither side gained a significant advantage. To the left of the Eighth Illinois Cavalry, General Burnside's command finally crossed the lower stone bridge, but the loss of life was sickening.

When night fell, Major Medill's cavalrymen withdrew a mile and a half back of their battle position, going into temporary camp, where many of the men spent the night caring for the wounded. Early on the morning of the September 19, orders were received to advance again, but Confederates had escaped across the Potomac. The regiment made a rapid march through the village of Sharpsburg, where every house showed the effects of heavy bombardment. The following day there was sporadic fighting along the banks of the Potomac, and the next day the Eighth Illinois cavalry remained in its camp at Sharpsburg, a respite from hard service.[39]

WILLIAM PRESUMABLY TO KATE

Sharpsburg, Maryland, September 22, 1862

Dear Sister:

I have time to write you a line and will improve it. Sammy has arrived and brought your letter and some little niceties also for which I am much obliged to you. His initiation into the regiment was on the morning of the great battle of Antietam Creek. The regiment was moving forward at the time he arrived and in twenty minutes after I shook hands with him, we were in advance of all the lines and under the most terrific storm of shell and shot I have ever experienced. Horses and men were blown to eternity on every hand, and yet we were compelled to sit quietly on our horses, supporting two batteries while they silenced three batteries of the enemy. Sam stood the fire first-rate, and I only saw him looking up wistfully occasionally when a shell would burst near. I don't think he was frightened much. I have no time to write any of the particulars of the battle, but I think it was by far the severest of the war.

The rebels have been driven from Maryland, but not without two very desperate battles and a great many skirmishes, in the latter of which our regiment has done more than all the others, and your humble servant has been in command ever since we left the Peninsula. I have had the pleasure of leading the regiment into every attack and have escaped without a scratch thus far, although I came very nearly going by the board in the last one. By the way, I have been promoted to a majorship, which was made vacant by the resignation of Major Dustin.

You speak of my soon getting a furlough, but as I am the only field officer with the regiment, I don't think there is much chance at present. We are expecting Major Beveridge one of these days, and I am in hopes the Lt. Colonel will also come. Our colonel is in command of a brigade of cavalry, which takes him away from the regiment.

My health is very good since we have been in Maryland. This state seems lovely in comparison with Virginia, which was a perfect desolation. The people are very friendly, and we get everything we want. I have also made the acquaintance of some very pleasant young ladies. I have almost wished to be wounded in order to receive their attentions for a while. They are wonderfully delighted to get the "Deliverers," as the rebel army styled themselves, out of their state. Well, I don't wonder for they are the most ragged, rude, filthy looking objects ever paraded as soldiers. Especially to a person of delicate feelings they are enough to produce the fits.

I presume we are to have another campaign in Virginia, which I very much dread. I detest the very name of Virginia, or anyone who lives there. I hope, if McClellan does take us in there, he will hurry matters up and make an end of things, for I am mighty tired of war.

Well, I must close. Sammy and I are very well and send much love to you all. Tender my regards to friends.

Yours, etc. etc. W. H. Medill

P. S. I enclose you a secesh envelope, which we captured. It contains the confederate stamps. The one this letter is enclosed in is also secesh. I have some rebel paper also but not at hand. Yours W. H.

William to Joseph
Sharpsburg, Maryland, September 22, 1862

Bro Joseph:

I have only time to drop you a line and let you know that Sammy and myself are quite well and enjoying ourselves—as well as constant riding and but little sleep will permit. Sammy joined the regiment on the morning of the great battle, and just as we were moving to the front. His initiation into the service was rather lively, but he behaved well. We did not have any fighting to do, but we did what was more trying on one's bravery, we took an advanced position beyond all our other troops, planted our two batteries of flying artillery and supported them until they silenced three batteries belonging to the enemy. Strange to say in all this fiery ordeal we did not lose a man although our horses suffered badly.

Well, we have driven the enemy out of Maryland and have fought two very severe battles. In both of which McClellan was successful.

Our regiment has performed a great deal of service—more than it ever did in the same length of time. We entirely destroyed two regiments of Gen. Ashby's celebrated cavalry and neutralized Stuart's efficiency. Col. Farnsworth deserves the credit of this as it was his command (he is acting Brigadier General of four regiments: the 8th Ill., 8th Pennsylvania, 1st Massachusetts and 3rd Indiana,) which accomplished about all that has been done. I wish you would, if you can, give him a good puff for he deserves it.

I will try one of these days to give you an account of our exploits. I am still in command of the regiment. Had command during all our fights and have been commended by Gen. Pleasonton. Suppose I am major or will be soon as the governor can send my commission.

As soon as the Lt. Col. and Major Beveridge return, I want you to try and get me a short furlough. By directing letters and papers as you always have, they are forwarded from Washington.

I am glad the pony reached and am much pleased to hear that Kate is so well. Tell Kitty that I called the pony "Nelly," but as that is the name of the other one, she had better name it "Kitty."

The weather is delightful, and our men are in good health. But I must close. With regards to all, I remain yours, etc. W. H. Medill

Dr. Hard's Account of the Eighth Illinois Cavalry at Antietam

On the morning of the 17th, a little after daylight, the battle of Antietam was fairly commenced. At first we were held in reserve, but were soon ordered to the front to support a battery near the center of the Union line. We had to cross the stone bridge over Antietam Creek, on the turnpike leading from Boonsboro to Sharpsburg, in direct range with the enemy's cannon, where but a few moments before several of the Fourth Pennsylvania Cavalry had been killed while crossing, among whom was the Colonel of the regiment; none of our brigade were injured although the fire was terrific and almost incessant. We were soon posted in support of Robinson's battery under cover of a hill, which afforded some protection from the enemy's shot and shell which, passing directly over our heads, would strike the opposite bank of the stream or dash into the waters. Our own guns were placed on the hill in our rear and also firing over our heads. The roar of the cannon of the opposing armies combined, produced an almost deafening noise.

Occasionally a slug from the cartridge would fall in our midst. In this manner several of the Third Indiana were wounded. At one time one of the rebel shells fell short without bursting, and striking the hill in our front came tumbling and skipping along, passing through our ranks into the creek some twenty yards in our rear. The men, as by instinct, suddenly opened their ranks and let the unwelcome messenger pass without doing any damage. After remaining in this position for several hours, we moved up the creek a distance of about half a mile, while the shells were passing over our heads from the front and rear, but almost miraculously none of them did any damage. On our right the battle raged with varying success. General Hooker was in command in this part of the field and was wounded, and General Sumner supplied his place.

To and fro the armies swayed over a field that was repeatedly won and lost, until the ground was strewn with dead and dying, and neither side gained very great advantage. On our left, at the lower stone bridge across the Antietam where General Burnside commanded, the battle was terribly sanguinary, the crossing was finally effected, but the slaughter was heart-sickening. In the center I think our success was probably better, but purchased with an almost inconceivable loss of life.

The "Irish Brigade" and One Hundred and Thirtieth Pennsylvania here made a desperate charge over an open field and dislodged the enemy from a lane, which had been gullied out by the rain, so that it made with the stones piled along its edge ready to be made into a fence an excellent barricade. They also drove them from a cornfield in front of the lane, from which a deadly fire had been kept up for many hours. Night closed upon a hard fought battle, wherein we thought the Union army had achieved a victory.

After dark our regiment was marched back half a mile and rested for the night, confidently expecting to renew the battle in the morning, as we knew the enemy had been forced from their position along the whole line of conflict. The night was spent in caring for the wounded. At a farmhouse used for a hospital we again met Miss Clara Barton.[40]

William to Kate
Sharpsburg, Maryland, October 3, 1862

Dear Sister:

I have neglected writing to you for some time owing to the fact that Sammy agreed to write, and as everything was new to him, he would be much more likely to write an interesting letter than I would, and he can write a first rate letter if he wishes to. But just as predicted, before he entered the service, he cannot stand it, and before he had been here on duty a week, he was so much crippled with the rheumatism that I made application for his discharge, and by special favor got it through immediately, so that he is no longer a soldier. Poor Sam, he is, I am afraid, destined to live a thorny life, unless he can effectually get cured. Since it has turned out as it has, I am glad he joined this regiment, for if he had got among strangers, it would have required two or three months in the regular course of events to procure a discharge. "Red tape" is very slow about business, especially when one is in a hurry. I have written to Joseph, telling him that Sammy was discharged, and as he has been talking about coming here on a visit, Sammy is still stopping with me, till I hear from him. We are yet on the battlefield of Antietam, and there is no certainty when we will leave.

During the past week we have been making some visits into Virginia and have had the pleasure of some sharp skirmishing. On the day before yesterday our brigade went as far as Martinsburg, which is about fifteen miles from here. Our regiment had the honor of taking the advance, and of bringing up the rear, as I am still in command, this duty devolved on me. That I conducted it well is evidenced in the fact that I received a letter of thanks from Gen. Pleasonton.

I had twelve wounded and four taken prisoners, while I captured about thirty and killed and wounded about one hundred and fifty and sent them flying in every direction. Of course, Gen. Pleasonton receives the praise of the affair in the newspapers as he was along, but he did not interfere nor give an order, and when we returned he thanked me for having conducted the affair so well. You can find an account of it in the *New York Times* and *Tribune* of the 2nd or 3d, I think. I rather like such little affairs for the excitement. The danger I care not for, although I was in close quarters a couple of times on the way coming back but escaped without a scratch.

Well, since writing to you I have been promoted to be a Major. Of course, I feel the dignity of my new position and will try and do honor to the double breasted coat and two rows of buttons. As I have no further use for keeping my commission as captain with me, I send it to you with Sammy and wish you would have it framed, and put away or hung up as an evidence that the Medill family was represented in the great war.

I rather think I will not be favored with a furlough this fall. All the field officers are absent sick and likely to be so for considerable time, which will keep me tied to the regiment. I hope to be able to get one so as to spend the holidays at home. When Sammy returns, he will give you the news more fully than I can write.

With much love to all I remain, Your affectionate Brother Will

The account William referred to in the *New York Times* is as follows:

> A dispatch from Gen. MCCLELLAN's Headquarters, dated last evening, informs us that Gen. PLEASANTON [sic], in the morning, crossed the Potomac at Shepherdstown, with a force of cavalry and artillery, for the purpose of making a reconnaissance in the enemy's rear. He came up with a force of rebels near Shepherdstown and drove them to Martinsburgh [sic], from which place he soon shelled them, with a loss on our side of only two men wounded. Some prisoners were captured. It is now believed that very few rebel troops are at Winchester, their main force being encamped between that place and Martinsburgh.[41]

Dr. Hard's Account of Sharp Skirmishing October 1, 1862

> General Pleasanton [sic], having gained all the information possible of the situation of the rebel army, made preparations to return. This move called for more military skill, caution and courage than it had required to advance. We were twelve miles from Shepherdstown, the nearest ford, with a force not to

exceed eight hundred men, (our regiment being very much reduced at that time) and with an opposition of five or six times our number on all sides, well acquainted with the country, of which we were comparatively ignorant.

On withdrawing, the Eighth Illinois was placed in the rear of the column, the rear guard being commanded by Major Medill. Scarcely had our pickets left their post before the rebel cavalry came pouring along in pursuit. The streets were filled and completely blockaded with them. A section of our artillery, placed on a slight eminence just outside of town, and trained to bear on a bridge, with a few well directed shots held the enemy in check for a short time and created considerable confusion in their ranks. This enabled our advance to move some distance ahead when the artillery was withdrawn, leaving Captain Clark with his squadron in the extreme rear. Ere long those in the front discovered that the enemy had taken advantage of Captain Clark's position and were sending terrific showers of shot into the midst of his gallant little band. The Captain sent word to Major Medill that it would be impossible for him to hold out much longer when one squadron of the Eighth Pennsylvania was placed in a commanding position to assist in repulsing the enemy, but their commander, seeing the situation of affairs and knowing that it would be a warmly contested point, abandoned his position without firing a shot. We then placed two pieces of artillery in position and opened fire upon the rebels to protect Captain Clark. It was, however, like firing against a tornado. The enemy by passing on either side of the road were enabled to rush madly on, seemingly determined to surround us at all hazards. Our artillery was obliged to fall back to prevent being captured.

Major Medill ordered his squadron commanders to form their men on the side of the road facing the rear "as quick as ever God would let them." Captain Southworth's squadron was on the right facing towards the advancing rebels. He scarcely had his men in line before they were upon him, but a couple of volleys from their carbines at short range checked the pursuit for a sufficient length of time, to allow Captain Clark's squadron to pass and take a new position, when the two squadrons, together with that of Captain Farnsworth, discharged such effective volleys into their very faces that they were repulsed and held at bay until the artillery could be placed in proper position, which sent such volleys of canister into their midst they were compelled to yield the field, leaving their dead and wounded behind them.

It was now dark, and after holding our position a short time, until it was thought the enemy did not propose another attack, the general withdrew his forces, and we were not molested again on our return to the Potomac, which we safely crossed a little before midnight.

General Pleasanton complimented the regiment very highly for the coolness and courage displayed, and also Major Medill for the manner in which he commanded his men. The discipline, which our men had undergone, was here fully displayed by our squadrons halting from a swift march and delivering their fire as regularly and coolly as on the parade ground, and by taking one position after another while retreating before a superior force and under a severe fire, in a manner which would not have been excelled by any troops in the world. Official reports showed the enemy's loss to have been one hundred and fifty, of which number forty were killed and buried on the field. The Eighth Illinois lost but sixteen men, twelve wounded and four missing.

October 2d was spent by the men in resting and recounting the deeds of daring and the narrow escapes of the previous day, and by way of variety an unpleasant misunderstanding occurred between Captains Hynes and Farnsworth in regard to the distribution of the horses, which had just arrived for the regiment. Such harmony had heretofore existed among the officers that a little "family jar" was looked upon as a serious matter, but mild counsels prevailed and all dissatisfaction was soon forgotten. Towards evening the four men who were missing arrived in camp, having been paroled. They reported that they were well treated by General Stuart, who led the rebel charge. The General said "he knew it was the Eighth Illinois Cavalry he was fighting, by the way they withstood his charges." General Fitz Hugh Lee told them that in our charge at Boonsboro, his horse was killed and he had to run into a cornfield and then walk ten miles to effect his escape. In the estimation of the Confederates, the Eighth Illinois was the best, and the Third Indiana Cavalry the next best regiment in the Federal army. One of the rebel officers sent his compliments to Captain Clark, saying "he liked his style—he was so cool—and that he would have been highly pleased if he could have made him a prisoner."[42]

William to a friend at the Chicago *Daily Tribune*
In Camp near Sharpsburg, Maryland, October 7, 1862

Friend Alf:

After a long silence, I find myself seated and commencing a letter to you. I should have answered sooner, but I have been so very busy of late as to preclude my writing to scarcely any of my friends. It was no great matter anyhow, as I observe by the paper, our whereabouts and movements have been kept posted.

Since leaving Yorktown I have been in command of the regiment, and I flatter myself it has been kept busy. I have never had a fair chance to test the fighting qualities of the men or of myself until we came into Maryland, but

I guess no one will dispute that the 8th will do its duty. My rule has been to charge the rebels wherever and whenever we have met them, and we have been successful. We have had a dozen hand-to-hand encounters and have had a good many killed and wounded, but never without doing the rebs three times as much damage as we received. We were not fighting raw troops but their crack regiments. I observe by a pictorial two of our charges are illustrated but like all pictures they are incorrect. The only thing looking natural is in the one where the flag was captured is the flag. It [the picture] should have shown a couple of hundred men all mixed up together, cutting and slashing, and one of our men with his pistol shooting the rebel flag bearer. There is another remark, the col. was present, and did not know there had been a fight until I presented him the flag, accompanied with a dozen prisoners and as many horses, arms, etc.

The last fight we had was the other day when we went to Martinsburg, Va. Coming home three regiments attacked me in the rear, but I can say with the nigger, "If ever I fooled a man in all my life, I fooled them secesh." I sent the battery ahead except one gun and had the five guns placed in a good position, sweeping the road, and by feigning weakness and apparently trying to save the single piece with me, drew them up to within a few hundred yards of the guns, by an understood order cleared the road and let the whole battery belch out grape canister and shells; and when they commenced running, we poured in some splendid volleys from our carbines and pistols. I never saw a more glorious sight in my life than when those guns opened. I jumped my horse over the fence and rode chase up to them, where I could see the effect. Horses and men were torn to pieces and knocked into "fire." We killed and wounded inside of ten minutes over 150! Our force being too small to follow them, night coming on, and ten miles farther to go home, Pleasonton thought we had better fall back. The rebs followed but at a very respectful distance. Gen. Pleasonton complimented me very highly and said it was the most scientific cavalry fight achieved by the cavalry in this army. To handle cavalry a man wants coolness, courage and a good horse. The latter I know I have, for I have tried him several times of late. On this occasion I jumped over a stone wall six feet high easily where I gained a splendid view of the affair and had an opportunity of emptying my pistol at short range among them.

At present we are in camp on the battlefield of Antietam. We occupy the ground fought over by Burnside and water our horses where the two sides fought so fiercely, and our men were finally driven back. Dead horses, fragments of wagons, cannon balls, shells, graves and trenches are seen on every hand near that place. In fact, for six or eight miles up and down that stream may be seen the evidences of the terrible havoc of that day. I never wish to be under such an infernal rain of cannon and musketry balls again, as I was on that occasion. I thought sometimes my final end was nigh, and that everybody else near me would share the same fate. But here I am, a living evidence of the folly of human speculation about life. To tell the truth I was not sorry when night came on and put a stop to the "dispute."

I don't know what we are going at next; probably going into winter quarters, and probably advance on the enemy. Hope the latter will be decided on—that is if we are allowed to follow them up. I think we can lick their army without doubt and probably drive them past Richmond. I fear, however, we will go into quarters this winter and make preparations for next Spring. All great generals, you know, do this, and of course "Little" Napoleon [General George McClellan] will keep up the rule.

What's the news with you? Our mails have come so irregularly of late that I have gotten behind badly. So John Fargahan finally accepted the exalted position of Sergeant Major in an infantry regiment. Guess he would have done much better to have enlisted in my company. He used to swear at Hynes and myself for our presumption in getting up a company. I feel more pleased to see the way in which Dennis has advanced than my own promotion. He is now Captain Hynes of Company G, 8th Ill. Cavalry, and there are but few better officers or braver men in the army. In our fight at Boonsboro he had two horses shot under him, then mounted a third and was foremost in the charge. Glory for Hynes. He said to me when I told him I was going to write, to give you his best regards and ask you to tell some of those cowards who have stayed at home and who have talked about him to look out when he returned. He and I are in hopes of getting a short furlough, if we go into winter quarters, to visit Chicago.

Can't you pay us a visit this fall? I'll guaranty you will be interested, and you may have an opportunity of participating in a scout with us. I am expecting Joseph every day. I wrote to him sometime since in regard to Sammy having the rheumatism and not being able to stand the fatigue, and as he intended visiting us, Sammy would remain with me until he arrived. Hope he will either come soon, or let me hear from him, for the reason that Sammy is pretty badly off and ought to be out of camp.

Please express to my friends my best regards and especially to Geo. Williston, White Smith, Ray Hickox, Ballantyne and the boys in the newsroom and to Mrs. Cowles. If you have time drop me a line directing it as follows: Major W. H. Medill, 8th Ill. Cavalry (To be forwarded) Washington, D.C.

P.S. I acknowledge the receipt of the daily *Tribune* instead of tri-weekly, for which accept my thanks. I get all the numbers notwithstanding they sometimes come in bundles of a dozen. W. H. M.

WILLIAM TO JOSEPH
In Camp near Knoxville, Maryland, October 12, 1862

Dear Brother:

I have been anxiously expecting a letter from you for some time but have been disappointed. I suppose the reason is our mail has strayed off to some other place and has not been forwarded yet. I have not had a line from you since the one you wrote on the 28th nlt [no later than]. I wrote you a letter about the same time giving you a list of the officers of the regiment and also some particulars of our doing; and also the fact that Sammy had been so badly afflicted with the rheumatism as to render his discharge necessary, which I affected. I waited an answer from you before sending him home until last Friday when I took him to Hagerstown where he could take the cars. We started from there on Saturday morning but owing to the raid of Stuart, the train was turned back, and he did not get away until Sunday or Monday. I understand the train he was on came very nearly falling into the hands of the rebels at Chambersburg, Pa. However, a "miss is as good as a mile," and he escaped.

The poor boy became worse as long as he remained and finally, he could scarcely walk at all. I took the very best care of him I could and would have sent him home sooner, but being nearly out of money, and nearly all the officers in the same condition, I had hopes that you might be able to procure a pass for him over a part of the distance at least, even if you did not conclude to come on yourself. But finding him getting so much worse I "strapped" myself and gave him $29.00 and told him to go as far as Mother's, and that you would, no doubt, get him a pass from there to Chicago. There will have to be great care taken of him, or he will soon be as badly afflicted as Father or Jim. I never felt more sorry for any person than for him when I saw the terrible pain he suffered in trying to walk. What an infernal disease this is and how our poor family have suffered from it.

I am still in hopes you may conclude to pay me a visit. You can come all the way by rail. We are encamped about a mile from Knoxville on the Baltimore & Ohio R.R. You can come right to the Knoxville depot, which is some three or four miles from Harpers Ferry. I also have some lingering hope that you might be able to procure me a short furlough through your friendship with [U.S. secretary of the treasury] Chase[43] or some member of "Old Abe's" cabinet. I think we will remain here for a week or two in order to recruit our horses and men and either prepare for winter quarters or a campaign in Virginia; in either case I would be pleased to pay my friends a short visit and have a little recreation. As long as I remain in camp most of the duty will be put upon me, and if Col. Farnsworth can trust the regiment to my command during active service, I need have no hesitancy about trusting it during its stay in camp to the senior captain present, Capt. Clark, a most excellent officer. There is no use applying for a furlough through the regular channel of the army circumlocution officer, for it never would be granted to a volunteer officer unless three or four doctors will certify that it is necessary for the preservation of life. Then it will *probably* be given. Their only chance is through outside friendship. We have just passed through one of the most active campaigns, as far as this regiment is concerned on record, and I have never missed a week's duty. I think I am entitled to a short respite. Besides, I must purchase some clothing for winter, as I was unfortunate enough to lose all my stock during the retreat from the Chickahominy to James River; and have never had an opportunity to replace the articles. I have only a jacket and a pair of pantaloons for a uniform as protection against the cold. Were my constitution not of the best materials I would be on the sick list now, having made the late terrible march after Stuart with no heavier clothing and a part of the time we were exposed to a very cold rain.

Well, I supposed you were not much astonished to hear of Stuart's raid. We all feel keenly the disgrace which our cavalry must suffer in the opinion of the public and our friends in particular. Your correspondent, Mr. Ingersoll, has written you the particulars of the part we played in the attempt to catch the rebels. In fact, we were the only cavalry that did anything. I hope you will make this a subject for an article on the cavalry. There never will be any success for our arms until our army is differently organized. We must adopt the European system of dividing an army into the three natural divisions of infantry, artillery and cavalry, putting each under the charge of the most competent man in his peculiar service. For instance, let the infantry be under the command of General Hooker, the artillery under the command of General Sigel and the cavalry under General Sumner. Of course, there would have to be subdivisions of each, but in this case there would be a man to assign to any position in the regiments, brigades or divisions best suited to the wants or necessities of the occasion. As at present in some places of vast importance there may be an inadequate number of cavalry or all of an inferior kind, or the same may be true of the artillery and infantry. This is what gives Stuart his advantage. He commands *all* the cavalry, and if he wants to make a raid or a reconnaissance, he knows where to find every regiment he wants, and he takes them. While we are cut up into half a dozen petty, little brigades under as many insignificant little brigadiers, each jealous of the other accomplishing something and in the end doing nothing. The cavalry in this army, with the exception of our regiment, the 3rd Indiana and the 12th Illinois are looked upon by the generals in command of divisions and corps as worse than worthless, for they are in the way. And they are right. We have maintained *our* reputation by over exertion against the natural prejudice engendered by the other regiments.

But I must close. It is getting late. I shall hope to hear from you soon if I don't have the pleasure of seeing you. Give my love to Kate and the children and regards to all my friends.

Yours, etc. W. H. Medill

P.S. Direct to Washington, as usual, W. H. M.

WILLIAM TO JOSEPH

Fredericksburg, November 8, 1862

[No salutation]

I have just been discussing an expedition which might be performed by this army. It is to take all the cavalry here and around Washington, amounting to nearly twenty-five thousand, add to that number about ten thousand infantry, ambulances and light wagons and about fifty pieces of flying artillery, place the command under Gen. Sumner and on some evening make a dash across the Rappahannock. We could gobble up all the pickets in our way and by morning be in the rear of Lee's whole army, destroy all telegraphic communication with Richmond and by evening be in that city. By destroying the railroads we could prevent their infantry from following, and we would be strong enough to capture whatever cavalry might attempt to retard us. I believe we could capture the city without much opposition, burn it, and retire by way of Petersburg and down the James River if pushed. If Burnside would pitch into Lee in the morning after we started, he could ship him and destroy that army and in that case after accomplishing our work, we could return and fall upon Lee's flying horde and finish all that remained of it. I suppose our generals would consider such a proposition visionary, but I am as confident of its being practicable as that Richmond is the rebel capital. Such an expedition, if successful, would end the rebellion as far as organized resistance is concerned. But our commanders never do anything which would hazard anything. We don't fight to kill but to conciliate our brethren of the South. Such an exploit would be likely to make our southern friends mad and prevent a reconstruction of the Union on a slavery basis.

Gen. Burnside seems to have left Stonewall Jackson away up towards Winchester, and I should judge it would be an easy matter to drive Lee or whip him. If necessary Siegel could join this army before Jackson could join Lee, and thus make victory a double certainty; then he could fall upon Jackson and disperse Jackson's army while Burnside could proceed to Richmond. We ought to do something of this sort before the campaign is ended. I hope you will not be hasty in committing yourselves to Burnside before he does something. He certainly has wasted a week here to the great detriment of his successful advance upon the enemy. I have heard a good many doubts expressed as to his ability to command an army of the size of this one, and his apparent hesitancy now looks queer. But I have yet to see the officer, outside of a few regulars, who were not pleased with the change from McClellan, for even if Burnside should fail, the apparent spell which bound McClellan to the President is broken, and a change could be made with less trouble. But Gen. McClellan must be laid out beyond any possibility of ever getting a command again.

Col. Gamble returned a few days since, and is now in command of the regiment. Col. Farnsworth having gone to Washington. I suppose the col. will return with his stars, as he carries a strong recommendation from Burnside and Sumner for his immediate appointment to a brigadiership. The commissions also arrive about the same time.

I am very much obliged to you for remembering the bridle, for I was in need of it, my other one being about worn out. I believe I told you in my last letter that there was no trouble about my going home. Col. Farnsworth was very kind. I should have mentioned the fact that I found the check you sent Sam when I returned and burned it. By the way, where is Sam? I want to write to him.

Our mails have not arrived but once since I returned, so that I have not seen but one copy of the *Tribune*. My stump of candle having about burned out, I am admonished to bring this to a conclusion.

Please give my love to your family and ask Kate to give my profoundest regards to the charming Misses C. and D. The recollection of these charming countenances make my hardships seem light, but tell Kate that I can't help thinking Miss C. the prettiest.

With hopes of receiving the mails soon, containing late *Tribune*s and other things to remind me of what is going on at home, I remain, Yours, etc. W. H. Medill

P.S. Find one dollar for which send me the value of it in three-cent postage stamps.

General Burnside started his campaign to Fredericksburg well. However, instead of moving straight south, using the vulnerable railroad through Manassas, he took the army to Falmouth. By moving quickly, he got two advance corps to Falmouth on November 17, but the pontoons needed for crossing the Rappahannock did not show up for more than a week. General Lee had the time to fortify the hills south of the river with 75,000 men.[44]

WILLIAM TO MARY
In Camp near Warrenton, Virginia, November 16, 1862

Dear Sister:

I arrived here yesterday and joined the command. I had a very tiresome trip and had considerable difficulty in finding the whereabouts of the regiment. Last night I had the agreeable pleasure of a bed in the open air under my blankets. I find everything in good condition, and the regiment, as usual, has been very busy since I left near a month since. I was engaged in all the fights through Virginia and I find the officers and men swearing loudly about the unfair reports made by the reporters, in giving credit to the New York and Pennsylvania regiments, which the 8th Illinois deserves. This has been our misfortune frequently. This army is moving and I presume we will proceed to Fredericksburg tomorrow. Everybody anticipates a battle soon. Hope public anticipation is correct.

Gen. Burnsides is accepted as McClellan's successor with great satisfaction by the army. He will do something even if that something is to get whipped. You can keep your eyes open for something in the way of war. News, of course, is a scarce commodity with me, and you must excuse the brevity of this note.

I want you to go to Orrin McIntire's and get six copies of the two small pictures and send them to me—three of each. Tell him to give you the bill of them, and I will pay it as soon as I receive it. When I left Canton I forgot all about his account. Send them in a letter, directing to me at Washington, D.C. to be forwarded just as my letters have always been sent.

Love to everybody. Write soon.

Yours, etc. W. H. Medill

This letter was in William's handwriting and filed amid correspondence for November 1862, but its opening page is missing.

William to an Unknown Recipient

[No salutation]

. . . We talked quite a while; he [the prisoner] was a captain of a Mississippi regiment, the number I have forgotten. When I told him I belonged to the 8th Illinois Cavalry, he remarked that "your regiment stand very high in the estimation of our army as being a good fighting regiment, and in fact," said he "all you western men fight well." I told him I thought the eastern men were just as good. He said, "d__n the Yankees, we can whip two to one." I asked him whether he was aware there had been a change in our commanders in this army, and he said he knew about the change two days after it took place. He said he supposed we soldiers of the Union army expected great things to come of the change, but he predicted that the Democrats of the North would soon be in as much rebellion as the South was. I told him there was no party opposed to the war in the North, but he said he knew better, as he had seen letters from Democrats at the North, saying that they had things about ripe for an uprising. We talked for some time in this same strain when we bid each other good day, and each turned and rode off.

I have no doubt that he told the truth about seeing letters from northern Democrats, saying just what he told me. Such men as Story[45] [sic] of the *Times,* the Woods of N.Y. and others of that stripe, are as great traitors as Jeff Davis and the leaders of what is called the Democracy, and I have but little doubt the scoundrels will attempt it, if there are not improvements in our mode of conducting the war and, to tell the truth, if we can't whip the rebels soon, there will be a good excuse for some change in the managers of this concern.

I am of the opinion there will be nothing more done here this winter. The rainy season has set in, and the roads are about impassable for teams, consequently transportation is about out of the question. Of course, I mean in a military way, the roads are impassable. To me, it seems as though we might manage to move as far as Richmond. I infer what I say about not doing anything more from the fact that we have stopped our march on this side of the Rappahannock when, if Gen. Burnside intended to go any farther, it is all important that we should cross the stream and occupy the hills back of Fredericksburg before Lee could get his army in position to dispute our progress. As it stands, Lee has taken up his position and will undoubtedly give us trouble in crossing. I would not be surprised if we should fall back to Alexandria for our winter quarters. If we are going into winter quarters, that would be as good a position as any, as the rebels could not place many men in our front, on account of the distance from their supplies and the impossibility of building railroads in winter. Should we be compelled to do this, Gen. McClellan ought to be hung for traitorism in not advancing when the weather was fit for that purpose.

WILLIAM TO JOSEPH

In Bivouac, near Bealeton Station, Virginia, November 19, 1862

Dear Bro,

We are in motion, and this time I hope in earnest. Gen. Burnside has commenced properly by doing away with the infernal wagon trains and substituted pack mules. Every regiment goes complete, ready for a march of one or twenty miles, as circumstances require. We are now covering the right flank and rear of our army against raids of the rebels. The mistake is to strike for Fredericksburg and then do what McClellan ought to have done, make a rush on Richmond.

My time for writing is very limited and therefore I cannot say all I desire. You may say to the people that all stories purporting to represent this army as dissatisfied with the change of commanders are infernal lies; that Gen. Burnside stands higher in the estimation of his men than McClellan ever did. The men are all desirous of demonstrating this in a battle with Lee. Depend upon it there will be no more uncertain victories such as Antietam. When we go into camp for a day or so I'll write a long letter.

I had some difficulty in finding the regiment, which I finally discovered at Warrenton. It has been very busy and has been with Pleasonton all the while. Col. Farnsworth has been in command of Averell's Brigade but is with his regiment at present. He says he expects to be appointed a brigadier one of these days. He was very glad to see me and said he was glad I had taken the chance of visiting home when I did. On muster day he reported me "absent with leave," and said he should have done so even if I had remained a month longer. Can't you manage to give him a puff. I rather expect to get a silver leaf on my shoulder before long, but I'll not say how at present.

As regards your correspondent, the col. says he don't amount to anything, and that you had better write to him saying that he won't do. I have spoken to our chaplain, Mr. C. K. Judson, about becoming your correspondent, and he said he would be glad to write for the *Tribune* if it were your wish, but I think he would expect some pay. Write to him if you think you want him.

You can write to me by directing as you have always done to Washington to be forwarded.

Give my love to your family. In haste, W. H. Medill

William to Kate
In Bivouac, Near Morrisville, Virginia, November 20, 1862

Dear Sister:

Well, I found the regiment after a long and tiresome trip at Warrenton, where it had arrived the evening before from Waterloo, a small town on the Rappahannock River. It had been, as usual, busily engaged in the advance of the brigade under Gen. Pleasonton. Col. Farnsworth was in command of Averell's Brigade, but only for a few days, and is at present in command of his own regiment. He was glad to see me, but said he expected I would have remained longer that I was a fool for hurrying so much when, if I had remained another week, I might have had another opportunity of seeing Miss C. or Miss D. In such matters I always was unfortunate and especially so in this instance, as I had a good opportunity. At home I had a good time until Tuesday when I packed my baggage and "off to the wars again."

Unfortunately, I did not have an opportunity to visit New Philadelphia, the weather being somewhat disagreeable. I regretted it very much, for I would have had a good time. The Lt. Col. failed to get along on Tuesday as he agreed to, and he has not arrived yet. I would not have started if I had known he was not onboard the cars.

From Capt. Hynes I learn that the 8th Pennsylvania Cavalry have been appropriating the glory belonging to our regiment. He says the Penn. regiment never made one charge, and that where Major Keenan of that regiment is spoken of as having led a brilliant exploit with the 6th Regulars as supports, [the action] was, in reality, performed by Capt. Forsyth at the head of Companies E & B and one squadron of the 3rd Indiana as support. When I read the account originally, I thought it strange that the 8th Pennsylvania should have suddenly become so brave, for I had known that same Maj. Keenan to break and run when I had command of our regiment. The reporters for the Eastern papers have always been anxious to gouge us out of our due share of credit.

A report has just come in stating that our pickets in the rear have been fired upon, and that three of our regiment, belonging to Company I who were out foraging, were captured by the enemy. We are covering the rear and right wing of the army. Stuart's cavalry have come up and are hovering around us for the remainder of our trip to Fredericksburg. I suppose we will be annoyed with them. For the past forty-eight hours it has been raining, and today we have been lying over, waiting for the rain to stop, and the infantry to get through to Fredericksburg. I wish Mr. Stuart would come up and give us a brush, as it is now over a month since I have seen any of his friends.

It seems to me that we are going to give the rebs a hard run in getting back to Richmond, especially Stonewall Jackson, who is staying somewhere in the Shenandoah Valley. I presume he intended to make a raid into Maryland and probably Pennsylvania. Gen. Burnside was not to be deterred from his plan, and I heard today that he was making tracks towards Richmond. This was the proper way of treating him, as he is nothing more than a guerrilla, anyhow.

I am much afraid the roads are going to break up and put an effectual end to our advance. If we do have to go into winter quarters, Gen. McClellan can be blamed, as he wasted all the good weather in fooling around in Maryland after nothing. The country can put him down as the man who wasted all the time since the Battle of Antietam without reason. His friends in the army are becoming few and beautifully less each day. They have gradually, or rather suddenly, come down from their swaggering attitude to that of meek apologists for their idol. I think in the course of a few weeks there will be "none so poor to do him reverence." The change came just in the right time for the soldiers, as they were mourning over the defeat of their friends in the recent elections. This change convinced them that President Lincoln was going to straighten himself up and assert his authority over his army. Gen. McClellan had about reached the point where he considered himself ready to jump into the presidency.

My advice would be for the Republican papers to pitch into him for this course, instead of bragging on Burnside. Burnside may fail, and unless McClellan is completely exploded he will, in that event, be foisted back on the army by the force of public opinion. He is standing in waiting to take his old place in case of a failure on the part of Gen. Burnside. This army is still under command of subordinates who have his return in their hearts far above all else. They owe all their greatness to him, and as certain as Burnside fights a battle they will endeavor to trip him up. With a few exceptions, such as Hooker, Sumner, Pleasonton and a few others, I have no confidence in their loyalty. They may be true, but I don't see it. As far as this army is concerned, there ought to have been a general change in commanders. If a reverse does take place, and McClellan is not completely exposed, you may expect to see him in command of the Army of the Potomac, and next either president or military dictator. Depend upon this. I wish you would urge this upon Mr. Medill. I thought of saying the same thing to him, but I was hurried so much when I wrote to him that I didn't have time. I am not alone in this opinion. When I mentioned it to Col. Farnsworth he said he would write to all his friends the same thing.

I can't help thinking of the difference between the way I am enjoying this evening and how I would put in this same evening in Chicago. I am writing on an improvised desk, formerly used as a pew in a church, which I have carried into my tent. My bed is neatly spread on one side and is softened by a nice little bunch of hay; my companions are Capt. Hynes, Lieut. Wing and Lieut. Warner of my old company. They have no tent, and so I accommodate them. Their conversation has been miscellaneous, and a portion of the time has been put in reading Orpheus C. Kerr's letters. They are very much obliged to you for sending it. Just at present Capt. Hynes is singing snatches of love songs. Our horses are all saddled ready for action, and we are about half expecting an attack tonight or tomorrow morning. It don't create any excitement, and we are all wishing that it may be so. If it keeps on raining as it is doing at present, there is little danger.

I have just learned that one of the men captured by the rebels got away and reached camp a few moments since. The particulars of his escape I have not learned. Col. Farnsworth sends word to pack up our effects and send lead horses and sick men to the rear, as he wants no encumbrances if attacked. This stops letter writing. Give my love to the family and don't fail to give my regards to Miss Carpenter, Miss Davis and such others as you may think proper. Please write soon.

Yours, etc. W. H. Medill

P.S. Please excuse all mistakes as there has been so much talking I couldn't write. W. H. M.

William to Joseph

Belle Plain, December 6, 1862

Dear Brother:

I am just in from a five days' tour of picket duty on the upper fords of the Rappahannock, and I feel in anything but good humor on account of receiving no mails. Since the letter you wrote me in regard to having sent the Commipions I have not had a letter from any source and not even a copy of the *Tribune*. Our mail has gone astray, and the Lord only knows when it will find us.

The weather just now is terrible. All yesterday and last night, the snow and rain fell in blinding torrents, and about four o'clock this morning the weather turned cold and froze up. Our poor horses suffered awfully. I think I never had a more disagreeable ride than on my return to camp last night, some twenty miles most all the way with the snow beating in my face and over the very worst sort of roads. This is serving one's country, however, and we must not find fault.

Having been away from the camp so long, of course, I have no news of interest to write you. The divisions of Sumner and Hooker remain quiet, while Franklin, who has the left grand division, is moving down towards King George's Court House, and I also observed on my return last night that the pontoon train was moving in the same direction. I understand the gunboats are all down there, which would indicate that as the probable point at which a crossing will be made. Our long delay has given the rebels time to fortify themselves back of Fredericksburg so strongly that to attempt to cross at Falmouth would be folly. Their earthworks are visible on every knob and available point, and they have mounted many heavy siege pieces. Our only chance is to strike them on the flanks. My hope is that Gen. Burnside will prove equal to the emergency, and if he gains a decided victory, keep them going until we reach Richmond. Winter is at hand, and we must be prepared for it. This is no place to quarter an army, and I know of none this side of the capital of rebeldom.

The army is in remarkably good spirits under the impression that there will be a fight soon. But, I assure you, unless Gen. Burnside moves shortly, there will be an immense amount of sickness among his men. The weather is very changeable. Our covering in the shape of tents very meager, and wood very scarce. Combined, and the result is a general cold, then a general fever and finally a grand funeral. He must move at once or retreat to better quarters. The former is the only practical one for Gen. Burnside for, if he retreats, off goes his head. I think he can overwhelm Lee, if he goes into the next fight with confidence.

There is a rumor in camp to the effect that we are going with Gen. Banks on his expedition. Were the rumor confirmed, there would be more rejoicing among the men of the 8th Ill. Cavalry than there was among the Children of Israel on their safe escape from Pharaoh. This army has been a deadweight on the country too long, and we feel that we have been persecuted by being in it. If praying would bring about the desired result then we would pray, but any faith in such good luck is small.

Col. Farnsworth is still in Washington. I presume on business connected with his promotion to a brigadiership. I observe there has been a list of Cols. sent in for promotion, and I expect he is one of the number. Hope so.

I am in expectation of receiving my letters and papers this evening, and I will write to you in a few days again, giving any information that I may obtain. With love to your family and regards to all my friends, especially to any of those charming young ladies who were at the party.

I remain, etc. W. H. Medill

President Lincoln chose Ambrose Burnside to replace General McClellan. In November when Burnside took over, he had 120,000 men plus several thousand more detailed to guard Washington, which he could use if absolutely necessary. General Lee had about 85,000 to oppose him. General Burnside needed to act, and contrary to McClellan's complaints, the Army of the Potomac was in good condition. Burnside decided to feint toward Lee's center then rapidly countermarch, cross the river at Fredericksburg, and open the route to Richmond. All went according to plan at first, but the pontoons needed to cross did not arrive on time. The leading corps under General Sumner arrived November 17, 1862, and Sumner wanted to push across and secure the town, but Burnside decided to wait. Pontoons finally arrived on November 25, but unfortunately Confederate general Longstreet had gotten there on November 21. Burnside might have moved back upstream and caught General Jackson isolated from Longstreet, but he chose to pursue the original plan, and then he compounded the difficulty by waiting for more bridges. When the Union army finally crossed, they met the full strength of the Army of Northern Virginia, dug into the hills behind the town.[46] Distraught by the disaster at Fredericksburg, General Burnside wanted to personally lead a desperation charge but came to his senses and withdrew the defeated army on the stormy night of December 15, 1862.[47]

William to Joseph

On the heights opposite Fredericksburg, Monday, December 15, 1862
Brother Joseph

While sitting here on the hill overlooking the City of Fredericksburg and in plain view of the two armies, I will acknowledge the receipt of your letter and also one from Kate, which were received on Saturday morning and right thankfully, too, for I had almost despaired of ever hearing from Chicago again. I also received a copy of the *Tribune* of the 5th. I don't understand why the paper doesn't come. Gen. Farnsworth does not receive his either.

This is the 5th day since the fight commenced, and we have been placid spectators of its progress so far. Each day we have been drawn up in line, on the hill opposite the city, waiting for the time when we were to sail in. From where I am sitting I can see the whole thing. Over on the hills back of the city can be seen the rebel earthworks from which an occasional puff of smoke shoots up, giving us an evidence of the presence of rebel artillery. A complete line of fresh entrenchments are visible this morning on the second range of hills, thrown up last night. They have a splendid position for defense, and my opinion is that Gen. Burnside can never take them without a most terrible slaughter; and, in fact, he has already had a taste of what is to come in his attempt on Saturday. There is no use claiming a victory on that day, for our men were apparently repulsed with ease and did not gain a single valuable position. The enemy still holding all his works and all the hills. What our loss was I am unable to guess; there are all sorts of rumors current as to the figures, some placing it at 6,000 while others insist that it was near 12,000.[48] It was certainly very heavy.

But what are we doing? That's the question. I cannot see. Our army seems to be lying on its arms, waiting for something to turn up. What that something is, no one knows. I think the rebels can be flanked very easily from above or right flank. The river is fordable at a dozen places, and men might be thrown across; this would be my plan. I am willing to trust Gen. Burnside, however, with an abiding faith that he knows what he is about. Rumor has it that Gen. Siegel has gone over, above here and will be heard from shortly. Hope so.

Later—he hasn't.

The grandest sight of my life was on Friday last on the occasion of the bombardment of the City of Fredericksburg. I have often wished to see such a sight, and now my curiosity has been gratified. About 175 guns opened upon it at once with a roar that made the very earth shake, and the air was full of iron. By close observation I could see stones and brick flying from the buildings in every direction and costly edifices crumbling down before the rain of shot and shell. The City was on fire in a dozen places at once, but owing to the perfect calm that existed, the conflagration was not so great as it otherwise would have been. Several blocks were consumed, however, and what the fire failed to do was accomplished by the shells.

Yesterday I went over and took a look at the scene. The City is a complete wreck. I looked into many houses, and the sight was awful. The occupants had fled, leaving their furniture and everything behind. Probably a dozen twenty-pound shells had struck and exploded in the building, tearing the whole into one mass of ruins. Costly pianos, glasses, china, crockery, chairs, sofas, pictures, books, marble statues, everything torn, smashed, destroyed! A few of the inhabitants were hidden away in cellars, crying, praying, wishing for deliverance from the crash and danger around and over them. Here and there could be seen the pool of blood on the streets where some unlucky person had been killed in trying to run away. I could not help exclaiming, "What a costly luxury secession is to the inhabitants of this place!" It would be about as cheap to burn the place up and then rebuild as to undertake its repair. I would have given twenty-five dollars could you have been here to have witnessed the bombardment, and money is scarce.

I sent you by mail on Friday last $200 in a check, which you will please dispose of. I should have sent more, but my expenses for winter clothing were pretty heavy, and as paydays come so irregularly I must keep a good supply at hand. I had to shave pretty closely the last time. I have been thinking that if you could see a nice lot somewhere near the park on the west side, not too dear, you might invest my money in it. Let it cost, say $1,000. I can pay the remaining $300 at next payday, which will occur in January or February. I consider such an investment about as safe as anything. But do as you think best, and I will be satisfied.

The weather is delightful, and we anguish to be moving while it lasts. The health of the army is good, and the men are in high spirits, confident of victory. Gen. Farnsworth is in command of our brigade, which consists of the 8th N.Y, 3rd Indiana and the 8th Illinois, but I understand that he will soon have command of our division, and Pleasonton will take over our brigade.

I am glad Sammy is going to school, and hope he will stick to it until he accomplishes what studies he commences. Tell Kate that I will write soon. Give my regards to all my friends and love to the family.

Yours, etc. W. H. Medill

William to Joseph
On picket near King George Court House, R.G. Co., Virginia
Wednesday eve, December 31, 1862

Dear Bro:

Thinking that a few lines from me might be acceptable and as this is probably the *last letter* I'll write *to you this year,* I'll make it brief.

Since Christmas Day our regiment has been on picket duty in this county. It's one of the best in the state, and our men have been living on luxuries since being here. The people are bitterly secesh and are mostly rich. They have or rather *had* a great many slaves. Since arrival upwards of 600 have immigrated to a more *republican* government, and as many more will be off tomorrow. You will see from this that the "Big Abolition Regiment" is pushing on our good work. Estimating the negroes to be worth $600 each you will see that we have reduced the value of the "portable property" of "Old Virginny" $360,000 and will soon make it as much more with a prospect of raising it to $1,000,000.

I don't know what will be the next move. We filled up our cartridge boxes and haversacks for something. I trust we will succeed better than we did at Fredericksburg. That was a shameful defeat through outright blundering. There is no use disguising this.

The weather has become suddenly quite cold and stormy. For a week previous we had splendid weather. It is shameful that we waste all the favorable times for moving and get ready when a change for the worse comes. McClellan always did this, too.

I have not seen a copy of the *Tribune* for two weeks, and only a stray copy previous to that. I wish you would try a few copies in single wrappers and prepaid and see if they would arrive that way. Having received but three letters since my return and no papers, I feel quite lost for want of news. I have written to both Mary and Ellen, but have not received a line from either of them.

You must excuse the brevity of this, for I am writing under disadvantages—on a piece of board with cold fingers, smoke blowing into my eyes, sitting on the ground with a pencil an inch long and no news to give. When we return to camp, I will try and do better. My health is excellent.

Love to your family and regards to all my friends is the request of your *cold* Brother W. H. Medill

CHAPTER FIVE

The Eighth Illinois, an Effective Cavalry Regiment, 1863

Small circumstances prevent great results.
—*William Medill, May 11, 1863*

WILLIAM TO MARY
In Camp near Belle Plain, Virginia, January 15, 1863

Sister Mary:

About a month since I wrote you a letter and some time previous to that I wrote Ellen a note. I have not heard a word in reply from either since. I have also written three or four times to Joseph and twice to Sammy, since my return from home, and have not had a letter from them, with the exception of a short one from Joseph on business matters. Now what does all this silence mean? Have I been disgracing the family? Are you all sick? Or have you been getting married? If no answer comes to this within a reasonable time, I'll take it for granted that all these inflictions have combined to prevent you from writing.

Since Christmas the regiment has been on picket duty on the Rappahannock, near King George Court House. We have had better living than at any time since being in the service. The people in this vicinity are generally F. F. V. [First Families of Virginia] and owing to our sudden arrival, the inhabitants did not have time to leave, and as a consequence we have found plenty of provisions and delicacies of all kinds. Chickens, turkeys, ducks, geese, etc. have become commonplace. Why, I had for my New Year's dinner a Mallard Duck, which cost a certain wealthy rebel the neat sum of twenty-five dollars and for dessert I started seventy-five of his darkies on their way rejoicing. During that day our regiment liberated and started near a thousand slaves into freedom. I never spent a New Year's Day to so much advantage, and

I shall long remember January 1st, 1863, and even if the war terminates in favor of the Confederates and slavery is never abolished, I shall feel satisfied with myself and the part I performed in the attempt made to put an end to the abominable institution. If every regiment in the army had accomplished as much towards that result as we have, there would have been a big hole made in the number of the "Peculiar."

The [Emancipation] Proclamation is well received in the army,[1] and will be used to good advantage if we ever make another advance. But our inaction causes considerable wonder, especially as the weather is so very fine; no better has ever been experienced for marching or fighting.

The recent operations of Rosecrans and his army causes a thrill of joy to pass through our veins; but Vicksburg and Galveston, with the loss of the noble little *Monitor* neutralizes the effect to a certain extent. When will the President see the folly of splitting our armies up into so many little factions. Supposing, instead of sending Sherman to Vicksburg he had been sent to Rosecrans, that terrible slaughter of Murfreesboro would have been turned to some account. Banks could have forced the rebs to retain their big army at Vicksburg. While Grant could have passed in rear of Bragg, and the result would have been either the capture or destruction of the latter, and then Rosecrans, Grant and Sherman could have sent as many men as necessary to swamp Vicksburg, Mobile, etc. while Banks could then turn his attention to Texas and that villain Magruder.[2] This army is large enough, strong enough and willing enough to eat up Lee and his whole army, if we had a commander willing and capable of it. The Battle of Fredericksburg was a great blunder and a great slaughter. I feel positive in asserting that it might have been won as easily as not. In fact there was no other way to fight that battle and be defeated, for we have nearly two men to their one.

But I must close. My time is exhausted. Give my love to the family, and to Hetta when you write.

Yours in haste Wm. H. Medill

Chicago Tribune, September 23, 1862

Antietam was not a decisive victory, but it stopped General Lee's invasion of Maryland and became the victory Lincoln needed to issue the Emancipation Proclamation. In response, the *Tribune* greeted Antietam as a triumph and touted another important victory—emancipation. The *Tribune* wrote, "President Lincoln has set his hand and affixed the great seal of the nation to the grandest proclamation ever issued by man. He has declared after the first day of January next all the slaves in the then rebellious States shall be free. . . . From the date of this proclamation begins the history of the republic as our fathers designed to have it—the home of freedom."[3]

At this point General Hooker, General Burnside's replacement, issued an order regarding leaves of absence, believing it would cut down desertions. The leave William had wanted for many months had to adhere to the following regulations, and he did not receive one until April 1863.

Leaves of Absence, Furloughs, Return of Absentee—Head-Quarters, Army of the Potomac, Camp near Falmouth, Va., Jan. 1863, General Orders, No. 3.[4]
    The following rules will govern officers empowered to grant leaves of absence.
    I. No leave will exceed fifteen days.
    II. Leaves to Commanders of Corps, Divisions and Cavalry Brigades will only be granted upon approval at these Head-Quarters. One Brigade Commander only in a Corps to be on leave at one time.
    III. Not more than one Field Officer of a Regiment to be absent on leave at one time, where the full complement of Field Officers are present. When less than that number leaves to be granted only in extreme cases.
    IV. Not more than two Line Officers to be given leave from any Regiment at the same time. Not more than one from any Battery or Detachment.
    V. Leaves not to exceed ten days except to residents of the following States, when it may be given for fifteen days, viz.: Maine, New Hampshire and Vermont; Ohio, Michigan, and the States West of these last named.
    VI. Furloughs to enlisted men must in no case exceed two for every one hundred men present for duty in the Regiment, Battery or Detachment and not to be granted to any men but those having the most excellent record for attention to all duties.
    VII. In case of the failure of any Officer or soldier to return before their leave expires, leaves will not be granted to others, from the same Commands until their return. All applications will by endorsement or otherwise state the number of Officers or men absent on leave from the Command, and the failure to return of any person will be notified immediately to the Provost Marshal General, with a memoranda of the leave, residence of the party and description of enlisted men. . . .
BY COMMAND OF MAJOR GENERAL HOOKER
JOSEPH DICKINSON,
    Assistant Adjutant General.

James to Joseph
Canton, Ohio, February 16, 1863

Brother Joseph:

Yesterday Mary received a letter from you, announcing that you had probably purchased a prairie farm near Onarga [in east-central Illinois.] As a matter of speculation, I think it would be a good bargain, but if you purchase with the expectation of making it a model farm, it will be dear at almost any price. It will be nearly impossible to ever put up a first-class barn and grain raising. Without one is a poor business. Feeding stock in a field don't pay, and a bleak prairie is not a place for fruit. There is no coal near Onarga, and wood must be dear. Again, "opening" a new prairie farm is about a ten years' job.

I was not aware that an improved farm could be purchased near Aurora for forty dollars an acre. If the land is good and contains timber, I should call it cheap. Of course, I infer that it is improved, and that there is no scarcity of water. I need not here repeat my remarks about the qualities of a good farm.[5]

I have now a private matter to write about. Ever since I came here, and for some time before, Mother has been hard pressed pecuniarily. The price of everything greatly increased, and there was also an increase in her household. I gave her all the money I had, and Mrs. M. sent me several remittances. These have ceased since the first of January, in consequence of sickness in Mr. Shriver's family, which has prevented her from teaching. So you can easily understand that she is pressed by a number of small but annoying debts. One thing more—please direct letters containing remittances to Mother in person; also, send the drafts in her name. She is thoroughly posted in business matters. In some future letter I will give you a few "contraband" items. At present I will only say that Mary has become intolerably overbearing in her manner, and Mother will no longer endure it. Do not mention this matter to anyone but relieve the necessities as soon as possible.

Yours very truly, James Medill

William Medill (Father) to his son, Joseph
Canton, Ohio, February 16, 1863

Dear Joseph,

This is the first letter I have attempted to write to you for a long time. My write [sic] hand has been greatly crippled, but of late it has been getting better. [Your] Mother prefers that I should write to you instead of one of the girls.

The fact is that she is very hard up for money. Our family is pretty large and out of things that we need. Market has greatly increased in price. Flour is $8 a barl [barrel]. Coal is ten cents bus [bushel]. Wood $3 a cord, and groceries of all kinds are got dearer. She has not been able to pay any money on wood or coal since last fall, and on them two articles she owes $20. She feels delicate in having to let you know our wants after you doing so much for us as you have done. We heard that you got a fall off your horse and was considerably hurt. We did not hear how you was getting along.

My own health, thank God, is greatly improved, but I am greatly crippled in my knees, so much so that I cannot make the least effort to help myself. I eat sparingly and my appetite is very slack. The health of the family, with the exception of James, is good, and we think he is getting better.

We all send our best respects to you and family. Direct your letters to William or Margaret Medill.

[This letter is not signed, but the envelope is marked "from James and Father."]

William to Ellen
In Camp, near Stafford Court House, Virginia, March 5, 1863

Dear Sister:

A pressure of business and bad weather has prevented me from answering your letter of last month sooner although, in truth, it has not been in my possession a great length of time. I am much obliged to you for writing and also for the pictures, and also for the good resolutions about attending more promptly to your correspondence, and also for anything else you have done for me.

Since I last wrote home, we have changed our location from the left to the right of this army, from King George C.H. to Stafford C.H.—from abundance and good living to poverty and hard living ("hard tack" and fat pork)—from little to do and no danger to constant duty and frequent alarms. It would appear that our regiment is moved about whenever there is any danger of an attack from Stuart. The Pennsylvania and New York cavalry get into difficulties, and we are "trotted" about to protect them. "Wind and Weather" do not appear of sufficient consequence to detain us when there is any work to be performed, for ever since we were ordered from King G.C.H.—some three weeks now—the weather and the roads have been most horribly bad. We have had three heavy snow storms, with as many thaws and as frequent rains. To a person not acquainted with Virginia soil, there can be no idea conveyed of its depth, its volume, or its adhesiveness. Language cannot convey an accurate knowledge of its destructiveness to horseflesh. Probably you remember the mud on the clay hills in "Pike." If you do, you have seen mud about one-tenth as deep and vast as this in

Virginia. No wonder it is called "sacred soil," so far as Northern white men are concerned, for I assure you it will always be too sacred to be trod upon by them when they can avoid it. Niggers; turkey buzzards; dirty, ignorant whites; crows; mules; vermin of all sorts; stunted pines; large chimneys with small houses between them; big gateposts and villainous mud are the products of "Old Virginny." So far as her land and people are concerned, I would not expend one life nor one day's time to reclaim them. The principle, I suppose, is what is looked at. Two-thirds of the country has been worn out and returned to nature to rejuvenate, and the other third would have been ready to be also turned over to the same source, ere this generation passed from earth, if this war had not commenced. The abolition of slavery, and consequent repopulation of the state by a different class will probably save it and reclaim some of that at present worn out. Every wrong act carries with it its own punishment. The Jews were at one time a rich, intelligent and respected nation. They became conceited and violated justice and humanity and now look at them. The same is true of the South. The retribution of justice is falling upon her, and her people will soon be cast forth to the world to be despised and kicked from door to door.

For a few days there have been frequent attacks made upon our outside pickets by the guerrilla parties. They have succeeded in capturing a number of our cavalry belonging to N.Y. and Pennsylvania regiments. We were sent out after one of these forays but only succeeded in breaking down a number of our horses,[6] getting terribly wet and disgusted. I had command of the regiment and was out three days and nights. It rained one day and snowed two. Our blankets were wet, too. Our clothes, and too the ground; the creeks were "swimmable" and numerous; forage and rations scarce. The men have nearly all been suffering with colds since. I did not escape the luxury either; the consequence is a bad headache, and a slight fever a part of the time. I feel dull tonight. which will excuse the brevity and non-interest of this. My head is so confounded thick, I cannot spell a word of over one syllable without stopping to think; and that appears to make matters worse.

I received a letter from Kate a day or two since, by which I learn that the family in Chicago is well. She sent me a real good photograph of little Kitty and Nelly. It is very natural, and I consider it a nice present. Speaking of pictures, I enclose in this one of myself and my horse, which I had taken a few days since. The likeness of my "charger" is perfect. He appeared to be aware of my wishes and looked his prettiest. Hope you will like the picture.

My commission as Major cannot be sent home just yet, as I will have to be mustered by it soon. When that is over I'll forward it.

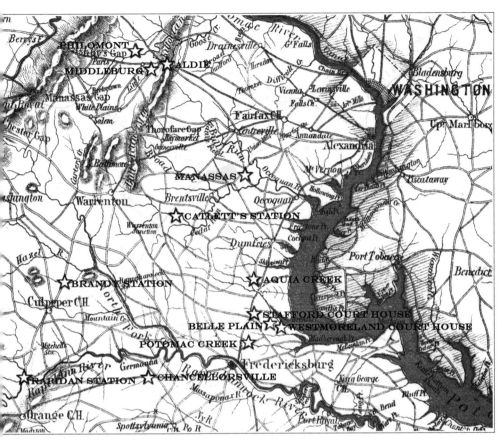

Action at Stafford Court House, Potomac Creek, Chancellorsville, Rapidan Station, Aquia Creek, Westmoreland Court House, Belle Plain, Brandy Station, Catlett's Station, Manassas, Middleburg, Aldie, and Philomont. (Library of Congress Geography and Map Division; adapted from Nicholson's *Map of Eastern Virginia*)

I hope Jim will soon be well enough to take charge of Joseph's farm, for I think I'll tender him my services when the war is ended. I begin to be tired of the unsettled, roving life I have been following and hope soon to marry and settle. Can't you pick me out a wife, among all your lady friends? She must be handsome, intelligent and cross!

Give my regards to my friends in Canton and in Pike, and tell Mary that when she next writes to Uncle Henry to give him my kindest regards and also his family. I will probably write to him myself soon. Give my love to Mother, Father, Mary, Jim, Amy and accept the remainder for yourself.

W. H. Medill

William to Kate

Near Stafford Court House, Virginia, Sunday, March 15, 1863

Dear Sister Kate:

I was thinking of home, my friends there, what they were doing, saying and thinking when I was suddenly awakened from my reverie by a peal of thunder and thereupon determined that I would answer your letter, which has been in my possession forever so long. By that thunder I was reminded that the springtime was really here, and that, although the atmosphere and the appearance of the ground did not give token of the approach of warm weather—for it is quite cold with snow on the ground—yet warm weather was at hand.

Other evidences of the change in the season of the year have been given, such as are known to an army. For ten days orders and circulars have been numerous, such as: "All wagons, excepting two, now in each regiment, will be turned over, at once, to the division Quarter Master, and the two remaining wagons will be used exclusively for carrying the books and papers of the regiment, and nothing else." "One pack mule will be furnished to each field officer, one to every three company officers, and one to each ten enlisted men in each company, for the transportation of three day's extra rations, which will always be kept on hand." "Officers and men will at once reduce their baggage to one suit of clothes with one change of underclothes, one rubber as poncho and two woolen blankets." "Company officers will see that their men have, at all times, one hundred rounds of ammunition on hand." "Regimental commanders will hold their commands in readiness to march at a moment's notice, and to have daily inspections of all arms, accoutrements, etc., and see that their men are in fighting trim." "All extra horses will be turned over to the brigade Q.M., and all worthless ones will be shot." "Surgeons will keep their instruments in readiness, and their medicine chests complete." "The ambulance corps will be in readiness to move whenever called upon." These are unmistakable evidences of Spring.

But how different from the admonitions we were in the habit of receiving in days gone. They do not bring up to the soldier visions of budding fruit, the rush of business, the planting of crops, the opening of navigation, the pleasant moonlit nights, the gayest, the happiest season of the year. What are the visions: *to the new soldier,* they are peculiarly exciting. His feverish brain always conjectures the worst, and he sees the *battlefield.* On that his whole thoughts centre, and what terrible phantoms he dreams of. Its roar is deafening and mingled with the screams and groans of the dying; the horrid sights of torn humanity make up a scene sufficient to set the poor fellow shivering, and wishing himself *honorably* out of the scrape. (What won't man endure to preserve his reputation for courage!) To *the old soldier,* there is a different prospect. He dreads the long weary march in the broiling sun under the weight of a knapsack and musket, the trouble of insects, stray shot of the murderous guerilla. But these hardships are offset with the idea of getting out of the dirty camp into the fresh air away from hospitals and hardtack, to the excitement of the skirmish after rebel poultry. He looks upon a battle as the farmer does a hard day's work, in harvest, and the groans of the dying are unheard. He talks lightly of death, and while drinking his cup of coffee with his messmates wonders what one will be hit in the next fight, or tells a story of the burial of some ragged rebel who was scarcely dead.

Although to a person at home the latter may be looked upon with disgust or horror, yet there is nothing bad about him. The terrors of war are more in the mind than in reality. Death is one of the necessities, and it is not so objectionable as it is represented. I have gotten over the notion, however, of thinking that dying on the battlefield is the most glorious way of ending one's days, since I see the small amount of respect shown to those who happen to fall. I am thankful that I am past my apprenticeship in being afraid of a battle. There can be nothing more disagreeable than thinking of danger when one knows it cannot be avoided.

There will be a forward movement soon of this army, but Gen. Hooker keeps his secrets as to the direction or way he intends to whip the enemy. We have no doubt about his ability to do so and if, by our exertion, we can assist him in doing so there need be no doubt of the result. Didn't he speak his mind nicely when he gave the reason for the failure of the Peninsular campaign of Gen. McClellan? "Incompetency" was the word, and that told the whole story. I have thought so ever since we failed to annihilate Lee at Antietam. McClellan was incompetent, and his advisers were traitors. Thank goodness we are rid of them now. Gen. Hooker took this army in its gloomiest moment when discouragement prevailed, when demoralization was apparent to anyone, when no one thought it could be rescued from being disbanded, when outside pressure of traitors and designing demagogues set their hearts upon its destruction and ruin, and by increasing toil, by severity and kindness, he has rebuilt its foundation, extracted the rotten beams and replaced them by sound ones. In a word, he breathed anew into its almost inanimate form the breath of life, and now he is ready to lead the Army of the Potomac forth to regain its lost glory. No one doubts that this army has been disgraced.

The Conscription Bill is popular in the army and were especially rejoiced when it was rumored that the President had appointed Gen. Butler to enforce it, but it seems he is going to put in one of those broken down defeated congressmen. Gen. Butler is the best man in the United States for such a position. If the Bill is carried out, all the conscripts should be filled into the old regiments or put into camps of instruction and kept to fill up from after each fight. I am afraid the politicians will get hold of it, and then goodbye to all hopes of any good coming from it. I see by the papers that the President is determined to fill up the number of brigadiers. Why not leave the positions open for competition among the officers in the service? There is no inducement held out to worthy men. Promotions are made without any reference to merit. I know of some in this army, who were promoted for reported service on certain battlefields, when the truth is they were not on the field at all. Col. Gregg of the 8th Pennsylvania Cavalry is an instance. He is made a brigadier for gallant and meritorious conduct at Fair Oaks, when he and his regiment were not near that fight. He is a coward, and I have always thought him to be a traitor. His talk would indicate that, and his officers are full of it. His regiment certainly is the poorest in the army, but was a regular and McClellan recommended him.

I have been compelled to fill this letter with military because I have no news to write. Rumors are not worth detailing, besides they are generally unreasonable. Stuart or Jackson are continuously reported to be hovering around us, and if they had taken all the prisoners that have been accredited to them, there would be but a few of us left.

I hardly know how to thank you enough for the picture of the children. Of course, I am proud of my nieces, and ever will be. Nelly's wish for peace and my safe return is just like her, dear little thing, and Kitty's wish for new dresses and riches is like her. The two opposites make them more interesting than were they alike in everything.

Your farm will always be a source of employment and will always be something to fall back upon. My mind is about fixed upon farming as my future occupation, and whether I marry or not, which I consider exceedingly doubtful, I will be most happy to retire after the war is over to your farm. I guess I'll leave it to Sammy to end the marrying in our family.

I have but little hopes of getting a leave of absence, for the reason that Col. Gamble and Maj. Beveridge are both away on sick leave, and another field officer can't be spared very well. When they return I may get ten days. I came near getting sick, too, from the effect of a cold but am up again. The boots have not reached me yet. I wish Sammy would go to the express office and try and find where the fault lies.

Give my regards to all my friends, and love to the family. Yours, W. H. Medill

> Hd Qrs. 8th Ill. Cavalry,
> Camp near Hope Landing, Va.
> April 1st, 1863.
>
> Sir—
>   I have the honor to ask that I be granted a leave of absence for the period of Fifteen Days, to enable me to visit my home in Illinois.
>   I have the honor to be
>   Your obt servt
>   Wm. H. Medill
>   Maj 8th Ill Cavalry
>
> Lt. Col. D R Clendenin
> Commanding 8th Ill Cvy

William's handwritten request for a leave of absence. (National Archives and Records Administration, Compiled Military Service Records in Volunteer Union Organizations)

WILLIAM TO JOSEPH

In Camp near Stafford Court House, Virginia, March 28, 1863

Dear Brother:

I am under the painful necessity of asking you to send me the sum of $100 in consequence of not getting our pay. The general commanding has revoked the order granting leaves of absence and paymasters are not permitted to come to the army. I am out of money and the commissary must be paid inside of two weeks. The government is now owing me the sum of $961, and yet it will not trust me $30 or $40 for victuals. I must now buy clothing at sutler rates and must have money to do it with. You can send it in two $50 bills. A check would be of no use for no one has money enough to cash it, except some robbing sutler at 50 percent discount. Send it in government funds; nothing else is good here. The boots have not come yet, and the express agent in Washington says they are not there. I suppose I will have to get a pair from the sutler. I wish you would also send me some postage stamps, I am entirely out.

This shutting off on furloughs looks like work, but the roads are still in a bad condition, and a movement will be exceedingly difficult. "Fighting Joe" ain't to be intimidated, however. I am willing to put up with some privations for the sake of a fight, for I am perfectly sanguine as to the result. There is even a satisfaction in getting wounded or killed in such a result and—when one thinks that—an advantage gained will be improved. If Hooker defeats Lee in the fight to take place, you may expect to hear of the 8th Illinois Cavalry being in Richmond in less than a week after the result. The cavalry of this army is now consolidated and ready to play its *legitimate* part of the future campaign. We can swallow Stuart if he dares to show us fight, and Stoneman only wants the opportunity to do it. This is not bragging.

I received a note from you the other day containing Mary's letter, for which I am much obliged. There is nothing of any further interest to write. We are glad to see the evidences of reaction taking place in the North and hope the Copperheads will be crushed in [the] future. Hurry up the return of deserters and put the Conscription Bill in force.

Give my regards to my friends and my love to the family. Hoping to hear from you very soon.

I remain, etc, etc. W. H. Medill

Headquarters Cavalry Corps, Army of the Potomac, April 4, 1863
　Special Order No. 50, Extract, II Leave of absence is hereby granted to the following name officer in compliance with General Order No. 3 r/o Headquarters Army of the Potomac current since
Major W. H. Medill, 8th Illinois Cavalry
for (15) fifteen days.
By Command of Brig. Genrl. Stoneman
"Signed" A. J. Alexander

William returned to his regiment in time to be present for the next major battle. Twelve miles west of Fredericksburg a small village formed at a roadway intersection, anchored by the wealthy Chancellor family's home. Early in May 1863, the village would be the site of a failed Union attack and Confederate triumph considered Robert E. Lee's greatest victory.[7] The prelude to the Battle of Chancellorsville was a planned cavalry action known as Stoneman's 1863 Raid. It is named after Maj. Gen. George Stoneman, who commanded the ten-thousand-man Cavalry Corps of the Army of the Potomac. Maj. Gen. Joseph Hooker, who replaced Burnside as overall commander of the Army of the Potomac after the carnage at Fredericksburg, wanted Stoneman to get between Lee and Richmond, cutting off the Confederate supply lines. Hooker also wanted to force Confederates out of Fredericksburg, so the Army of the Potomac could attack a weakened enemy out in the open. Stoneman's Raid gave the Union cavalry a newfound sense of self-respect. They proved cavalry could operate as an independent force against the enemy. Hooker, however, faulted General Stoneman for not following his orders and inflicting less damage than expected.

At the Battle of Chancellorsville, 97,000 Union troops engaged 57,000 Confederates. The Confederate victory resulted in 14,000 Union casualties and 10,000 Confederate, including Stonewall Jackson, who suffered a mortal wound.[8] In this campaign William served under Gen. William W. Averell, and in the following letter he charged Averell with failure to engage the enemy.

> WILLIAM TO JOSEPH
> Hd. Qtrs. 8th Ill. Cavalry, In Camp near Potomac Creek Station, Virginia, May 11, 1863

Dear Brother:

First, let me say I am well and have again passed the chances of getting killed without even a scratch, if I except a slight abrasion on the bridge of my nose received in passing through a piece of thick woods, and secondly, I'll talk a little about financial matters.

You will find enclosed in this two checks, one for $250, which you will place to my credit, and the other one for $50 I want you to place in safekeeping for my little servant boy, James Williams, and send me an acceptance of yourself for the amount that I can give him, so that he can send for this money whenever he desires. Make this acceptance in his name but send it to me, for he might not get it if directed to him. I feel a real satisfaction in sending this money. The little fellow ran off and joined the regiment the day after the battle of Williamsburg and has been working for one of the lieutenants ever since. He has saved most of his wages but lent it to different men in the regiment, and he has not been able to collect quite all, which would have amounted to some $80. Since he has been in the regiment he has learned to read and makes a very fair attempt at forming letters and figures. My orderly hears his lessons. He is much elated with the notion of going North with me when the war is over and working on your farm. He says that he will have $100 to send to you next payday.

What an infernal institution slavery is when, had it not been for a mere accident of war, this boy would have been doomed to have served as a slave, but a little above the station of the brutes all his life, and he is but 14 years old. His mother, father and two sisters are scattered in different states, having been sold away when our army advanced on the Peninsula. Jimmy and one brother of his were kept by the rebels at work on the fortifications at Williamsburg and managed to make their escape to our lines. The brother is also with an officer in the regiment. They are intelligent, honest boys and, though quite black, are handsome. Please acknowledge the receipt of this letter as soon as it is received.

The fifty dollars you sent me and the express receipt Sammy sent were received by Lt. Col. Clendenin during my absence and were placed in a drawer in his desk. During a late movement the wagon containing the desk was ordered to the rear, and while there was opened by some person, and the two letters purloined. I am thus the loser of the $50 and the amount of the boots, which you will please subtract from my money in your possession. If you mention the matter in the letter, do so in such a way as to let Lieut. Irving know that you have been paid. Probably you can trade up the boots and get them. It is too bad to lose them.

And now for a few lines in regard to our late affairs which will be very brief for I know but little about it.

I presume Gen. Hooker has failed to whip the rebels, but that there is any blame attaching to the general or to the bravery of his men, there is not the least truth. He failed through a combination of circumstances, some of which were treachery, cowardice, want of numbers, etc. Which is chief I am unable to say. If I had time to narrate the facts, you might judge. My opinion is that Gen. Averell is as much to blame as anyone. He is under arrest for his part. Through cowardice or something else he failed to join Stoneman at Gordonsville, and by this means the supposition was that Stoneman had failed. In fact, we heard that the general was killed and the whole expedition destroyed. Stoneman wasted three or four days in waiting for Averell, who had the greater portion of the force intended for the expedition, three brigades numbering in the aggregate over 4,000. Our regiment was with him during those three days, then rebs overwhelmed Hooker. Averell reported his failure to join Stoneman after two days and also sent him word that he learned from good authority that Stoneman's force was destroyed. The thing was likely, for the rebels had only to concentrate on him and destroy his little command. Hooker, finding that his force was inadequate to whip Lee, recrossed the river. Through prisoners taken, Stoneman heard that Hook had been whipped, and he at once prepared to return. In doing so, however, he took his time and destroyed many bridges and much property of other kinds. As to the causes which prevented Averell from joining Stoneman there is but one hypothesis. He did not wish to do so and was afraid to fight a couple of regiments and two guns, although he had 4,000 cavalry and a full battery. We remained one day and a half at Rapidan Station and then marched back, having accomplished nothing. We lay all the third day within three miles of the left flank of the rebel army that was whipping Gen. Howard and never moved. When, if we had pitched into their flank, I have no doubt we could have destroyed their force, for such an attack could have been entirely unexpected. But the great blunder was in not joining Stoneman, for in case Averell had done so Stoneman could have captured and burned Richmond! I heard Gen. Stoneman say this himself, and he moreover asserted that Gen. Averell should be shot for not joining him. Just look at the things that might have been accomplished had it not been for this failure. With our force joined to Gen. Stoneman's, he could have destroyed the great bridge across the Anna River, thus breaking Lee's communications for a week. He could have hunted up Stuart's cavalry and destroyed him, which was a part of the program after destroying the bridge spoken of and the telegraph. He could have captured and burned Richmond; he could have opened the James River to our gunboats and permitted Dix to rush his troops up the Peninsula with impunity, for he was guarded on both flanks by navigable rivers. He could have remained in [the] rear of the rebel army as long as he pleased and communicated with Hooker either by way of the Rappahannock, or at Yorktown he could have had force enough to have destroyed the whole subsistence and all transportation sent forward for the rebs. In a word, the infliction of injury could have been prolonged indefinitely, for the rebs had no force to oppose—infantry could do us no harm.

What are the results? Stoneman wasted three of his most precious days in waiting for Averell to join him. During those three days the rebels forwarded more than 50,000 troops to the bridge over the Anna River so strongly as to repel the attempt to burn it. They whipped most of their stores along railroads within their lines and withdrew their transportation trains from the way of danger. Stuart, though he dared not attack Stoneman, watched him so closely that he was unable to separate his command and thus inflict damage at different points at the same times. Stoneman was without information from Hooker, except what came from rebel prisoners, and Hooker was similarly circumstanced with regard to Stoneman. For want of numbers Stoneman was compelled to abandon his position in the rear of Lee, while for want of this same force to destroy a R.R. bridge. Lee was reinforced sufficiently strong and soon to enable him to force Hooker to withdraw his army from the favorable position he occupied and, in reality, after outgeneraling, out fighting and out marching the rebels to fall back to his former position and thus tacitly admit a defeat. Small circumstances prevent great results and especially in great and sudden military operations. You ask the cause. I answer that Gen. Averell, like Fitz John Porter, was made by McClellan, and to Mc was due his first allegiance. Besides, I believe he is, like his master, a dirty coward. He got scared while making a reconnaissance by a small party of rebels dashing across the Rapidan and nearly capturing him and his staff. He never stopped running until he reached the rear of his division! These things can be proven.

Unfortunately for us, our brigade was detached from Pleasonton's command, and was along with Averell, and thus we are deprived of all participation in the late affair. We did nothing but march, break down our horses and listen to our army fighting superior numbers. We disgraced ourselves by coward-like failing to throw our force upon Jackson's flank. We could have saved the disgrace that befell the 11th Corps, for our position was on the rear and flank of Jackson's lines. As regards Hooker's battles, I know but little, except that though he was compelled to fall back, he out maneuvered Lee and did him more harm than our force suffered. If Hooker's army is whipped, his men do not know it. I have conversed with many officers and men belonging to different corps, and they all claim that they never felt more confidence than at present. They scorn the insinuation that they were beaten, and are confident that another movement will soon occur, and a victory will certainly result. I understand that we have received a large addition to our army since the late battle, and also that the enemy has withdrawn a number. The whole army is held in readiness to march with haversacks and cartridge boxes full. Gen. Hooker has not lost anything in the estimation of his men; we are proud of him.

We are at present at Potomac Creek Station on the Aquia R.R., and the command was paid up to the first of March. The men are very healthy, in good spirits and are sending home a goodly amount of money.

I received your letter of April 30th today. I hardly know what to think about the hint you give me in regard to Miss C. Although I may have talked considerable about matrimonial matters, I have not, since I passed my boyish love, thought very seriously of marrying. I have never felt exactly certain that I would make a first-rate husband. Besides, my confidence in being able to win a first-class girl to loving me is not over-great. I have thought as seriously of Miss C. as I ever did of any girl, and were I placed where I could meet her frequently I'd no doubt fall "head over heels in love," but I am not so placed. As to writing to her, why, I never even hinted to her about a correspondence, and I rather guess she would take it as an insult—at least a great presumption—for me to do so without first asking the privilege. She is smart and fond of fun, and I doubt not a little flirtation would not be disagreeable to her at least. If not, she is very different from others of her sex. I have had so little to do with the ladies that I really feel more fear about opening an attack on the affections of one of them than I should to charge with my battalion on a brigade of rebels. But really I think I have said more in regard to this matter than it will bear, for I never met the young lady but twice and then nothing occurred between us to warrant me in thinking she could possibly think of me other than as a passing acquaintance. You may give her my profoundest regards when you see her and pardon me for writing you so extensively in regard to this matter. My apology is that I know you think better of Miss C. than of most young ladies of your acquaintance, and so do I.

I am glad you intend spending the summer pleasantly and hope to see you down this way sometime. Say to Kate that I will write to her in a few days and the same to Sammy. Give my love to the family, and I remain

Yours, etc. etc. W. H. Medill

P.S. When I commenced this letter, I did not intend to write more than a few lines, which will explain the apparent contradiction in regard to details, spoken of in the opening.

Joseph warned President Lincoln about the political consequences of drafting soldiers and advocated changes to the legislation. In the second half of his letter, Joseph urged the swift organization of black regiments and revealed goals for the Union League of America (ULA), a group of men's clubs established to promote loyalty to the Union. The Medill papers verified Joseph played a prominent role in Union League programs. For example, the Illinois Grand Council ULA certified Joseph as its representative to the National Grand Council held in Washington on December 9, 1863.[9] The ULA supported organizations such as the United States Sanitary Commission and the Republican Party, which benefited from its funding, organizational support, and political activism. The Union League of Chicago still exists, although it has become nonpartisan, pursuing economic and social goals.

Joseph to Abraham Lincoln
Willard's Hotel [Washington, D.C.], May 15, 1863

President Lincoln

Not having either time or inclination to hang round waiting rooms among a wolfish crowd seeking admission to your presence for office or contracts or personal favors, I prefer stating in writing the substance of what I would say verbally.

Your army is melting away rapidly by battle, disease and expiration of term of service, and there is great delay in putting the conscription act into effect. The hot weather is at hand, to be followed by the sickly season.[10]

The act itself will not furnish you with soldiers if you construe the 13th sec. as obligatory on the Gov't to receive $300 commutation for personal service. You will get but few men under it, and they will consist of the poor, penniless, soulless, ragged loafer class who have neither credit, money, or stake in the perpetuity of the Union. The attempt to enforce will do your administration immense harm and cause it to [lose] all the state elections next fall. The Copperheads are gloating over the prospective harvest of votes they will reap against a bill that "puts the rich man's dirty dollars against a poor man's life."

A law ought to be construed in harmony with its obvious purpose. The conscript act is not a revenue measure, but a law to raise men. What is the Sec. of War to do with twenty or thirty millions of dollars that may be paid over to his agents? They are under no bond nor is he. What is to be done with the money? The law makes no provision, except that it is received for the *procuration of such substitute*."

I contend that the Sec. of War is not bound to receive any conscript's money unless he has a substitute standing ready to receive it and to take the conscript's musket. If you put this construction on the law, you have plain and safe sailing. You will get exactly as many men as you call for—either as conscripts or substitutes. The country will sustain that construction of the law . . .

The country is impatient at the slow progress making in raising colored regiments. The blacks of our state are clamorous for the privilege of raising a regiment. So they are in Ind., so in Ohio. If you would give commissions in the West to white officers, they would raise in the western free states, in Missouri and West Tennessee, ten to fifteen thousand able-bodied, robust and brave colored soldiers. The opposition to colored soldiers has passed away. The Republicans are all loudly for them, and the Democrats have withdrawn their opposition. A hundred regiments of blacks can be raised between Chicago and New Orleans if you will resolve to have them. Transportation and rations ought to be provided for each colored volunteer as soon as he takes the oath. If blacks are to be used at all, why not let the Union cause have the full benefit of their powerful aid? The war is dragging too slowly. It is now in the *third* year. Twelve months hence we shall be in the midst of another presidential struggle. If the Copperheads elect their ticket, all the fruits of this bloody and costly war will go for naught, all will be undone and the plans and policy of the rebels will achieve perfect triumph. The value of time and concentration of our armies I fear are insufficiently appreciated.

In order to rally the Union sentiment and prepare for the great presidential struggle, I have organized a Union League somewhat secret in its action but at the same time strictly patriotic. I wrote the ritual and the forms and devised lots of the signs and set it going. I have worked hard and zealously on it for eight months. It is now spreading in every state. There are 4,000 members in this city, and there are 75,000 in Illinois. A national convention of my calling meets in Cleveland on the 20th inst. With any sort of decent success on the part of the army, the League will keep the people up to the support of the administration. My labors and services may not be appreciated by you now, but no matter. If the Union is saved the rebellion crushed and the principles of liberty established, I will be content and die happy.
Very Truly Yours J. Medill[11]

William to one of his sisters (Mary or Ellen)
Hd. Quarters 8th Il. Cavalry Camp at Potomac Creek Station, Virginia, May 15, 1863

Dear Sister:

I have had so little time and opportunity for writing since my return that I have omitted to notify my friends even that I had escaped all harm during this late terrible battles. I knew you would be uneasy about me, but there was no help for it, until within a few days our regiment has neither sent nor received any mail. We were on the front and there were no facilities for communication. Enough that we neither had a fight nor were in much danger. Under command of Gen. Averell, we started to join Gen. Stoneman in his raid, but our commander being either a coward or a traitor failed to connect. We got as far as Cedar Mountain, met a brigade of rebels, halted two days and then returned. Thus we were prevented from all participation in Stoneman's glorious achievements. Had we been with him (Stoneman) I have no doubt we could have captured and burned the city of Richmond. We feel very much aggrieved at the failure. It has always been our desire to lead the cavalry in this army, and Gen. Stoneman promised that we should have the post of honor in his raid. We were within hearing of the battles all the time, and our division commander was afraid to attack the enemy. Well, there is no use crying. Next time we will have a better opportunity.

I am unable to give you any of the particulars of the different engagements, not having been present, nor having witnessed them either. All I know is, that our men feel as though they had won a victory. I never knew the men to be in such high feather with their achievements. Everyone is willing to renew the battle whenever Hooker gives the order and the sooner the better.

At present we are in Camp at Potomac Creek Station about half way between Aquia Creek and Fredericksburg. Our horses were pretty much worn out, and it will require a week to recuperate sufficiently to move again. At the end of that time we are at Uncle Samuel's disposal for any purpose he may desire us to perform. The health of our regiment is very good, but there was so much filth accumulated during the winter that the air is very impure and will soon produce sickness. Hope we'll get away before the evil effect is manifested.

I saw Abe Keel just before the battle but not since. That corps run during the fight and I suppose he was not hurt, however, his col. (Meyer) was captured by the rebs. I heard that the 4th Ohio lost seventy or eighty in killed and wounded. Have not seen the regiments yet, and consequently not received those little articles Mother sent by Dr. McAbee. I will go over there one of these days.

I will endeavor to write a long letter one of these days when I will give more of the particulars. My health is excellent. Hope all the family are well. Give my regards to my friends and love to the family.

In haste. Yours affectionately, W. H. Medill

An unidentified friend writes to William

Philadelphia, May 20, 1863

Friend:

Yours came to hand a day or two since and hardly know what to say in reply. The repulse of Hooker seems to have done more to unsettle public opinion than any recent event, and during the last week [I] was in Washington and found a general uneasiness pervading almost all I met. Among them I found your Bro. J [Joseph] and had quite a pleasant hurried chat with him. He seemed to have little confidence in Abe as he expressed it—"he is a weak man," he said he had not been able to see you. What to say at present puzzles me.

Will write you again soon. Am expecting to go to Wash. into the Treasury Dept. and hope to be better posted then. May go this week, will write from there.

Val—seems to be in for Fort Warren,[12] it is not right, Medill, nothing but out & out measures will answer for the times, and these I am almost confident Old Abe don't mean to take. We have had a deputation from the Union League Clubs here to the Prest. in reference to this very matter, but the result seems to be more of this leniency, which has been our misfortune so far and which even on the approach of the draft seems to be continued.

I am almost positive that we shall have an armed resistance, to the conscription law—and it will do us more harm than any postponement of the war.

You have seen the cavalry raids in the west, good ain't they?

I am so much engaged in my own immediate affairs that the humor is hardly on me to write a long letter so with best wishes from my friends and mine to yours, I am

Your old friend St M

Joseph to William
Office of the *Daily Tribune,* Chicago, May 24, 1863

Brother William:

I returned home yesterday having stayed three days in Cleveland and one in Canton. James is still in a very bad way, but thinks he is a little better than when you saw him. It is doubtful whether he ever will recover. I found wife in rather poor health on my return and must take steps to improve her health—horseback and open air. I was very sorry that I could not get a pass to Falmouth, and particularly now I learn the trouble you put yourself to on my account. If I could have remained another week in Washington, I would have asked Lincoln himself for a pass, but I was obliged to leave there on Saturday.

How do you like the glorious news from Vicksburg? The river opened, the rebel army destroyed, millions of property captured or burned, 24,000 prisoners taken, Louisiana conquered, Mississippi to be conquered and slaves all freed in a few weeks, the rebellion nearly played out in the whole Southwest.

I tell you the Kingdom of Jeff Davis totters to its fall. A victory by the Potomac Army would give it the finishing blow. It looks to me as if you will be able to join my family at Newport in August.

I believe the war is hastening to its close. When we get the devils going downhill, the velocity of their fall follows the rule of other falling bodies. Rosecrans and Burnside will now deliver the blows, one at Murfreesboro and the other near Knoxville. Hunter will shortly go in on his muscle at Charleston. Banks has Louisiana nearly cleared of rebels and is raising a large army of blacks to garrison the conquered territory. A powerful cavalry force will be sent into Texas.

The policy of the government now is to mount 100,000 of the infantry in order to give them speed and to make tremendous raids into all parts of secession, cutting up and destroying their railroads and canals and telegraphs and stores of all kinds, and driving them into two or three Atlantic slave states.

Cotton will begin to come forward from the South in great abundance and must fall In price. Gold will also go down to near par and greenbacks go up to the value of gold.

Emigration from Europe is already pouring into New York at the rate of 1,000 per day, which will fill up the gap made by the war in our labor population. When the rebellion is crushed and slavery abolished, there will be a great rush of population into the South from the North and from France, Italy, and Southern Germany, while half a million a year of emigrants will pour into the North from Great Britain, Russia, and Scandinavia. The niggers in the South will all float off into the Gulf States like blackbirds when the frost comes. There is a great, grand, and glorious future to our country when the slaveholders' hellish revolt is crushed out. There will never be another rebellion. There was but one in heaven, and there never will be but one in North America. The Almighty put the revolted Lucifers into hell, and the loyal people will put the revolted slaveholders into as hot a place.

But it is very possible that we shall have two wars when this one is ended—one to clear the British out of Canada and the other to clear the French out of Mexico. This continent belongs to the free American race, and they are bound to have it—every inch of it, including the West. We have got a taste of blood and learned the art of war and our own tremendous strength and resources. Our navy will domineer the seas and our army the continent. The insults received from England must be wiped out, and the only reparation she can give us is to vacate North America. Peaceably if she will—forcibly if we must.

And as to France, she has taken a mean and cowardly advantage of this nation to crush poor Mexico, which will not be allowed. We shall permit no nation to abuse Mexico but ourselves. We claim the right to turn her up on Uncle Sam's knee and spank her bottom for not behaving herself, as in 1846, but will permit no one else to touch her. Louis Napoleon will get his eyes blackened within six months after our rebellion is put down and will find himself kicked out of that country.

In future war black and yellow men will be freely used to fight. England holds India with Sepoy troops, who hate her. How easy for us to hold the South with black troops who love the North and are devotedly loyal. Old Abe says: "Bring on your niggers. I want 200,000 of them to save my white boys as soon as I can get them." Our people are learning sense. The war has pounded new ideas into their heads and old—out. It is a great teacher, and great progress is never made by a people except thro' war. The tree of Liberty must be watered by [the] blood of patriots at least once in every three generations.

I have not lost my faith in Hooker a particle. He came within an inch of destroying Lee's Army and will do it next time. The fates were against him, but better luck next trial. Your army inflicted far greater loss on the rebs than it suffered. Two more such victories, and there will be no rebel army left to boast of victories won. The draft will soon fill your ranks full of men.

I have been looking over your account and find it as follows, as nearly as I can recollect the dates, my first memorandum book being stolen a year ago:

Cash paid to and for you from August to November 1861 towards raising company, buying horse and outfit. & etc $365.00 4 percent premium . . . To your Credit $1,237.40

I will immediately invest your last remittance in 4 percent bonds. In this shape the money is perfectly secure, drawing interest and can be converted into cash at a moment's notice at any bank. You perceive that your money has already produced $67.75 of interest since last September.

Very truly yours, J. Medill[13]

WILLIAM TO JOSEPH

Hd. Quarters 8th Illinois near Brooke Station, Virginia, May 30, 1863
Bro Joseph:

I received your letter of the 24th and one from Kate of the 21st yesterday, and I assure you they were both welcome. Since I returned from my visit last month, our regiment has been nearly constantly on the move and away from all communication. We were in camp four days after the battle of Chancellorsville and were then sent down the Neck after guerrillas and smugglers, and I think we put an end to some of them for a while. Since the return of the army to this side of the Rappahannock, the 8th Pa. Cavalry has been doing picket duty down in King George Co. where we were last winter. Through their lax manner of doing duty, the guerrillas have been sniping and killing their pickets. In one case they picked up a lieutenant and five men who went outside of the lines to see some girls. Smuggling and spying became the trace of all. Finally Hooker asked Pleasonton if he could not stop it, and the little general thought the 8th Illinois competent to the task, so we were sent down the Neck with instructions to destroy smuggling and capture guerrillas and end all contraband business as far as practicable, and were given ten days to do it in. I can't pretend to give you the details in *exterisco* of our doings but will give the results: We burnt one hundred boats of nearly every size from a schooner down to a dugout; we captured and destroyed thirty smuggler establishments with goods valued at (in Dixie) $300,000; captured 325 horses, 212 mules and 100 prisoners. But the loss of all this property did not produce the squirming as the relieving from bondage of one thousand slaves. I think the 8th Illinois maintains is preeminence in this respect over any other regiment in the service. We had the grandest train it has ever been my privilege to see on our return. The negroes were jubilant over their freedom and when they were shipped at Belle Plain for Aquia Creek such a shout was passed up from the men and waving of handkerchiefs from the women to our boys [that it] was cheering. They cried, danced and prayed in the fullness of their hearts, and I saw many of our men who came into the service pro-slavery men wipe a tear from their eyes at the sight of these poor people. They were kept in a horrid condition by their masters. Clothing is so scarce and dear that planters cannot afford to buy for their slaves, and as a consequence, they are kept as nearly naked as possible. We returned to camp at the end of ten days and are now taking a rest from our labors. We had two men wounded, one slightly and one seriously. We also captured two Confederate flags, which we found flying in Heathsville, the C.H. town of Northumberland County. Lt. Col. D.R. Clendenin [David Ramsay Clendenin] commanded the regiment and deserves praise for the manner in which he conducted the operations.

Happens that you were a little premature in announcing the capture of Vicksburg, but I hope and believe Grant has it by this time. If he has, and Rosecrans and Banks move as suddenly as they ought, the effect on the rebellions will be awful. I am afraid, however, we will waste our time as usual in waiting for the enemy to concentrate and neutralize the good effect of this victory by winning a battle somewhere else. My impression is that Lee contemplates attacking this army soon. What the result will be I know not. We have been greatly reduced by the withdrawal of those N. Y. regiments, and I doubt whether reinforcements have filled their places. I have confidence that Hooker will smash Lee to pieces if the rebel army crosses.

Congratulate me on receipt of the *boots*. They reached the camp yesterday, and I am now sporting them. Tell Sammy they are a perfect fit, but Lieut. Wing's were a size too large. He sold them, however, very readily for what they cost. The fifty dollars sent me was stolen, I have no doubt, and I have no hope of ever seeing it.

I was much disappointed at your non-arrival. You would have been just in time to have gone with us on our raid down the Neck and could have had a splendid opportunity of seeing slavery and our mode of abolishing it, which would have paid you better than attending all the Union League Conventions that were ever, or ever will be, held. You would have gained flesh every day. The weather was pleasant, the roads good, country rich and slaves plenty. We subsisted our men and the slaves on the people during the trip and as a consequence we lived well.

You omitted to send me the paper I mentioned for my boy "Jimmy." He wants to have it. I was not aware that I had so much money in your hands. I'll have enough, if I keep on another year, for quite a spree. I intend to save $100 per month, and as I have some 15 months to serve, I'll have a respectable sum at that time. I hope, however, then I will have my discharge, so as to join you at Newport in August. I will write to Kate tomorrow. Give my love to the family and regards to friends.

Yours, W. H. Medill

William to Ellen

Hd. Quarters 8th Illinois near Brooke Station, June 5, 1863

Dear Sister:

Yours of the 29th was received today. I intended to postpone my answer until tomorrow, in hopes that my head would stop aching, and I would be in a better trim for writing. The weather has been exceedingly hot and sultry, and with the amount of travel, of horses, the camp has been full of dust, this produced a heavy headache, which sticks to me. We are promised a shower of rain tonight which will cool the atmosphere, lay the dust and cure my aching head—I hope. But, since your letter was received, an order has come directing us to hold ourselves in readiness to march at any moment, and to have three days of cooked rations on hand. My impression is that we will move tonight or tomorrow morning—where to I have no definite idea. I hope to make another attempt to advance on Richmond, but I fear to repel an advance of rebels on Washington. They are threatening some sort of move, probably to cover the sending of reinforcements to the West, probably to prevent us from doing so, but more likely to attack us. (While I write, heavy firing is in progress up the Rappahannock, towards Fredericksburg. I guess the fight has commenced.) Under these circumstances I will drop you a line today—brief, however, it must be.

I was very sorry Joseph could not get a pass to the army. He would have enjoyed the visit, I think, and we of the 8th would have shown him every attention. He could have accompanied us on our trip down the Neck, on the occasion of so many contrabands being relieved from bondage and so many horses joining our regiment. We made quite a cleaning out in this Neck. How the people do hate us. I succeeded in capturing a very nice little horse, which I have purchased from the government. I hope to take him home with me when the war is over, and give him to you and Mary for a buggy horse. He is one of the nicest kind for that purpose—being a very fast trotter.

Since the battle of Chancellorsville this army has been resting and watching the movements and battles of Grant and Banks. We had great hopes that Vicksburg would have fallen sooner, and with less loss to our brave boys, but it seems as though there would have to be a long, protracted siege before it can be taken. I am afraid something will cause a failure. If Johnson is not watched, he will go for Grant some night. Banks has an easier job on his hands. Port

Hudson has a much smaller force garrisoning it, and there is no one to interfere with our rear. Although an army is supposed to contain nothing but fighting material, yet there is scarcely anything so easily deranged, and so easily destroyed. A flank attack or a rear attack seems to leave no recourse but a run for it. A battle is the most trying thing on men's nerves. While men feel confident or hopeful, they will stand or advance, but let them lose these, and at the first discharge a panic seems to take possession of them, and courage departs. The bravest will act as though they were the meanest of cowards. No persuasion can stop a rout under those circumstances. I have witnessed one such catastrophe—at Gaines Hill on the Peninsula last summer—and hope I may be spared from ever seeing such a sight again,

A report comes from the front that Hooker has commenced crossing at Fredericksburg again. There certainly is terrible firing over in that direction. Although we are some four miles from the river, we can distinctly hear the musketry, while the sound of artillery is incessant. I hope this may prove true, for it shows that Hooker is confident. His army is well pleased with him. I believe that he can whip Lee and will do it. I trust that we will have something to do this time. The sound of battle revives me already, and my head is getting better fast.

I would be much pleased if Mother could remove to Illinois, and I know of no place so attractive for a residence as the location you mention at Hyde Park. It is just far enough removed from the city, the land is high, rich and dry, there is always a breeze from the Lake, and the scenery all about is beautiful. But the difficulty lies in disposing of her Canton property for its value. I presume lots are not selling very readily just now. I am glad you will probably go there in the Spring. The West is the place for young and aspiring people. The East has no attractions for me. I think I will become, after the war, one of those Western Provinces so much spoken of and each year pull up stakes and advance another step westward. A roving life will suit me best hereafter. With no wife to trouble or retard me, I will move when the humor suggests a move. Our family has been altogether too domestic, too much wedded to one spot. I will be the exception. I believe I have always been an exception.

While I should be exceedingly happy to open a correspondence with Miss Griswold, I am afraid she would not consider it just the thing prudence would dictate. If you have no hesitancy about asking her, I certainly have no objection, and if she is willing, will endeavor to make my letters as interesting to her as possible, and not insult her with any impudent matrimonial insinuations. I have scarcely any correspondence outside of our family, especially among the ladies. Letters are highly prized in the army, and we try to do the best we can in making ours valuable.

Tell Mary I am much obliged to her for the papers. The magazines did not come. Don't fail to give my best regards to Miss Sarah Keel and her parents when you see them and to all my friends in Canton. Whenever you have time write, whether I do or not. Tell Mary to write and that, if we don't move tomorrow and I have time, [I'll] write to her. Give my love to the family.

Yours, W. H. Medill

After the Battle of Chancellorsville, William came down with a fever, aggravated by diarrhea. At the same time, Lee's army commenced its march on Pennsylvania. Union cavalry continually engaged with the rebel cavalry and picket forces, hoping to discover the enemy's intentions. The next great battle was only a month away.

By 1863 Gettysburg citizens had been on edge for months. The war always felt close because the Mason-Dixon line was just a few miles to the south. In September 1862 residents had heard the rumble of cannons at the Battle of Antietam, and if Lee had won—Gettysburg was just across the state line.[14]

Now General Lee invaded again, marching from Fredericksburg beginning June 3, 1863, with Lieut. Gen. Richard S. Ewell's Second Corps following that of Gen. James Longstreet. Ewell was a nervous man with a bald head, protuberant eyes, and a jutting nose, a combination that gave him a curious bird-like appearance. He had lost a leg at Groverton in August 1862 and left Fredericksburg riding in a buggy with a pair of crutches beside him, but when action started he strapped himself onto the saddle. Left behind for the time being, Lieut. Gen. Ambrose Powell (A. P.) Hill faced Union troops under General Hooker. Hill was a slender, weak-framed man, who was chronically ill, yet maintained the will to be a furious fighter.[15]

Union general Hooker promoted Alfred Pleasonton to major general on June 22, 1863, and placed him in command of the cavalry corps. Pleasonton was thirty-nine years old, small statured, furtive-eyed, neat, and dapper with a straw hat worn at a jaunty angle. A man of quick perception and generally good judgment, he was not above coloring his battle reports to enhance his reputation. His subordinates included experienced regulars John Buford and David McMurtrie Gregg, the young Hugh Judson Kilpatrick, and British soldier of fortune Sir Percy Wyndham.[16]

General Pleasonton led the Cavalry Corps June 9, 1863, against J. E. B. Stuart's cavalry at the Battle of Brandy Station,[17] which was the largest cavalry battle of the Civil War. General Stuart and his staff had spent the night camped about a half mile northeast of Brandy Station. Men sleeping on the ground were awakened that morning by the sound of small arms fire and cannon fire. Early in the melee the Eighth Illinois Cavalry's commander, Maj. Alpheus Clark, was shot in the hand, requiring his evacuation. Almost immediately, the next ranking officer, Capt. George Forsyth, was shot in the thigh. At about the same time, Capt. Benjamin Foote, commanding Company E, Eighth New York, was shot and killed. Lacking leaders, the Federal attack stalled.[18]

After the grueling combat, Pleasonton ordered his men to break off their attack. Stuart was left in possession of the field but in no shape to pursue. The battle is considered a narrow Union defeat, but it had a great positive impact on the morale of the Union horse soldiers.

Although Pleasonton's cavalry fought their counterparts at Brandy Station, the Confederates fended off the Union's multiple attempts to push through and locate the main body of Lee's army as it tramped northward through the Shenandoah Valley.[19] The Battle of Brandy Station did not stop Lee's campaign into Union territory, but it delayed General Stuart's move northward. General Pleasonton acquired intelligence about Confederate movements but did not provide Hooker with enough information about what was happening—discovering Stuart's movement did not prove that Lee was launching a major invasion.[20]

One of the hard-fought cavalry engagements took place June 9, 1863, near Warrenton Junction, where officers of the Eighth Illinois were wounded—Captain Smith and Major Clark mortally and Major Forsyth severely. When William heard of the fight, he got up, sick as he was; ordered his horse; and joined his regiment. Excitement enabled him to persevere. He wrote on June 10: "My sickness has not troubled me half so much as to be left behind my regiment when there is warrior's work to be done. I cannot submit to this fever and shall mount my horse and join my regiment if it takes two men to hold me on."

William to Joseph
In Camp near Catlett's Station, Virginia,
Head Quarters 8th Ill. Cavalry, Sunday, June 14, 1863

Dear Brother:

We have changed our base of operations and taken up the line of the Orange & Alexandria Railroad. The cavalry came up some days since, and the infantry are moving up at present. The 11th Corps reached this point last night. Hooker is keeping himself in Lee's front with his fists extended ready for a fight. One corps (I believe the 12th) is left to guard government stores at Aquia Creek. My impression is that this is the proper place for defending Washington or moving upon the enemy. The country back from the river here is very good for fighting. The land is level and even. Whether Lee will attempt to cross and attack at this point is doubtful. He may move up into the Shenandoah Valley. In fact, a scouting party from this regiment went up there yesterday, moving to ascertain whether any movements of the enemy are being made.

The late cavalry battle near Rappahannock Bridge was made in order to check a big raid, which Stuart had formed and was ready to commence. From papers found in the rebel camps, it is developed that there were 12,000 cavalry and one division of infantry in the expedition. The infantry were to be mounted as soon as the expedition got into Maryland. The animals to be taken from the people. I haven't the slightest doubt but Stuart, once past us, would have been able to go all over Maryland and far enough into Pennsylvania. But Gen. Pleasonton with a command of less than 7,000 attacked and crippled Stuart so much that he gave up the proposed trip.

The fight was a terrible one, much the severest that has ever taken place on this continent. It was a close fight where the men met face-to-face and was a succession of charges, commencing at 5 o'clock a.m. and continuing until 5 o'clock p.m. You can judge the severity of the engagement by the loss sustained. Our whole footings of killed, wounded and missing show 931 of men and over 1,500 horses. We only lost about 50 prisoners. What the rebels lost we cannot tell, but it was much heavier than ours. We captured upwards of 250.

The loss in our regiment was 41 men killed, wounded and missing and 100 horses. From accounts given of the fight (I was too unwell to be present) I understand that every man did splendidly. When the 8th New York broke in wild confusion through the ranks of our men, the boys never wavered nor faltered notwithstanding the commanding officers were shot one after the other—Capts. Clark, Forsythe and Smith. These men took command of the regiment in succession and were each severely wounded. The latter Capt. Smith will most likely die, as he had his leg shattered and amputated. The others were not so bad. I have no doubt I would have been hit had I been with the regiment. Col. Davis was killed at the head of our regiment. When he found his old regiment breaking, he came up to ours and cried out, "Eighth Illinois! Charge! My regiment won't stand!" Just then a ball pierced the center of his forehead, and he fell. He was an exceedingly brave man, and his death was a severe loss to the service. Col. Gamble commands the brigade now.

About all that is doing now is changing the organization of the cavalry. Pleasonton is in command, and the whole is put into two divisions under Buford and Gregg. Ours is still the 1st Brigade of the 1st Division. Our regiment is still the right of the whole. Stoneman is assigned to infantry.

I am still quite unwell and have made application to be sent to a hospital in Georgetown, D.C. I have the diarrhea very bad, and it keeps me down. The fever is not bad, only a little during the afternoon. I think ten days or so in a good hospital will cure me. I am very sorry I could not have been in battle and am afraid that unless I get cured, I'll miss the next one.

Gen. Farnsworth is here at present and last night at dress parade made his old regiment quite a pretty little speech. The men rushed about him as eagerly as though he was a parent. He is looking quite well.

Vicksburg still holds out. I guess it is better to starve Pemberton into surrender than to try to storm and capture the place. The loss of life, in that event, would be awful. Farnsworth seems to feel hopeful that this rebellion will soon end, and we will be home before winter sets in again.

Well, I must close. My head aches. Give my love to the family and regards to my friends.

Yours, etc. W. H. Medill

JOSEPH TO WILLIAM
Written on letterhead from the Offices
of the *Daily Tribune,* Chicago, June 19, 1863

Dear Bro,

I am sorry to hear of your continued illness. If you find yourself getting worse, telegraph me, and I will go out to see you. I am in doubt where to direct this letter. Don't let your sickness run on without acquainting me of how you are.

Yours Truly, J. Medill

After William rejoined his regiment, they took part in desperate cavalry contests at Aldie and Upperville. The Eighth Illinois rode in the advance, charged on the rebel force drawn up in front of the Aldie Gap of the Blue Ridge. The Third Indiana acted as skirmishers, and the Twelfth Illinois as supports. Early in the fight, Lieutenant Colonel Clendenin, who commanded the Eighth Illinois, had his horse wounded and retired from the field. Major Medill, next in rank, took command. In charge after charge he led his men on the rebel ranks, routing and scattering them. His regiment defeated, successively, two Virginia and one North Carolina cavalry regiments. His favorite weapon, in making a charge, was the revolver.[21]

Before General Lee could cross into Maryland, he had to deal with the Union outpost at Winchester, twenty-five miles southwest of the Potomac, a garrison of nine thousand soldiers, covering Harpers Ferry and the upstream crossings at Shepherdstown and Williamsport. An old-time U.S. army regular, Maj. Gen. Robert H. Milroy, commanded the occupied territory. Because of uncertainty about Lee and Hooker, Milroy's immediate superior urged him to abandon Winchester and fall back down to Harpers Ferry, but Milroy put him off with assurances that he had the place well fortified. Confederate general Ewell drove Milroy's troops, both cavalry and infantry. In a three-day action, at a low cost to Ewell, Milroy lost nearly half of his command. For not retreating until disaster loomed, Milroy's action was analyzed by a military court of inquiry that reached a verdict placing no blame for Milroy's actions. Milroy himself maintained that his resistance at Winchester delayed Lee's invasion by three days, giving the North extra time to prepare.[22]

In order to learn about Confederate movements, General Hooker turned Alfred Pleasonton's forces leftward toward the Bull Run Mountains on a scout. As Stuart's Confederates rode north on the western side of the mountains, two columns of Pleasonton's troopers approached the mountains from the east, starting through the gaps that Stuart's divided forces were moving in position to cover. Two simultaneous engagements erupted late in the day on June 17, 1863, one at Aldie and the other at Middleburg, just five miles apart. The greater fight took place at Aldie, where Pleasonton, seconded by Gregg, led the advance. Stuart was at Middleburg instead. The fight ended with Confederates withdrawing, not because they were beaten but because orders came from Stuart, who wanted to gain firmer control after the jarring news that Union troops were near.[23]

The encounters at Aldie and Middleburg didn't give Hooker the information he wanted about Longstreet's movement. As a precaution, part of the Army of the Potomac went northward to Leesburg, Virginia, to cover Edward's Ferry and other Potomac crossings in the area. Rumors from Pennsylvania were too confused and contradictory to depend on. Union general Pleasonton's force was not seriously diminished by his losses, but until he had more infantry support from Hooker, he moved from Aldie cautiously on June 18, making a push through Middleburg.[24] General Stuart gave up less than a mile of territory, but his position went unchallenged by Federals. It rained the next day, and action was limited to skirmishing.[25]

In two days of fighting General Pleasonton had lost about eight hundred men. Stuart's loss was about five hundred, but he had kept Pleasonton from learning much more than that the Loudoun Valley was free of Confederate infantry. Federals fell back to Aldie in the Bull Run Mountains. Hooker had wanted Pleasonton's reconnaissance to penetrate the Shenandoah Valley and obtain reliable intelligence, but Pleasonton fell short of that goal.[26]

William to Joseph

Headquarters 8th Ill. Cavalry near Aldie, Virginia, June 23, 1863
Dear Brother:

Since last I wrote you I have been kept busy, and nearly the whole time we were outside of mail facilities. When my last letter was written I was sick, but by good luck and the desire to join the regiment my health rapidly improved, and I was able to join our regiment for duty in a few days from that time. I caught up with the command at Catlett's Station. The long ride and excessive heat were almost too much for me, and I came near having a relapse of the fever. It was so near that I asked for a sick leave to go to the hospital, which was granted, but feeling much better when the regiment marched from there, I remained with it. I have had a diarrhea since, with that exception I am feeling quite well at present. The weather changed very materially from the terrible heat we had the past eight weeks by a succession of heavy thundershowers, commencing on Saturday last and at present. Though the sun shines hot, a strong breeze keeps one cool.

We are now near Aldie in Loudoun County, which is situated in the Bull Run Mountains at the junction of the Catoctin Mountains. We marched from Catlett's to Manassas on the 16th, and from there to Aldie on the 17th. We arrived at Aldie, and we found Gregg's Division just finishing a very severe fight with Fitzhugh Lee. Although Gregg whipped Lee our loss was the heaviest, the rebs having fought behind stone walls, which abound in this county in great profusion. Our principal loss was in Col. Kilpatrick's Brigade, which very foolishly charged the enemy with sabers instead of using carbines and pistols.

On the 18th our brigade went on a reconnaissance to Philomont six miles from here towards Snickers Gap in the Blue Ridge. We met but few of the enemy. On the 19th Gregg moved towards Ashby's Gap and at Middleburg, 4 miles from Aldie, he found Stuart's cavalry in force. He fought all day but failed to gain any decided advantage. On the 20th we all remained quietly in camp and rested. On Sunday the 21st, Pleasonton moved both his divisions to the front on the Ashby Gap Road and commenced driving Stuart. The rebs fell back slowly, fighting as they went. We moved in two columns, our division taking a side road to the right of Gregg. We had some severe fighting to dislodge the enemy from behind the infernal stone fences. By two o'clock we had driven the rebs a distance of 12 miles and within a couple of miles of the gap. Here in a splendid position in a number of fields fenced with stone we came suddenly on their line of battle.

It seemed to me as though I never saw so many cavalry. Our force was but a handful in comparison. The 3rd Indiana was acting as skirmishers to our brigade. As soon as Gen. Buford saw the enemy, he ordered our regiment to make a charge. I tell you it was exciting. The enemy was massed in columns of regiments in our front, ready to advance as soon as we entered the field their column occupied. Their artillery was advantageously posted and reserved its fire till we came within range of grape and canister. Col's Gamble and Clendenin had their horses shot as soon as they came within range, and I took command. I discovered the reb artillery and saw that our only safety lay in getting so close that it would fire over us. I formed a line and charged, using carbines and pistols—our boys being much more proficient with those weapons than sabre. We drove our brigade clear out of the first field in haste. Their cannon, just as I expected, firing over us but still sufficiently near to make the position rather unpleasant.

Some more fresh regiments of the enemy came forward to the rescue of their friends. By this time a few squadrons of the 3rd Indiana and 12th Illinois came up to our support. We quickly formed our ranks and prepared to receive them. Every carbine was loaded, and our line formed behind the fence. As soon as the rebs came into the field, I again charged them. Again they were run out, but not, however, without hard fighting. They seemed determined to whip us. In this charge we killed and wounded a great many and lost a number wounded. An attempt was made to get on our flank, but Capt. Hynes with a battalion of our regiment moved to our left and effectually spoiled the attempt. They made three more attempts to drive our brigade but in each were beaten.

Everyone who was in this fight agrees in saying it was by far more severe and fierce than the fight at Beverly Ford. I never saw anything like it, and so say all. Gen. Buford says it beats all cavalry fighting he ever witnessed. He especially compliments our regiment and the 3rd Indiana. If you could only have been present, it would have been worth a whole age of peace. Men never stood up in the face of such odds and under such fire of grape and canister as did our boys. None floundered or showed the white feather [behaved in a cowardly manner] with *one exception*.

I don't know how to describe my feelings during the whole fight. As quickly as I saw the enemy, all nervousness if I felt any before vanished, and I felt a desire to rush at him. After the first volley, I lost all care about the bullets or the shots from the cannon and devoted my time to my men in rallying and charging and encouraging. I saved all our men who were captured by charging into the rebel ranks. We did not lose a man as prisoner. My horse was struck twice, but both times by spent balls, which only bruised him. How I escaped I know not.

While we were rallying after one of the charges, I saw a rebel officer chasing our Sergeant-major Sam'l W. Smith, who had got mixed up with the rebs. I gave my horse the spur and in a few bounds was near him. When he saw me, he raised his sabre and ordered me to surrender. I brought my pistol to the aim when he threw his sabre down and surrendered. He proved to be a major in the 11th Va. Cavalry and big enough to have whipped two like me in a fist row. But the battlefield recognized one man as equal to another if armed with a shooting iron. There has long been a desire on the part of our regiment to meet the 9th Va. Cavalry, which is the crack regiment in the reb army, while they have made many brags about what they would do with us. We met on Sunday. The result was that we routed them just as we did all the others, wounding and capturing their Lt. Col. Lewis, who commanded the regiment & also a number of prisoners. We captured upwards of a hundred prisoners all together, losing none. We killed and wounded upwards of 200. Our loss was upwards of 40. None of our officers were hurt.

While we were fighting on the right, the 2nd Division was engaged on our left, near the town of Upperville. They were also successful and killed a large number. I have not learned what our whole loss was. We killed and wounded over 500 of the enemy. The fight only lasted about an hour. You can guess how savagely it was conducted. The whole country was covered with dead horses and men. Two pieces of artillery were also taken from them. Their rout was so complete that they ran completely through the gap without trying to defend it, although two hundred men and a section of artillery ought to defend the place against ten thousand. There were many instances of bravery, but taken as a whole I don't believe the war will show where a regiment stood up against such odds as the 8th Ill. Cavalry did on this occasion. It was not like being surrounded and fighting for life or death, not waiting to defend a position till supports came up. We could have fallen back a quarter of a mile and taken a position, which was almost impregnable, but we remained in the open field and formed in face of their sharpshooters and under a murderous fire of grape and canister. Even the rebs themselves were astonished at the coolness of our men.

The 3rd Indiana having been deployed as skirmishers were so much scattered as to be able only to collect two small squadrons to our support, and with the exception of about 100 of the 12th Illinois, which was attached to the Indiana regiment, no other assistance came to us. These men did nobly. They mixed up among our men, and all acted together. The 8th New York was left in the rear to support a battery and did not come up at all.

I have spoken of having had command all through. Lt. Col. Clendenin had his horse slightly hurt in the beginning of the skirmishing, and he failed to come on the field though he rode his horse all the time during the engagement. It has been the impression in the regiment for some time that he is a coward. Now it is confirmed.

Col. Gamble is in command of our brigade. He had his horse killed by a shell when the fight began. He is brave, but drinks too much. In fact, he is becoming notorious. I am very sorry for he is an excellent officer and a good man. Major Beveridge has never been under fire, and there are many who think he doesn't intend to get hurt. You can see, by this, my position. Besides this, there is continually ill-feeling between those officers, and they are all the time back-fighting and abusing each other. It is very disgraceful. I have never mentioned these matters before, for I dislike to see these quarrels among officers in a regiment, but when position cowardice comes to be apparent in our superiors, then I can stand it no longer. Gen. Pleasonton says he will try and make matters straight, but when Beveridge returns, he will take command, and the change is but a slight improvement. Now what do you think the chances would be to get transferred to some staff in the West, say Hutchins for instance? Some cavalry commander would suit me best. I don't like to leave the 8th Illinois, but a change or a resignation is fast becoming necessary. I have the blues about half the time. It is not agreeable to run all the risks and do the work and not receive the credit. Think of this matter and let me hear from you, if you please.

I cannot give you any news from any other portion of our army. The corps are divided. The 5th is here with us; the 12th is somewhere near Leesburg. Hooker is, I understand, at Fairfax C.H. I have not seen a newspaper later than the 18th, so that I am not posted at all. Your letter of the 12th and a few copies of the *Tribune* came along yesterday by some accident. *We are quite anxious about what is going on.* My policy would be to use enough of our men to make a nucleus for the new troops for the defense of our states and with the rest of the army destroy Richmond and the rear. We could go clear through the Confederacy before Lee could get back. We can raise enough at home to defend ourselves, while Hooker's army devastates and destroys the

Confederacy. We can carry off every nigger in Virginia in two weeks. I can clean a county in two days with our regiment. But what's the use talking? There's not enough enterprise in our commanders.

I should think you had earned the right to drive a matched team and a fancy carriage after twenty years of hard toil. I hope to take my ease at an earlier period of life. By remaining single in blessed repose I will not have need of so much worldly treasure. So the preacher is ahead again. Well, congratulate him. He is evidently an ambitious, persevering chap, or he would have given up long ago. I know I should have failed if it would require as much hanging on as it does for him.

I have not heard from Sam although I wrote to him a long while ago. I presume I have tired your patience sufficiently and will quit. This letter is strictly private, especially the personal part.

Give my love to the family and regards to friends.

Yours, etc. W. H. Medill

Four other sources clarify statements William made in the preceding letter. First, the regimental history Dr. Hard wrote does not confirm or deny Clendenin's conduct during the action, ignoring any rumors or suggestion of cowardice. Secondly, Dale Price in "Rally Around the Flag" 8th Illinois Cavalry Guidon Presentation, for the DuPage County Historical Museum[27] provided details about Colonel Farnsworth and William Gamble, stating that Colonel Farnsworth did not have the military acumen to train troopers, so he sought out the "most under-appreciated member" of the regiment's leadership, William Gamble, a fiery Irishman who provided necessary discipline and training, shaping men with little military experience. Gamble could "swear the pants off a lazy trooper." Thirdly, Dr. Hard's regimental history praised Major Beveridge, writing that on "November 4th Major Beveridge and Samuel Smith left the Eighth Illinois Cavalry. The Major's leave-taking was a touching scene. I venture to say that no officer in the army ever possessed the confidence and love of both officers and men to a greater extent than did Major Beveridge. He resigned his position to accept the Colonelcy of the Seventeenth Illinois Cavalry."[28] Fourth, charges against Colonel Clendenin sidelined him for a while, but he was later restored to command.

> Major John Beveridge, a jealous competitor for promotion in Clendenin's regiment had leveled accusations of three instances of cowardice toward the end of June of 1863. Allegedly . . . [he] called into question Colonel Clendenin's conduct during actions at Kelly's Ford (May 8th), Beverly Ford (May

9th) and Upperville (June 2nd). Deeply angered and humiliated, Clendenin had to endure the shame of being ordered to Alexandria to command dismounted cavalry. These serious charges cost him the chance to participate in the Battle of Gettysburg, where his regiment, the 8th Illinois, performed creditably. When his case was finally brought to trial, Colonel Clendenin was exonerated of all charges. He regained his command in time to participate in the 1864 campaigns.[29]

The letter William wrote June 23, 1863, was the last one the Colonel Robert R. McCormick Research Center contained. However, William wrote a final letter, which the *Tribune* published in a front-page article November 22, 1863, when the consecration of the National Cemetery and Lincoln's Gettysburg Address once more made the Battle of Gettysburg newsworthy. William's letter, quoted by the *Tribune*, explained the significance of the Union cavalry's defensive stand and feint on the first day of fighting.

Illinois' Share in the Mighty Struggle[30]

Eighteen loyal states were represented on the battlefield of Gettysburg. Among the number was Illinois, which had three regiments engaged in the mighty struggle—the 8th and 12th cavalry and Hecker's (82nd) infantry. The latter regiment fought desperately, and suffered terribly. It lost truly one half of the men taken into the fight, but behaved to the last as bravely as the best regiment on that bloody field. It composed a part of the 11th army corps and fought through the whole three days of the battle. Ex-alderman Salomon of this unit is its Lieutenant Colonel. The regiment mainly composed of citizens of Chicago. On the first day's fight the 8th and 12th Illinois cavalry bore a conspicuous part, and made repeated and furious charges on the rebel infantry, disordering their ranks, delaying their advance and capturing many prisoners. We had never seen any account of the part in the battle of Gettysburg by these regiments; the following extract from the letter written by Major Medill, supplies the deficiency, and may be interesting—at least to the friends of the regiments. It is dated Westminster, Md., July 4, Evening. Since my last letter to you which was written the day after our big cavalry fight near Upperville, June 23d, our brigade (composed of the 8th and 12th Illinois, 3rd Indiana, 8th New York, and a battery of flying artillery under command of Col. Gamble) has been continually on the march. Our Division under Gen. Buford marched from Aldie to Williamsburg; thence to Jefferson, Md; thence to Boonsboro, Md; thence to Fairfield, Pa., where we had a sharp fight with the rebel infantry and drove them from the village; thence to Emmitsburg; thence to Gettysburg where we arrived on the 30th of June, and charge on two rebel regiments of infantry belonging to Hill's command which we whipped with ease and drove back on the double quick. The next day we lay in camp with pickets out, watching the enemy. On the morning of the 2nd [sic] of July the rebels advanced in force and gave battle. Our infantry—the 1st and 11 army corps under General Reynolds . . . were in our rear between Gettysburg and Emmitsburg, and did not arrive to our support until 9 a.m. The attack commenced at 5 a.m. So that we had to take [the] head against the rebel army with two small brigades of cavalry and two field batteries, number less than 3,200 men all told under Gen. Buford. We held our position, however, and had captured a rebel flag and quite a number of prisoners before the infantry came up. This was done by successive charges on their front and flank, while our flying artillery played on them from every point. We actually compelled them to halt and change their line of battle several times. The prisoners we took said they supposed that our whole cavalry force was on their front and flanks. In these charges we lost a good many men and horses, but inflicted ten times as much damage on the enemy as we received.

When the infantry came up at 9 a.m., our regiment (8th Illinois) and brigade were ordered to the left of the line, to prevent a flank movement on the part of the enemy. From that time until the battle ended, we gave him great annoyance, and materially retarded his advance by making frequent bold dashes on him, obliging him to halt and change front to prevent us from sabering his flank and rear. In this way we saved a whole brigade of our infantry and a battery from being captured and cut to pieces. The rebels had them nearly surrounded and hemmed in, perceiving which, we made a detour to the left, gained their flank, and charged right on the rear of one of the living walls that was moving to crush our infantry. The rebel line halted suddenly, faced about, formed to receive us, and fired a volley that mostly went over our heads. We returned the fire with our carbines and galloped away. But during the time, they were thus delayed our infantry brigade escaped.

Our line was whipping the rebels until Longstreet came up to Hill's aid with 30,000 men and a powerful train of artillery. His corps was put on to the rebel right, in line of divisions—the line being a few hundred yards apart. These new lines overlapped our left more than half a mile. Our men both infantry and cavalry had been standing up gravely and successfully for eight hours before Hill's and Ewell's corps, but when this fresh horde of butternuts came up the fate of the day could easily be guessed. They advanced in long lines, they seemed to roll over the ground like great logs, that could not be checked, and yet moved slowly. I never saw anything like it. Our brigade's battery belched forth grape and canister at short range, making gaps in the advancing line at each discharge, and our infantry and cavalry poured volley after volley into the rolling mass, but still it came steadily on, closing up the spots as fast as made. On it rolled, in three long parallel lines, about 500 yards apart, their muskets gleaming in the sun and pouring forth volley after volley of fire and leaded missiles at our lines. Our regiment was posted on the extreme flank, and partially on the rear of those logs advancing. Hues of 30,000 solid infantry making a grand charge. I could see the whole thing as plainly as you can a revue in McVicker's Theater, as we were not 400 yards from the moving columns. When the rebels got near the thin, weak lines of our infantry, the latter of course had to give way and fall back. Then the rebs rushed forward on the double quick, with loud cheers. Our brigade then formed [a] column of attack and charged after the screaming devils. When close on their heels, we gave them a volley that sent scores of them headlong to the ground. Their lines halted, changed front, and delivered a volley after us as we fell back. By this means our infantry had time to take up another and stronger position and succeeded in checking the further advance of the enemy. The battle ended about half-past four o'clock p.m. The fighting was exceedingly desperate, and the losses very heavy on both sides.

During the night Gen. Meade arrived with three army corps. He ordered our cavalry division to fall back to this place (Westminster) and take positions on the railroad to guard our left against an apprehended flank movement of the enemy to cut off our communications and ammunition trains, but nothing except light skirmishing has been done. Here we have been two days listening to the roar of a tremendous battle that is being fought a few miles to our front. The thunder of the battle was heard all yesterday and this afternoon. It has now ceased. How we have ached to take part in it. Word has just come that the rebels have been repulsed at all points, and orders are received to mount our horses for the pursuit. In an hour we are off. We shall give the rebels a hot chase to the Potomac, no matter who lives to relate it.

And so they did. Next morning by daylight the two Illinois cavalry regiments commenced sabering the rebel rear guard, capturing trains, taking prisoners, and they kept it up until the rebel army stood at bay at Williamsport and Falling Waters with its back to the river. In this pursuit these regiments captured 2,000 prisoners and 800 rebel army wagons, and fought with the enemy's rear guard at every mile of the way. On the afternoon of the 6th, the gallant officer, from whose letter we extract, received his death wound while leading his regiment in a charge on a rebel brigade of infantry at Williamsport. The fight at Falling Waters, a few days afterwards, was the last contest of

Illinois soldiers with the rebels on the north side of the Potomac. It was the parting kick after the great battle of Gettysburg to the vanishing enemy.

Events after the Battle of Gettysburg left scant time to write. To complete William's story it became necessary to turn to the pocket journal he wrote in 1863, the journal Joseph kept when called to William's deathbed, and to accounts written by other individuals embroiled in these great events.

CHAPTER SIX

The Last Full Measure of Devotion

Immense number of slaves running off from different plantations.
—*William Medill, January 1, 1863*

WILLIAM MEDILL POCKET DIARY 1863
January 1863

Thursday, January 1, 1863, on picket near King George Court House at Taylor farm. Immense number of slaves running off from different plantations. Should judge the number to be as high as three hundred. Weather clear and cold.

Friday, January 2, Dr. McKinney and Dr. Noel below C.H. Capt. White very sick of C.H.

January 5–9, 1863, All of the Burgess family are extensively engaged in violating the blockade. Bad men. Beaterly has persecuted the few Union people in those parts badly. . . . Fred Toomey can be heard from at any of these places. Is a well known contraband trader.

Friday, January 16, 1863, Attended the court-martial of Tras K., which was postponed indefinitely. Returned to duty on picket at K.G.C.H. after a tiring ride through mud. Pontoons moving to front, Pleasonton's cavalry ready to move, indicative of an advance. Weather turned clear and cold.

Saturday 17, Nothing has occurred today. The weather has cleared up and is quite cold. Have been reading Handy Andy's blunders.[1] No news from Hd. Quarters. No papers. Received two letters—one from Jos. and one from Mary.

Sunday 18, Eight darkies belonging to Dr. Granlow and Mr. Dishman passed on their way, rejoicing. Weather clear and cold.

Monday January 19, 1863, The day passed quietly until night when the 8th N.Y. Cav. arrived and built fires along the hills—a feint evidently. The army

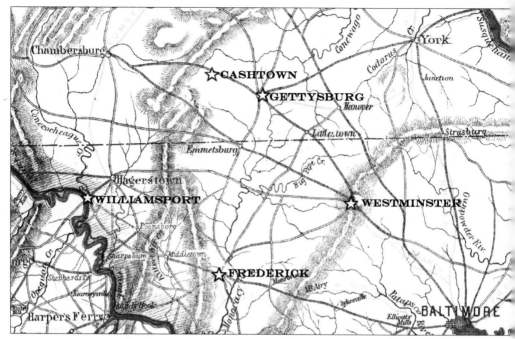

Action at Cashtown, Gettysburg, Westminster, Williamsport and evacuated to Frederick, Maryland. (Library of Congress Geography and Map Division; adapted from Nicholson's *Map of Eastern Virginia*)

is evidently on the move. Weather became warmer and clouded up. Rec'd letters from Sammy, dated 11th.

Tuesday 20, Were relieved on the river by the 3rd Ind. and assisted Cols. B & M at Edge Hill. Order No. 7 from Burnside announcing another battle about to be fought. We are ordered to be ready to march at a moment's notice. Weather rainy.

Wednesday 21, Weather continues rainy. After a ride of six hours' duration, I got the picket line established. My Bat. has ten posts. No news from the front. Infantry are at Falmouth. I fear bad weather will prevent the advance.

Thursday January 22, 1863, weather continues wet and disagreeable, roads fast becoming impassable. Heard reports of some guerrillas being seen near our line. Doubtful.

Friday 23, Weather cleared up and the sun came forth in all its effulgence. No news of importance.

Sunday, January 26, 1863, Captured two deserters from the 8th N.Y. Cav. and two negro spies. Saw 22 deserters at H. Qts. Large number of them running off. Captured two rebel soldiers and two citizens who were secreting them. Weather clear and warm.

Monday 26, Weather continues clear and warm, but I apprehend rain. Many deserters continue to be gathered up. Demoralization is inevitable if action is delayed. Col. Taylor's negroes run off in the night.

Tuesday 27, Started at daylight and rode to the Hd. Qtrs. 6th N.Y. Cav. to attend a court-martial of Col. Griffiths. Weather warm and rainy—roads awful. Remained overnight at Belle Plain. Fresh news in regard to the change of Burnside, Sumner & Franklin.[2]

Wednesday January 28, 1863, Weather cold and snowy, wind northeast. Returned from Belle Plain to Edge Hill. Roads were worse than I ever saw them. McClellan reported to have superseded Halleck.[3]

Thursday 29, Nothing new today. The weather has cleared up and turned quite cold.

Friday 30, An alarm was carried along the lines today by a party of guerrillas attacking Co. A. Two of our men were wounded, one in the breast & one in the shoulder.

Dr. Hard's regimental history clarified this entry:

Sometime in January, while out on a foraging or scouting expedition, a party of our men were fired upon by a number of rebels who were concealed in the brush by the roadside. Elijah Hall was shot in the shoulder, the wound proving very severe, and Samuel Peterson was pierced by eight buckshot, one of which broke his arm near the shoulder. But after a tedious convalescence both recovered. Upon learning the sad news of their being wounded, a party was dispatched in pursuit of the enemy. A number of citizens, suspected of being concerned in this murderous assault, were taken prisoners, as it was well-known that on the appearance of our men in force, they would assume to be quiet citizens, but no sooner did they think they could escape detection than they would prove themselves to be the most lawless guerrillas.[4]

February 1863

Sunday February 1, Made application for a leave of absence for ten days. Had considerable fun with a pack of young ladies, who were very desirous to enter our lines.

Monday February 9, 1863, Was notified to get my battalion ready for a scout to Westmoreland & Richmond Co.'s. Force consisting of my Bat. and one squadron of the 8th N.Y. We reached Oak Grove at daylight Tuesday where I left the N.Y. regiment as pickets.

Tuesday 10, Reached Westmoreland C.H. at 10 a.m. Caught two rebels belonging to the 7th Va. Cav., one conscript and run down one of the pickets belonging to the 15th Va. Cav. was too late to catch the conscript commissioners. Got seven horses. Encamped at Westmoreland C.H. [illegible name] let two prisoners get away.

Wednesday 11, Started out two parties. Hynes took one road and I the other. I reached Warsaw at 11 a.m. Captured two prisoners belonging to the 40th Va. Inf. Col. Bowen caught several horses and mail. Hynes captured a cav. picket. Encamped at West. C.H.

Thursday February 12, 1863, Returned to Edge Hill and at night relieved the 8th N.Y. on pickets. I captured, in all, twenty horses, mostly good.

Friday 13, Another party under Cap. Wadsworth of Gen. Reynolds staff has gone out to Westmoreland & Richmond Co.'s.

Monday 16, Were relieved by the 10th N.Y. Cav. and encamped at Caman.

Tuesday 17, Moved to Belle Plain. Roads awful muddy. Snowed all day.

Wednesday February 18, 1863, Moved to this place near Aquia Creek, a terrible march at night. Rained all day and night. No feed for horses.

Thursday 19, Bad weather continues. Procured some forage for horses by carrying it on their backs. An order detailing 125 men from the regiments to repair roads is received. Shameful proceeding.

March 1863

Wednesday March 25, 1863, At two o'clock we were suddenly ordered out and I was placed in command.

April 1863

Tuesday April 21, 1863, Returned from leave today.

Monday April 27, Caught up with the regiment at Warrenton today. Glad of the privilege.

Tuesday April 28, 1863, At 12 midnight the cavalry moved. In command of one squadron of Indiana, covered rear to Kelly's Ford.

Wednesday 29, Crossed over at Kelly Ford on the pontoon bridge. Skirmished with rebels at night.

Thursday 30, Marched at 6 a.m. Reached Culpepper at 12; passed Cedar Mountain at 3 p.m. and halted at Rapidan. Enemy in force across river. Disagreeable rainy day.

May 1863

Friday May 1, 1863, While at Rapidan a party of rebs crossed and captured Capt. Waite, but his men recaptured him. Two men badly wounded. Crawford's horse killed. Maj. Beveridge's horse wounded. Object accomplished— forced the enemy to burn R.R. bridge. Brilliant!

Saturday 2, Left the ford at Rapidan Station at 9 a.m. Marched 30 miles to Ely's Ford on some stream. Fighting going on between infantry on other side. Rebels fired into camp of the 16th Pa. All moved back from river at 11 p.m. Cannot tell who commands. Supposed to be Jackson against Howard.

Sunday 3, Heavy battle in progress this morning [Chancellorsville]. The firing is receding toward Fredericksburg. Afraid we are whipped. 6 p.m. have moved to W.S. Ford. Hooker's whole force across. Gained a victory this a.m. Sedgwick fighting now. Hopes high that Hooker will win. Formed our division. Reported death of Jackson and A.P. Hill. Gen Berry killed.

Monday, May 4, 1863, Lay in camp all day. Picket firing all day but no serious engagement until towards evening when a serious fight occurred. Gen. Whipple was killed.

Tuesday 5, Sedgwick recrossed at Bank's Ford. Said to have been whipped and lost one whole brigade. Things look dubious. Nothing heard of Stoneman. Our brigade was marched to Deep Run; too deep to cross; heavy rain today swelled it. Weather very disagreeable.

Wednesday 6, Rained all night and cold. Built bridge across Deep Run and marched to Kelly's F. Rifle pits dug to guard ford. All the infantry have recrossed to this side. Can't understand what is up. Hasn't been fight enough to be whipped. Weather cold and wet.

Thursday, May 7, 1863, Headquarters at Mt. Holly church, ½ miles from Kelly's Ford. Rifle pits all complete. Gen. Stoneman arrived at ford. His raid was eminently successful.[5] He [Stoneman] destroyed 12 miles of R.R. and was 4 miles from Richmond. The reg't. gone to Yorktown.

Friday 8, Stoneman's cavalry crossing, one man drowned. Rec'd Lt. and Mrs. Wing's card.

Saturday 9, Left Kelly's Ford this a.m. and marched to Deep Run and encamped.

Sunday, May 10, 1863, Marched to camp near Potomac Bridge. Will be paid tomorrow.

Monday 11, The regiment was paid up to the 1st of March today. Rec'd my pay up to 1st of May.

Tuesday 12, Sent $250 to Bro Joseph today.

Saturday, May 16, 1863, Have been in camp at Potomac Creek Station. Since Saturday [illegible] inst.

Sunday 17, Received an order to scout the Northern Neck.[6] Marched to [illegible.] Five of the 8th Pa. Cavalry were gobbled this morning by rebs. My Bat. takes the left going down.

Monday 18, Marched to Westmoreland C.H. and encamped. Mattox bridge burned by rebs.

Tuesday, May 19, 1863, Camped overnight at Westmoreland C.H. During the day burned one boat near Federal farm and a quantity of sail at the Hague. Camped at Hall Creek near Kincaid.

Wednesday 20, Camped at Fellow's Mill, and I took eighteen men and marched to Smith's Point. Captured 6 horses and 14 mules and ten niggers.

Thursday 21, Made an excursion and captured a number of criminals.

Friday, May 22, 1863, Lay in camp all day. A dispatch reports two regiments of rebs coming over to capture us. 3 regiments of infantry sent down to capture them. Will move in morning. We have over 100 contrabands. Camped at Fallon's Mills again.

Saturday 23, At 9 a.m. marched from Fallon's Mills and passed through Union Village at 11 a.m. Maj. Beveridge joined up at 6 p.m. He has 325 niggers and 200 horses and mules. Camped at Union Village.

Sunday 24, Continued march to Westmoreland C.H. and encamped. Found a brigade of infantry awaiting us. In united caravan of "nigs" amounted to 715.

Monday, May 25, 1863, Continued the march and encamped at Edge Hill, K.G. Co. Terrible tribulations among citizens in reference to their "nigs." Saw Miss Brown and Mrs. Colton's had a good visit.

Tuesday 26, Marched to Belle Plain. Shipped the "nigs" on steamers to Aquia. Glad to get rid of them. The darkies were jubilant and gave us three cheers. I am very sorry this raid ever occurred. Disgusted.

Wednesday 27, Reached camp at 12 p.m.

The regimental history written by Dr. Hard, explained the outcome of this scout:

> On returning from this reconnaissance, the negroes belonging to the plantations along the line of march, joined the emancipating column, coming in squads of from five to twenty, until there were finally accumulated fifteen hundred men, women and children of the contraband persuasion. They brought with them all their personal property, horses, mules, carts, clothing, &c., and doubtless some that did not legitimately belong to them, but which they had confiscated from rebel masters, under the "sequestration act." We also found some very loyal citizens who rendered most valuable assistance to our troops.
>
> Not the least important result of this expedition was the addition of five hundred valuable horses and mules much needed in the service. These animals were with few exceptions far superior to those purchased by the Government for cavalry service. The stories invented by the rebel citizens to induce our men to leave their horses and mules, were very touching and affecting. In

most cases, the men being in the rebel army, the women of the house would appear as a widow with "nine small children, and this animal was the only thing on which they had to depend for support" when, not unfrequently, three or four fine horses would be found secreted in a clump of pines nearby.

The regiment reached camp near Brook's Station on the 27th, and a more ludicrous procession was never seen than this cavalcade of cavalry, negroes, captured horses, mules, carts, wagons, oxen, rebel soldiers, trotting sulkies, top carriages, &c., &c. Not unfrequently a small mule would be harnessed by the side of a large horse, ox or cow, and when the wheel of a cart or carriage would give out, the negroes would "confiscate" one from the nearest plantation, whether it was smaller or twice the size of the one broken. Three or four children would be mounted on a single mule, all of which added to the laughable appearance of the procession, which was three miles long.[7]

June 7–21, 1863

Sunday, June 7, 1863, Col. Farnsworth left today.

Monday 8, Remained in camp all day. No news.

Monday, June 15, 1863, Left Catlett's Station at 7 o'clock p.m. and marched to Bristow Station.

Tuesday 16, Marched to Bull Run and encamped. Heard of Stuart's raid into Pa. Humiliating to be compelled to fight and march over the same ground each year.

Wednesday 17, Ready to march at 5 a.m. Marched at 10 a.m. and reached Aldie at 5 p.m. Found Gregg's Division had been fighting and lost 180 killed and wounded. Killed about the same number of rebs. 61 prisoners. Went on picket at night.

Thursday June 18, 1863, Our brigade made a scout to Philomont and drove the rebs ahead of us. Returned to Aldie at night. Heavy thunderstorm this p.m. First rain for six weeks.

Friday 19, Was ordered on picket at dawn this morning. Gregg's Division's fighting at Middleburg today. Hard work and heavy losses on both sides.

Saturday 20, Remained on picket today.

Sunday, June 21, 1863, At two o'clock was relieved. The regt. moved to the front beyond Middleburg. Prospects for a fight good, at dark. Had a splendid fight this p.m. near Ashby's Gap. Punished them finely. Camped near Upperville.

Confederate forces under J. E. B. Stuart were defeated June 21, 1863. Union general Pleasonton fought a day-long engagement, and four officers fired deliberately at Stuart. Upperville was a defeat and a narrow personal escape for Stuart. However, his men prevented Federal troopers from pushing through Ashby's Gap into the Shenandoah Valley.[8]

Confederate generals A. P. Hill and Longstreet hurried toward the mouth of the Shenandoah Valley to follow Ewell into Maryland. Ewell's column had orders to proceed toward Harrisburg and the vital mission of requisitioning supplies. General Early of Ewell's corps accompanied a brigade of dirty, ragged troops, some of whom were barefoot, into Gettysburg and demanded the borough provide sugar, coffee, flour, salt, bacon, whiskey, onions, pairs of shoes, hats, or—in lieu of provisions—five thousand dollars in cash. Representatives of the town council replied the demands were impossible to meet. No attempt was made to enforce the demand and only a few houses were robbed.[9]

After the cavalry fight, Jeb Stuart's new mission was to proceed to Pennsylvania and position troopers on the right of Lee's advance, keeping alert for Federal countermeasures. He was given two route choices—through the Shenandoah and Cumberland Valleys, or a southerly arch to the east between Hooker and Washington, damaging Federal communications along the way. He decided to use the more spectacular path, believing Federals were stationary and occupied a relatively tight area, not understanding that Union troops were spread out and beginning to march toward the Potomac.[10]

June 22–25, 1863

Monday, June 22, At 4 a.m. returned to near Aldie. ½ past 6 a.m. we are attacked in our camp. Excitement high. rebs in force on all sides. Rebs driven off by 2nd Brigade whose camp was entered. Camped on same ground.

Tuesday, June 23, Weather pleasant. Everything quiet. Same camp.

Wednesday, June 24, 1863, Another pleasant day. Capt Hynes made a reconnaissance toward Philomont. Found a regt. of rebs camped there.

Thursday, June 25, Remained in camp all day. Col. Clendenin was ordered to the rear. Officers had a meeting and expressed a want of confidence in him. Weather looked rainy.

Events on June 25, 1863, became a day of reckoning for Stuart. He had two options—either wait for Union forces to pass or head southeast and then north. He decided to head southeast, a long, hard route, and his decision cost Lee and his staff valuable information.[11]

June 26–27, 1863

Friday, June 26, An order to move at five promptly. Destination unknown at these quarters. Weather quite wet. Reached Leesburg at 10 p.m. Distance 10 miles. Very pretty town. Camped at Leesburg.

Saturday, June 27, 1863, Marched at 5 a.m. Crossed the Potomac at Edward's Ferry. Will go through Poolesville. Camped near Jefferson at foot of mountain. Infantry ahead of us.

The Eighth Illinois Cavalry marched over poor roads and crossed the Monocacy River at a wretched ford on June 27, 1863. Union forces wanted to stay within observation distance of Lee's army, maneuvering in ways that also protected Washington, D.C. General Reynolds, senior commander of the First, Third, and Eleventh Corps, moved up from Frederick to Emmitsburg, used the cavalry well out to the north and west to track Confederate movements on either side of South Mountain. Union soldiers endured long marches with alternating periods of baking, dry heat, and heavy rains.[12] The Army of the Potomac covered sixty miles between Fredericksburg and Edwards Ferry in four days and the next fifty miles to the Pennsylvania state line in three—with no concessions to fatigue, weather, or equipment.[13]

In spite of the punishing trek, when the Eighth Illinois followed the First Corps into Maryland, cheering residents welcomed them into an Eden with pretty gardens, neat farmhouses, and whitewashed fences—stark contrast to where they had been in war-ravaged Virginia. Troopers had suffered through fights at Aldie, Middleburg, and Upperville, some of the most vital cavalry actions to date. In Maryland bright-faced girls, watching from windows and doors, reminded them why they endured hardship. The army's most advanced, and most vulnerable, units were three infantry corps around Emmitsburg: John Reynolds's First Corps, Otis Howard's Eleventh Corps, and the Third Corps of Dan Sickles.[14]

Every report of the Confederate advance generated swells of fear and caused inhabitants of Pennsylvania and Maryland to flee, urged on by the danger. Pittsburg citizens dug fortifications. In Baltimore people expected Lee to come in a few days, so they barricaded every street and filled them with artillery.[15]

When reports reached Governor Andrew Curtain of Pennsylvania that Robert E. Lee was concentrating the Army of Northern Virginia on the state's southern border, Curtain issued a call for men to defend Pennsylvania. Newspapers confirmed northern citizens' worst fears—Confederates had invaded. Governor Curtain was a handsome, talented administrator, who kept the state in line with Lincoln's policies. Even as Confederates invaded northward, Pennsylvania Democrats were nominating a man to challenge Curtain at the polls. The paltry response to the call for militia to defend Pennsylvania increased Curtain's anxiety. He issued a second proclamation for 60,000 emergency militia to serve only 90 days, but by June 29, 1863, only about 16,000 ill-sorted volunteers were on hand to defend Harrisburg. More refugees left the capital than came in to defend it.[16]

June 28, 1863

Sunday, 28, Marched at 5 a.m. Reached Middleton at 8 a.m. Camped overnight. 3rd V. 11th Corps passed towards Frederick. Hooker has resigned Meade in command. Lee's headquartered at Gettysburg, Pa.

In the early morning hours of June 28, 1863, a messenger from President Abraham Lincoln arrived to inform Meade of his appointment as Hooker's replacement. Meade was forty-seven years old, six feet tall, with a grizzled beard and Roman nose. He lacked dash and glamour; his face was often obscured by a low-drawn hat brim. His nervous temperament resulted in fits of ill humor, but he had proved dependable as a commander and did not share the fear of Lee's talents that made other Union generals unsure of themselves. Meade must protect Washington and Baltimore, a vital command under dire circumstances, and this time Lincoln and Halleck gave Meade freedom of decision, which they had not given Hooker. Soldiers of the Army of the Potomac, however, did not have a great degree of confidence in their new commander because he was unknown except to his own corps. Meade did not care for pomp or parades. His own soldiers respected him for a willingness to endure hardships. After being informed of his promotion, he showed no elation and, on the contrary, seemed weighed down with responsibility, standing silent and thoughtful by himself.[17]

The evening of June 28, 1863, General Lee headquartered at Chambersburg, Pennsylvania, with Generals A. P. Hill and Longstreet, unaware that Federals were moving along his inside track. It had been a busy day for the sidetracked Jeb Stuart. He found and captured a train of two hundred Federal wagons, an impressive feat in itself, but one that did nothing to enhance Lee's campaign. As Stuart continued northward, the captured items encumbered his progress. About ten o'clock that night, Longstreet received a reliable scout's report that Federals had crossed the Potomac and were positioned on the right at Frederick City. It was at this moment that Gettysburg assumed military importance because Lee must concentrate his forces quickly.[18]

General Meade disapproved of changing commanders so close to a battle but spent June 29 expediting movements of the various Union columns. Admitting that he lacked knowledge of the army as a whole, he decided to leave cavalry movements to General Pleasonton.[19]

The day General Hooker was relieved of command and General Meade took over, concentrating the Army of the Potomac in the Frederick area, the Eighth Illinois Cavalry held its position—even though reports said Lee's army had advanced into Pennsylvania and Maryland.

June 29, 1863

Monday 29, Called up at 11 a.m. Stuart reported to be advancing. Ready to move. Marched to Fountain Green across South Mountain. Crossed the mountain at Reno Pass through Brantboro and Cavitown. Entered Pa. at 5 p.m.

Confederates under Stuart took possession of Rockville, an important direct wagon route from Washington, D.C., firmly astride Union army communication lines, and they captured a wagon train eight miles long, carrying much-needed feed for their horses as well as other vital supplies.

Federal cavalry and Battery A of the Second U.S. Artillery under John Buford left Middletown on June 29, 1863, took the National Pike to Boonsboro, Maryland, then the road to Smithsburg, and from there up to Monterey Pass. As Gen. John Buford stood at the opening of Monterey Pass through South Mountain, overlooking the Cumberland Valley, he saw the dust in the background toward the mountains in the Greencastle area. At this time it was evident to General Buford that a major battle would soon erupt in south-central Pennsylvania.[20]

The march took men and horses thirty miles over two mountains, finally resting at night in a valley, fifteen miles from Gettysburg. Pennsylvania militia that had been called out to defend their homes skirmished with the advance of the enemy, captured but then lost some prisoners. When questioned, fearful natives failed to give reliable details about the position of the enemy.

At first light two brigades again moved, this time on the Hagerstown and Gettysburg road to Fairfield. Spirits rose.

When the Eighth Illinois proceeded, fog concealed the countryside and skirmishers ran unexpectedly into Confederate pickets. Shots were rapidly exchanged, and one struck Thomas Withrow, Company C, in the stomach, but hit a button or buckle and did not penetrate—just knocked him off his horse. This made Tom angry, and he swore revenge. He ran behind a barn and fired on his own responsibility. At first Union men drove in the rebel pickets, but when they were reinforced, General Buford ordered the men to fall back, not wishing to bring on a general engagement. Withrow's horse followed the Eighth back to the column, leaving its dismounted rider at the barn. Tom kept firing until he heard a rebel officer give orders to search the barn, then he hid in some hay. Rebs entered the barn, searched every part, thrust their bayonets down through the hay but missed him. Tom could have killed a rebel colonel but was not willing to commit suicide.

Rebels brought their wounded into the barn and he overheard their conversation, from which he learned that the skirmish had killed one man and wounded three.

After the rebels left, a citizen entered. Tom asked, "Is there a chance of escape?"

The frightened fellow answered, "I don't know." But admiring the adventure of a brave soldier, he took Tom to his house for a good dinner. That night Tom Withrow rejoined the regiment.

The last day of June dawned calm but cloudy and drizzling. Cavalry withdrew to Emmitsburg, reaching it about noon. There they met advancing infantry and proceeded to Gettysburg, filing through town over Washington Street. Tired, dirty men rode without pomp, but schoolchildren lined the streets singing "The Battle Cry of Freedom," and cheering citizens handed buttered bread and cold water to their "deliverers." Some Confederate cavalry had been there foraging, but they left as the vanguard entered. Union pickets were stationed a few miles in advance of the town, and headquarters for General Buford's Division became the Eagle Hotel, kept by Mr. Tate.[21]

Cavalry pickets, or using their term *videttes,* had a restless night under lowering clouds that released drenching rain—in sight of the Confederate outposts. Captain W. C. Hazelton was in charge of a reserve outpost near a farmer's house. The old man offered them dinner and to stand watch while they ate, but, being on duty, Hazelton refused. Before dark, a patrol of the Ninth New York captured a prisoner from Ewell's corps, which meant another problem existed to the north, and a farmer passed through the videttes of the Seventeenth Pennsylvania to warn the Union that Ewell's corps meant to march on Gettysburg the next day. Therefore, one advantage General Buford had—which Confederate generals Hill and Heth did not—was Buford knew what was coming.[22]

Headquarters Army of the Potomac, Taneytown, July 1, 1863

From information received, the commanding general is satisfied that the object of the movement of the army in this direction has been accomplished, viz, the relief of Harrisburg, and the prevention of the enemy's intended invasion of Philadelphia, &c., beyond the Susquehanna . . .

The time for falling back can only be developed by circumstances. Whenever such circumstances arise as would seem to indicate the necessity for falling back and assuming this general line indicated, notice of such movement will be at once communicated to these headquarters and to all adjoining corps commanders. . . .

The cavalry will be held on the right and left flanks after the movement is completed. Previous to its completion, it will, as now directed, cover the front and exterior lines, well out.

The commands must be prepared for a movement, and, in the event of the enemy attacking us on the ground indicated herein, to follow up any repulse. . . .

All movements of troops should be concealed, and our dispositions kept from the enemy. Their knowledge of these dispositions would be fatal to our success, and the greatest care must be taken to prevent such an occurrence.

By command of Major-General Meade:

S. WILLIAMS, Assistant Adjutant-General[23]

General Meade needed to leave his choices open and deployed the army so that each corps had support nearby, but the circular he issued upset soldiers who needed no reminder they were now defending Union soil. Every back stiffened. General Reynolds came from a leading Lancaster family; his father was a friend of former President Buchanan. He needed no prompting to defend northern soil, but by nature he was a private, quiet man. As the army prepared to meet Confederates, his moods by turn became "inflamed" and "depressed." Pennsylvania was his home. He was born in Lancaster in 1820 and his family held some of the largest land holdings in Lancaster County. He graduated West Point in 1837, served in the Mexican War artillery, went back to West Point in 1859 as commandant of cadets, in 1862 commanded one of the brigades in the Pennsylvania Reserve, and then went to the Army of the Potomac to command the First Corps at Fredericksburg and Chancellorsville. No better man than Reynolds could be in place; in the eyes of soldiers he was alertness personified.[24]

Reynolds knew Confederates Longstreet, Lafayette McLaws, and Richard Anderson from West Point. Reynolds was an outdoorsman, fine horseman, well-matched to field service with twenty years' solid military service. He had advanced grades above many of his contemporaries. General Buford sent a dispatch to Reynolds that Hill's army was massed at Cashtown. Reynolds and the left wing were in position to support Buford where the enemy showed its strongest force, but abundant, conflicting messages from headquarters, scouts, and alarmed citizens reached Reynolds.[25] Ultimately General Meade had to rely on Reynolds's judgment.

On the morning of June 29th General Lee ordered Confederates to concentrate at Cashtown. Hill's corps was in the advance and reached Cashtown June 30. That night Hill and Heth heard that a force of Federals was at Gettysburg. Early the next morning Hill, with Heth's and Pender's divisions, started down the Gettysburg Pike. General Lee was then west of the mountain with Longstreet. Buford's cavalry was holding Gettysburg as an outpost.[26]

June 30, 1863

Tuesday, June 30, 1863, Left camp at 3 a.m. and marched to Fairfield, had a skirmish with rebs infantry and drew them out. Then marched to Gettysburg through Emmitsburg. A.P. Hill's Corps were headed off and driven back to the mountains, remained at Gettysburg all night.

Dr. Hard explained the role the regiment played on the first day at Gettysburg:

Early next morning, July 1st, our pickets brought word that the enemy was advancing in force. Captain Dana was in command of the picket line on the Chambersburg road where they first made their appearance; and here, as in many other of the great battles, the Eighth Illinois received the first fire and shed the first blood. The pickets fell back slowly, making all the resistance in their power, and arrangements were made to hold the rebels in check until the infantry could come up. The First Corps, under General Reynolds, and the Eleventh Corps, under General O. O. Howard, were known to be between Gettysburg and Emmitsburg, to whom notice of the situation was given with a request to hasten forward. Two colored servants of rebel officers had been captured, who gave valuable information as to the position of their forces and who was in command.

The long line of the enemy came in full view, and their batteries rained upon our men showers of shot and shell, but our brave boys stood firm and fell back only when ordered. The Eighth New York, on our left, was wavering some, but the Third Indiana, on the right, never flinched. About this time it began to be warm work. Sergeant Goodspeed, of Company H, was wounded and taken to the depot where a temporary hospital had been established, and soon after Williams, of Company M, had his arm shattered by a ball, which required amputation.

The battle raged with great fury, our division of cavalry being all there was to impede the progress of the overpowering numbers of the enemy, for several hours. About eleven o'clock A.M., General Reynolds and staff arrived on the ground, and soon after, the advance of his corps. As they came upon Seminary Ridge and deployed in line the cavalry was withdrawn. General Buford told me that he never saw so daring and successful a thing as was done by one of the Eighth Illinois men.[27]

For the first hour of fighting, cavalry forces were Gettysburg's only defenders. John Buford set up a defense of greater consequence than he knew. His troopers met the Confederate advance staunchly. General Reynolds sent word to Meade at Taneytown that Buford had found a place suitable for a definitive battle and sharp fighting had begun. When James S. Wadsworth's division of two brigades, including the "Iron Brigade," were thrown across Buford's mile-wide front, cavalry troopers were permitted to fall back.[28]

July 1, 1863

Wednesday, July 1, In camp at Gettysburg. Report says Gen. Farnsworth got badly whipped at Hanover yesterday. The rebs are all round us. The reg't. advanced and gave battle. Our forces were driven back through town. Camped back of Gettysburg. Maj. C. Demon killed, Capt. Follett, Lt. Conrad, Capt. Morris wounded.

On the morning of July 1, the actions of Buford's cavalry division were textbook examples of a delaying action. His troopers bought the time needed for the Union First Corps to arrive. Troopers made multiple stands. Col. William Gamble commanded the First Brigade under Maj. Gen. Alfred Pleasonton at Gettysburg. Maj. John L. Beveridge led the Eighth Illinois Cavalry, and records show that 470 men were engaged with 2 percent losses.[29]

A stand was made just south of the town on Cemetery Ridge, which the enemy did not assault with much vigor. During the day General Buford received an order from General Doubleday to charge the enemy in a certain position, but seeing at a glance the inconsistency of ordering cavalry to charge upon infantry, who were protected by a stone fence, he ordered a part of the Eighth Illinois and Third Indiana to dismount and drive the enemy from their position; which they did in the most gallant manner, and to the entire satisfaction of their General, who referred to the incident as being a brilliant affair. Night found the Union army driven from half to a mile back of the position it had taken in the morning, but still holding a prominent and strong line.[30]

At the end of Gettysburg's first day of fighting, rebels halted, rested, and rejoiced while the Union First and Eleventh Corps fell back undisturbed to the strong, natural positions of Cemetery and Culp's Hill. Lee gave orders to Ewell to pursue if he found it practicable, but the order was not positive. The Union army on those hills was the barrier between Confederates and large cities of the North. The outcome of the battle decided not only the character of the war but that of the nation. Even privates understood that this was a pivotal battle, and the men steeled themselves to do their best.[31]

July 2, 1863

Thursday, 2, 5 a.m. Prospects for a battle good. Our troops arriving rapidly. Gen. Meade present. Left camp at 8 a.m. and marched to Taneytown. Camped overnight. Fighting very light. Mere skirmish on left.

Brigadier General Buford's cavalry division was withdrawn on July 2, 1863, because J. E. B. Stuart's cavalry had arrived and was now riding behind the Union army. Union cavalry was needed to protect the new Federal base at Westminster.[32]

> The Surgeons had but little rest, as the wounded men occupied nearly every farmhouse and barn for miles—the enemy having possession of the city of Gettysburg and the battlefield.
>
> The morning of July 2nd broke upon the two armies lying as quiet as though they were friends. Much of our infantry had arrived during the night, a council of war had been held and all were preparing for a desperate struggle: The cavalry were in line between the enemy and Round Top. General Sickles' division was advanced across the Emmitsburg pike, and all the movements betokened a renewal of the engagement, when it was rumored that our supplies were in danger of being disturbed, and General Buford's division was ordered to protect the train. We left the field of Gettysburg about one o'clock P.M. (just as the battle was being renewed,) and marched to Taneytown, where we encamped for the night.[33]

On July 3 cavalry continued to Westminster—the terminus of the railroad from Baltimore and the base of supplies.

July 3, 1863

Friday July 3, 1863, Marched to Westminster, Md. Will remain for some days to recruit horses and men. Terrible battle fought today at Gettysburg, Pa. Many prisoners captured. No reports of the result.

The Battle of Gettysburg progressed while the Eighth Illinois Cavalry was stationed at Westminster. Thousands of rebel prisoners marched past on their way to Washington. Next day, rebel prisoners continued to arrive, along with cheering news of the result of the battle. Dwight Sabin, an old friend engaged with the Christian Commission, received permission to accompany the cavalry. After procuring a horse, Sabin joined the medical staff, caring for the sick and wounded.

Late in the day the regiment broke camp and marched toward Frederick City. It was hoped that by going round and crossing the South Mountains, cavalry could intercept and harass Confederates and delay them until the infantry could fall upon the rear of Lee's shattered army. Torrential rains muddied the roads, but troopers reached Frederick City at noon the next day, where General McReynolds of Michigan commanded.

The Battle of Gettysburg ended after three days with the disastrous Confederate assault on the center of the Union line, named Pickett's Charge. Two armies stood at bay, watching for a stroke or motion to signal a continuation of the struggle. General Meade did not venture out against the Confederates after defeating Pickett, and General Lee would not undertake further fighting—unless he was attacked. Few sights or circumstances match the state of these two armies on Friday afternoon, July 3, 1863. Thousands of wounded men were scattered over a five-mile area, unattended, mingled amid broken gun carriages, exploded caissons, hundreds of dead and dying horses. As night came, survivors lit small fires, made coffee, and ate hardtack and salt pork, the only food available. A band in the rear began to tune up. A full moon looked down, unclouded, on surgeons severing limbs.[34]

July 4–6, 1863

Saturday 4, My third 4th in the army. Buckamore, Va., Harrisons' Landing Md., and Westminster, Md. Marched to Union Village and encamped. Gen. Meade won a brilliant victory at Gettysburg.

Sunday 5, Marched to Frederick and I encamped. An aid of Gen. Forrest was taken captive.

Monday, July 6, 1863, Marched at daylight on South Mountain found lots of prisoners and wagons. Heard Stuart was following. Kilpatrick near Boonsboro.

Notation in William's pocket journal: "This is the last entry. My uncle was shot some hours after this on July 6th 1863. Died July 16, 1863 in hospital, Williamsburg,[35] Va. Surrounded by the officers of his regiment. My father [Joseph Medill] also with him. Military Funeral Incar. 266 W. Washington St. Chicago."

The Retreat from Gettysburg

After three days of brutal fighting, General Lee remained in position, but General Meade's troops were exhausted, and Meade allowed a majority of his corps commanders to talk him out of attacking. The weather deteriorated July 4, according to eyewitness accounts. Showers began at 6:00 A.M. and became a hard-soaking downpour. Under cover of the storm, Robert E. Lee's army set out for Virginia. Their wagons stretched over seventeen miles, and the drivers struggled to navigate the mud. In town, wary citizens heard a commotion on Baltimore Street, which turned out to be the welcome sight of Union soldiers marching down the street, fife and drum corps playing, the Stars and Stripes fluttering at the head of the lines.[36]

The town was one vast hospital, and homes, barns, and other buildings for miles around were filled with over twenty thousand wounded men. Father James Francis Burlando escorted twelve Sisters of Charity from St. Vincent de Paul in Emmitsburg to Gettysburg, a distance of less than twelve miles. The Sisters were the first outsiders to try to provide aid, food, and bandages, but thick mud also made their travel difficult, and they did not arrive until late in the afternoon of July 5.[37]

Gen. George Meade waited until Sunday, July 5, to send one cavalry brigade after Confederates on the Chambersburg Road and detail Sedgwick's corps to follow Confederates on Fairfield Road. Hard riding and fighting lay ahead for cavalry units on both sides. Confederate cavalry flanked Lee's columns to protect against attack. Meade left Gettysburg on July 7. Subsequently, Union forces found Lee's army waiting for the flooded Potomac to recede near Williamsport, Maryland, but Confederates managed to cross into Virginia on July, 13, 1863.[38]

> Report of Brig. General John Imboden, C.S.A.
>
> Shortly after noon of the 4th the very windows of heaven seemed to have opened. The rain fell in blinding sheets. The meadows were soon overflowed, and fences gave way before the raging streams. During the storm, [Confederate] wagons, ambulances, and artillery carriages . . . were assembling in the fields along the road from Gettysburg to Cashtown, in one confused arid apparently inextricable mass. As the afternoon wore on there was no abatement in the storm. Canvas was no protection against its fury, and the wounded men lying upon the naked boards of the wagonbodies were drenched. Horses and mules were blinded and maddened by the wind and water, and became almost unmanageable. The deafening roar of the mingled sounds of heaven

and earth all around us made it almost impossible to communicate orders, and equally difficult to execute them.

About 4 P. M. the head of the column was put in motion near Cashtown, and began the ascent of the mountain in the direction of Chambersburg....

Our situation was frightful. We had probably ten thousand animals and nearly all the wagons of General Lee's army under our charge and all the wounded, to the number of several thousand, that could be brought from Gettysburg. Our supply of provisions consisted of a few wagonloads of flour in my own brigade train, a small lot of fine fat cattle, which I had collected in Pennsylvania on my way to Gettysburg, and some sugar and coffee procured in the same way at Mercersburg.

The town of Williamsport is located in the lower angle formed by the Potomac with Conocochesgue Creek. These streams enclose the town on two sides, and back of it about one mile there is a low range of hills that is crossed by four roads converging at the town. The first is the Greencastle Road leading down the creek valley, next the Hagerstown Road, then the Boonsboro' Road, and lastly the River Road.

Early on the morning of the 6th I received intelligence of the approach from Frederick of a large body of cavalry with three full batteries of six rifled guns. These were the divisions of Generals Buford and Kilpatrick, and Huey's brigade of Gregg's division, consisting, as I afterward learned, of 23 regiments of cavalry, and 18 guns, a total force of about 7000 men.

I immediately posted my guns on the hills that concealed the town, and dismounted my own command to support them and ordered as many of the wagoners to be formed as could be armed with the guns of the wounded that we had brought from Gettysburg. In this I was greatly aided by Colonel J. L. Black of South Carolina, Captain J. F. Hart commanding a battery from the same state, Colonel William Aylett of Virginia and other wounded officers. By noon about 700 wagons were organized into companies of 100 each and officered by wounded line officers and commissaries and quartermasters, about 250 of these were given to Colonel Aylett on the right next to the river, about as many under Colonel Black on the left, and the residue were used as skirmishers. My own command proper was held well in hand in the center.

The enemy appeared in our front about half-past one o'clock on both the Hagerstown and Boonsboro Roads, and the fight began. Every man under my command understood that if we did not repulse the enemy we should all be captured and General Lee's army be ruined by the loss of its transportation, which at that period could not have been replaced in the Confederacy. The fight began with artillery on both sides. The firing from our side was very rapid, and seemed to make the enemy hesitate about advancing. In a half hour J. D. Moore's battery ran out of ammunition, but as an ordnance train had arrived from Winchester, two wagonloads of ammunition were ferried across the river and run upon the field behind the guns, and the boxes tumbled out, to be broken open with axes. With this fresh supply our guns were all soon in full play again. As the enemy could not see the supports of our batteries from the hilltops, I moved the whole line forward to his full view, in single ranks, to show a long front on the Hagerstown approach. My line passed our guns fifty or one hundred yards, where they were halted awhile, and then were withdrawn behind the hilltop again, slowly and steadily.[39]

Union Cavalry Reports

Point of Rocks, Maryland, July 5, 1864, 8th Illinois Cavalry Lieut.-Col. David B. Clendenin with his regiment arrived at Point of Rocks from Washington at 2 p.m. to find Mosby with two pieces of artillery and 200 men, posted on the south bank of the Potomac. A skirmish of half an hour ensued, during which Clendenin lost no men and the enemy one killed and two wounded. Later in the evening the same regiment frustrated an attempt on the part of Mosby to cross the river at Noland's ferry.[40]

History of the Eighth Illinois Cavalry

Forced march took troops through Middletown, back over the South Mountains through Boonsboro, from there on to Williamsport, where Federals hoped to cut off Lee's retreat and destroy his wagon train. General Kilpatrick's division marched via Hagerstown to cooperate. The morning of July 6 within two miles of Williamsport, the Eighth Illinois Cavalry came upon General Imboden's rebel infantry in charge of their trains and a crossing at that point. A severe engagement ensued. Union batteries came forward to match those of the enemy firing on the Federals. Troopers from the Eighth Illinois went forward as dismounted skirmishers, and pressed the enemy, who held defensive positions in a cornfield, behind barns and outbuildings.[41]

Major William Medill, while exposed on the picket line, was shot in the abdomen, and Sergeant Richard C. Vinson and Alfred C. Bailey received critical wounds. Gale Carter, of Company G, was killed. Captain Sullivan was shot in the head, but not seriously wounded, as the ball only fractured the outer table of the skull. Comrades brought the wounded back to ambulances, which took them to a barn, designated as a hospital.

As this battle progressed, General Kilpatrick was driven back and forced to retreat. His division, falling to the rear, blocked the only road of retreat, and

Telegraph from Frederick, Maryland, July 7, 1863, says "Maj. Medill is very dangerously wounded in the abdomen. Come to Frederick City, MD immediately he is anxious to see you. D.J. Hynes, Capt. 8th Ill. Cav." (Courtesy Colonel Robert R. McCormick Research Center)

thus left the Eighth to resist the entire force of the enemy, but they succeeded in keeping Confederates in check until night, when they fell back, covering the retreat of General Kilpatrick and bringing off all their wounded except Carter, who had to be left dying on the field. Troopers went back some six miles to Stone's Corners, put the wounded soldiers in a church, and attended them during the night.

It was evident that Major Medill, Bailey, and Vinson could not survive. The major had endeared himself to his men by many acts of kindness, and by his coolness and undaunted courage in the midst of battle.

On the morning of July 7th the enemy made their appearance in force, and we were ordered to fall back to Boonsboro. The men carried Major Medill on a litter the entire distance as the roads were too rough to admit of his riding in an ambulance. Vinton and Bailey died at Boonsboro, and Medill was taken to Frederick City, where he survived nine days of extreme suffering; then expired like a true soldier—calm and composed. Before dying he gave his brother Joseph full directions as to his funeral and place of burial. . . . Bailey knowing his hour of departure was near, wished me to inform his parents that he had tried to perform his duty faithfully and did not regret having entered the army. Vinson was calm and composed and met his fate in a soldier-like manner. Better, or more noble soldiers could not have been found in the army.[42]

His brother Joseph rushed to his side and helped care for Major Medill. Before dying, William gave his brother Joseph directions as to his funeral and place of burial, which took place at Joseph Medill's home in Chicago on July 22, 1863. Two companies of the 15th Illinois from Camp Douglas escorted the body through downtown Chicago, past the *Tribune* building on Clark Street and north to Graceland Cemetery. After serving his regiment in nineteen engagements, William Medill had died.[43]

Death of Major Medill

Captain Waite, in a letter to his father, writes of Major Medill's fall.

> Major Medill went to the front and took charge of the three squadrons of dismounted men fighting as skirmishers. They moved forward at a quick step, and with a "hip," "hip," in the very best of spirits. In a few minutes the sad news came back to us that our noble major was mortally wounded, and soon after several soldiers came slowly along, bearing in their arms the gallant officer. A ball had entered his breast, and we believed him past recovery. I cannot describe the sadness and gloom, which this misfortune cast over the entire regiment and brigade. Officers and men all felt that we had met with a severe loss. The Major had been with us through many a hard fight. His conduct at the late desperate cavalry battle near Aldie had particularly won for him the confidence and esteem of all the officers and men present. The gallantry, bravery and coolness displayed by the Major on that occasion were very highly spoken of by all. His genial, kind-hearted and generous nature had made him a favorite with the officers of the regiment, while his integrity of character and strict discipline as an officer had won our confidence and respect. There is not a man in the regiment but mourns his fall.[44]

Diary of Joseph Medill Kept at Major William H. Medill's Deathbed, 1863

Front plate: William died easy at 10:20 a.m. July 16, [18]63 in presence of his brother Joseph, Capt. Hynes, Gen. Farnsworth, Surgeon Stull and several others of the 8th Ill. Cav. besides Sister of Mercy O'Keefe, who closed his eyes. He is now free of pain & misery forever. He looked wonderfully natural in the face until the breath left him.

1863, July 7, Rec'd a dispatch from Capt. Hynes dated 7th July, saying Major Medill was very dangerously wounded in the abdomen; he wants you to come immediately.

July 8, Started July 8, 7:20 a.m.

July 9. Reached Pittsburg July 9, 2:30 a.m.; Phila. July 9, 6 p.m., delayed to midnight, reached B&O junction 6 a.m.

July 10, Got to Frederick City at 2 p.m. Friday. Met Capt. Hynes, who showed me where the Major lay. Shook hands long and tenderly. He was exceeding glad to see me. Looked at his wound—it was a frightful hole nearly in the center of his body, 2 inches long, 1 broad, unknown depth. *Looked mortal.* He was in fair spirits, quite hopeful; believed he would live; experienced not much pain. Had suffered greatly at first. He gave me a full history of how it happened and the difficulty of carrying him from the field—14 miles on ambulance over bad roads at night. Stayed in a church. Surgeon had examined wound after administering chloroform—could not tell where [the] ball went. But gave his opinion that it was [a] mortal wound.

He was carried on [a] stretcher 14 miles to the hospital where he arrived on the 8th a.m. Soon after Capt. Hynes came to him on the 6th. When he thought himself dying, he made his will—giving his watch to his Sister Mary, one horse to his Sister Nellie, one horse to his orderly Miller, and his battle horse to his constant friend Capt. Hynes. His money and other effects he left for me to dispose of according to a previous letter will to me.

He conversed with me very freely on general questions. Enquired about my family, very closely about social matters, about his mother, sisters, brothers. Talked about the war and had me read the newspapers. Read the abrv. information of the 8th containing notice of his wound. He had not much acute pain. I sat up with him till 10 p.m. and then lay down on a cot near him. He spent a middling night under the aid of opiates. Slept some. Pulse at 90 & middling strong. His color was natural—but rather flushed.

July 11, Had his wound dressed—he thought it looked some better, but I did not. The surgeon talked rather hopefully, but vaguely. Weather hot and oppressive. Used cold cloths external on chest, neck & sides and ice water internally. Saturday. I wrote home a long account of his wound, its acumen and his condition, stating his condition I fear unfavorable. He talked considerable with me during the afternoon on various subjects. His spirits good. His appetite weak; difficult to ease his bowels—passages slight, but ascribes this to the large and frequent doses of opium. Asked some questions about Miss ***, but did not betray much feeling or solicitude. Said he would give something nice to be in [a] chamber of my house with Kitty and Nelly to talk to. This night he rested rather worse than last night.

July 12, Sunday. His eyes looked duller this morning, which he detected in the mirror. I thought his breathing was rather more difficult & shorter than yesterday. The weather very hot. Same treatment as yesterday. Conversed less freely today—was rather more irritable and sulky caused perhaps by the morphine.

At 3 p.m. order came to remove him to another building where the ventilation and air were better. He was much displeased with the order and protested against it. Sent for the surgeon to have it countermanded. Chiefly he cared it separated him from a favorite nurse—an old soldier called "Peter." But the order was carried out. He was very petulant [the] remainder of the day. His bed did not suit him; the waiters and nurses were inferior. He sent me out to find a private place. Searched with Hynes & others—found a comfortable place, but it was difficult to procure a good surgeon. I was also afraid to remove him, as he seemed worse. Talked despondingly somewhat. Wrote to wife to advise about him.

KATE TO JOSEPH
On letterhead from the Office of the *Daily Tribune,* Chicago, July 1863—Sunday

My Dearest Husband,

With a mind very much relieved by your dispatch, I sit down to write. It came on Friday evening between eight and nine o'clock. I immediately telegraphed to your mother and also sent the dispatch down to Smith who published it next morning.

Everybody was inquiring about him. Thank God! The boy will not die by a rebel bullet—altho' he could not *die* more noble than for his country, yet we would all prefer he would *live* for it. *Live* to enjoy the blessings of a government for which he has sacrificed so much, almost life itself. He must live to wear his laurels. Tell him the warmest corner at the hearthstone, the pleasantest room in the house is waiting for him. We are looking for another dispatch as a letter asking some of us to come and take care of him. Perhaps you have already written for Mary. I hope you have, and I do hope you have written me a good long letter telling me all about him and your journey. I want to know just how he is situated. Whether he has proper care—he needs every attention. I know you will do the best you can, but you are *no nurse*. You must be so careful he does not talk or exert himself in the least. He must be kept very *quiet*—and not moved too soon. Where is he staying—is it at a private house—is there an efficient nurse to be had? Has he a good surgeon? Who sits up with him at night? You certainly need a woman around. What is a sick room without a woman in it? Just think—great men walking around it squeaking boots, banging doors, sleeping so soundly that nothing but a breakfast gong awakens them. Imagine yourself sick without *me*. To be sure Jim is sick without his wife, but that is an exceptional case. Your Mary is a capital nurse. She could lift Will and be so efficient every way, and I hope you have written for her—unless you intend to remain a month and would like me. I can talk more than Mary. Tell Will I believe Ann Moffett and I could talk him well in a week. I have such a lot of gossip on hand.

You and I, the Major and Anne Mc. have all received invitations to a wedding next Thursday. It quite took my breath away, such a display of silver-edged envelopes—and one to Major Medill—unkindest cut of all! As Will has such a pain in his breast now poor boy, I will not make it worse by telling him who the fair one is. It was _____ made the highly original remark that there was as good fish in the sea as ever came out. Willy can do the same.

But seriously, my beloved, do you not think that we ought, some of us, to come and take care of Will? As we were going east anyhow, I could take the children and Anne to Massillon, send them on in the hack and come on to you—I know I could travel alone if I would try. I would be happy to come. Lou and Edward can sleep here, and Julia can keep house—on the other hand I would not like to *intrude*. *I am only a sister-in-law*—tho' Will is as near as are either of my own brothers. So for that reason and that only, it would be better to send for Mary. Do what you think is best. Your judgment is better than mine.

We are getting along very well. Captain [a horse] was taken sick the day you left. Avery's Harry came up and said we must send for a doctor. Mr. Avery came up and looked at the horse at ten o'clock at night and started himself after one. They went for two but did not get one until next morning. Morgan Avery's doctor came, bled him and took him home. I was afraid Prince might take the disease. It is a kind of fever of which several horses have died lately. Avery's horse has it. He sends Edward over every day—the horse is better and will be home in a day or two.

Chicago has gone back to its normal condition again since the jubilation is over. We are all waiting anxiously to hear of Lee's defeat by Meade.

Everything is going all right in the office, I believe. I think it fortunate you are so near the seat of an account of dispatches—the news [is] yours this morning I suppose—unless you should be taken prisoner when it would not be so agreeable. Is the army near you? Do be careful of yourself. You spoke when here of removing Will to a hospital in Washington. Do not—I beg of you—it is so hot there in summer, and the sight of so many wounded men would of itself retard his recovery. How long will it be, if his wound progresses favorably, before he can come home? He has a good constitution, which is everything in his favor. Have you plenty of medicinal stores—old linen, lint etc.

Sol. Scott died on Wednesday—he would not keep quiet, or he might have saved his life. Nelly sends so much love to Will and is almost reconciled to his being wounded since I told her he would *never* go back to war again. With the hopefulness of children they look forward to his speedy arrival.

The weather is very cold—there was a terrible gale commenced on Friday night, raged all day yesterday and until far in the night. The *Times* this morning reports forty vessels lost on the Lake. We have a bright fire in the grate while I suppose you are suffocating.

Sammy says I must hurry on. I want to get this in time to the office. Goodbye, dear husband. We all send our best love to Will and pray every night and morning for his speedy recovery.

Goodbye, Your own wife, Kate

JOSEPH TO KATE

Fredericksburg, Sunday July 12, 1863, p.m.

Dear Wife,

I wrote you yesterday at some length describing William's wound & condition. Since then a more careful inspection by the surgeons have been made,

Telegraph from Joseph Medill to the editor of the *Tribune* in which Joseph writes, "Tell Mrs. Medill to remain. The Maj. will be no more before she would arrive. She can do nothing for him." (Courtesy Colonel Robert R. McCormick Research Center)

and I regret to say that their conclusions are not as favorable as before. They think the ball penetrated thro' the diaphragm and turned to the left under the ribs and that is not in the flesh but below it. This being so narrows his chance of recovery.

He does not look so badly in the face as you would suppose. His color and skin look natural; his pulse is not very strong. He drinks a little milk & the like, but has not much appetite, and last night was nervous and restless. He has considerable strength and not very much pain. The wound does not seem much inflamed. Today the doctor put on a poultice to draw it and to keep down inflammation as much as practicable. I'll see tomorrow how this looks. Will's case is critical. There are more chances against recovery than for it. It will take two or three more days to arrive at a correct idea of the result. He is in worse spirits today than yesterday—is more fretful and nervous but this may be in consequence of removing him last evening to another ward where he lost the services of a favorite nurse and was not so gently handled and there was more noise but the air is better with a freer circulation. . . .

Write to Mother from my letters. If he grows worse, I'll telegraph. The weather is hot. What a difference in my feelings between this and last Sunday. A battle expected tomorrow or Wednesday. Hynes is still here.

Your affectionate husband, J. Medill

Diary of Joseph Medill, 1863

July 13, Monday. He was clearly worse. Had more fever and pain and breath shorter. Wound was poulticed with flaxseed [a traditional remedy for sores]. It looked badly. His hopes of recovery still strong.

About noon he had some more twangs of pain. Surgeon looked serious after examination of wound, took me to his room, said he feared inflammation would set in, which would necessarily be fatal. I wrote home stating his case cautiously, but admitting he was worse.

About 3 p.m. after I had read the Baltimore paper to him, and he had read the Phila. paper, he was suddenly seized with most terrible pains in side and near heart, which cut his breath. He growled greatly and called for the surgeon. Various applications were made. The spasm lasted half an hour. When it partially ceased at 6 p.m., he was cupped over the region of the pain but without much relief or satisfactory results. Mustard plaster was applied to [his] side—thought it helped him a little. At 5 p.m. two surgeons closely examined him. At six p.m. the regular surgeon took me aside and informed me that inflammation of the bowels had commenced, which caused the pain. That it would increase in frequency and perhaps severity—that he could not live more than two or three days longer and advised me to break the matter gently to him. William discovered from my countenance the nature of the news imparted to me and broke out rather sharply against the skill of the surgeon. Said he would live he was sure—that after surviving the first day he was quite confident of ultimate recovery, and requested me not to write or telegraph home alarming his folks. I said, and indeed could say, but little in reply.

Capt. Hynes came in about 7 p.m., whom he requested to send a messenger to Surgeon Stull [First Assistant Surgeon Theodore W. Stull] of the 8th. Ill. Cav. to come and attend him a few days. He also expressed a wish for Surgeon Crawford [First Assistant Surgeon Samuel K. Crawford] of St. Charles, Ill. to be sent for, but this was out of the question, as C. could not get here if he could come at all until too late. Besides he could do nothing more than is being done. Mental help can avail little now.

I wrote home at noon before his worse symptoms came on.

July 14, Tuesday, The Major slept a little last night in brief winks—suffered considerable pain all the time but not those terrible spasms. I remained by his side all night with two nurses to fan him by turns.

At 10 a.m. the surgeon dressed his wound and made some prescriptions. He told me privately that his fever was higher, his pulse faster and further that the inflammation was spreading—that the ball had penetrated the lung, as he heard the air . . . pass thro the wound. My feelings for the last 24 hours have been terribly tortured. I have felt an inward sinking and experience blank despair. But there poor "Billy" lies flushed, hectic and hopeful—told Hynes that his pains were mere pleurisy—that he felt considerably better and would live though he expected a long siege of sickness and much pain & suffering. Also spoke hopeful to me. Had Hynes read the *Herald* to him; read the *Times* a little himself. Talked about the progress of the war.

The surgeon asked me whether I had informed him of his danger. Ans. in the negative. He thought I ought soon. One of the Sisters, a sweet faced, gentle young girl also asked me some questions. She feels deep solicitude for him. His firm, open, sincere, manly face and youth arrest the sympathy of all who come in contact with him. I have not seen him for an hour, having been writing today and yesterday's observations. Sent a dispatch to [illegible] announcing him worse.

1:30 p.m. Stayed with him from 12 to 1 p.m. fanning him. He declined to talk as it hurt him. Slept for a minute or two at a time. Discovered he was flighty. His mind running on military subjects. His hands and arms look paler—his face continues flushed, and his breath short. He holds his hands over his left side when the greatest pain exists. How much better—as it now seems—if the bullet had proven instantly fatal? Preventing this dying by inches. It is hard to look at a strong, healthy man succumbing gradually to the savages of the disease caused by his wound. I think I suffer in mind almost as much as he does.

4 p.m. The Major seemed brighter this p.m. He made Capt. Hynes and me read him all the news about the great riot in N.Y. and the army news and talked considerable on different topics. Ate some rice and milk and has a little appetite. Had eaten nothing before for two days. Still considerable pain but looks and acts better. Strange, if there were hope of recovering or even of getting him home.

7 p.m. Appearance of improvement at 4 p.m. illusory. Surgeon examined him at 6:20, found pulse at 145 and weak. Nostrils fluttering. Breath short. Some pain constantly. A little flighty. Hands and feet somewhat cold. No hope for improvement. Wound looks worse and smells badly. Yet strange to say he does not and will not realize his actual condition. He says that I am too easily alarmed. Capt. Hynes has engaged to talk with him on the matter. Sad. Sad.

8 p.m. Introduced the subject of his impending dissolution. He talked very calmly about it. Said he was prepared to die—had no sort of fears. Could die perfectly content. Would leave home free of scorn or reproach. Had no dread of the future life. Died in a good, patriotic cause on the field of battle with his face to the enemy of his country. Wanted to be buried in Graceland Cemetery because it belonged to a good and true loyal man and was near Chicago.

Wanted me to settle a couple of small debts: $50 to Geo. Armstrong and $25 to Henry Maxwell in St. Johns N.B. Owed nothing else. Wanted to be buried in his battle uniform. His body to be shown to his relations in Canton before taking it to Chicago. As to his effects, he wanted his money given to his mother—also his pension of $25 per month so long as she lived. His bay horse to sister Ellen. The large horse to Capt. Hynes and the grey one to orderly Miller for faithful dedication to him for 2 years past. His dress sword to his brother, Samuel, his pistols to me. He desired his commissions framed and hung in my house as a family relict [sic]. He had some pictures which he directed me to dispose of without specifying particulars how.

His vest bearing the murderous bullet hole he wanted preserved by Mother. Asked me how much longer he would probably live—gave him my opinions. Was glad to learn surgeon's opinion that his pain would soon abate or the disease get worse, but that he might become flighty and should therefore give his directions while his mind was clear.

I held his hand in mine while talking and promised to stay with & by him to the end. He was solicitous about this.

July 15, 4:30 a.m. William called me to his bedside at daylight. His mind was clear but his voice feeble and breath short. He had slept some but was suffering considerable pain. Pulse very feeble and fluttering.

5:30 a.m. Spoke about paying his black boy [the] small bal. due him. Reconsidered the propriety of giving a horse to his sister Ellen; talked about giving her the proceeds of the horse. No definite conclusion came to, undecided. "Poor Jim," said he, "what can I do for him? He will not long survive me." He then named some articles to remember him by. He talked a little on other subjects when his mind became flighty and wandered. He looks much weaker than last evening. He seemed quite resigned to die and spoke very calmly and with no symptoms of uneasiness or dread.

At 8 a.m. he asked to see his carpet sack. It was opened and contents shown him. One photograph he tore up. Said give the others to Kate. His larger ring requested me to give Kate and the smaller one to his mother as keepsakes. His commission he wanted framed & hung in his bed chamber. Made a present of coat & pants patern [sic] to me, which he had in his carpet sack. Said I did not dress very well.

9 a.m. Requested me to find his field glass left in Washington for repair (with sutler) and keep it for his sake. Gen. Farnsworth visited him and talked for some time on many subjects. His hands & feet very cold. Surgeon administered a little whiskey to rally him.

He requested me to tell James that he died firm as a soldier should—without dread of the future and in the belief in which he lived. He died a philosopher believing that his misery ended with this life, and happiness began in the life to come.

He wished his body embalmed if it can be done conveniently. Desires a marble slab of plain monument with some patriotic inscription, and nothing of rank, date of death and wound—all of which I promised.

10 a.m. He wants Sammy to keep out of the army—as he cannot stand it. If drafted, thinks I had better pay his commutation. Requested his handkerchief to be given to Sammy, which he got from him. Tell him he used it to stop his heart's blood when wounded. Keep it to his memory.

Sends his dearest love to his mother. Tell her he did not suffer very greatly after the second day. Thanked me for the little favors I had done him. Called me, next to his poor mother, his best friend. Spoke very affectionately of Kate whom he loved as one of his own sisters.

Is very feeble and grows pale. Extremities cold. Mind still clear. Hopes that pain will decrease as he draws near his end. Surgeon says he can hardly live till night, but he may last a little longer as his constitution is strong. Requested his boots blacked, his coat buttoned full up, a clean shirt or shrowd [sic], his face shaved.

10:30, His heart beat most violently. Called me to him, thought his last moments were come. Held his hand and felt the terrible throbs of his heart. He was quite sensible. Wanted his nieces to plant flowers on his grave—he kissed their picture very warmly and smiled sweetly on them. His mind then wandered and he gave many military commands as if in battle. For last three days, when dreaming, he talked of military matters, exclaiming almost:

"What a glorious charge that was

"done to my full satisfaction

"you are brave men

"Two companies to the center

"String them at night—

"Forward charge!

"Glorious!"

Thus he talked. When he came to himself and was rational. His black boy, Irving, called to see him, shook hands and wept. One of his old soldiers also called and bid goodbye, saying to me there is as brave a man as ever drew a sword.

10:45, We kissed and he bid me goodbye in this world. I wept.

July 15, Wed. 1 p.m. The Major has been flighty since 11 a.m. but has been rational several times for a moment, disliked to talk. Voice still strong. Color of face nearly natural—but extremities quite cold. Heart beating strong and quick—pulse weak and flickering. It was a struggle of a strong man with death. I am full of sorrow, and copious tears would be a great relief.

The day has been cool and breezy, but he calls out, "Oh, fan me faster." Says that his breast is hot. (The result of inflammation.)

3:20 p.m. William's breathing harder. Mind wavering & flighty. Slept and dreamed for 2½ hours—all about the army and the good news rec'd. couple hours since. At his request I read all the dispatches, partial capture of Charleston, defeat of Johnson, capture of Port Hudson—more of Lee's rebels captured. Grand result at Vicksburg. When I finished, he said he feared it was too good to be all true. I assured him, when he remarked he could now die happy, he had almost lived to witness the end of this accursed rebellion. That he saw the day breaking—had done his part towards putting it down—was part of the price paid for the salvation of the Union.

He has been kept upon stimulants today, but the lamp of life burns feebly and flickers in the socket. It will soon be over and poor Willie will have rest from his labors and pains. His legs and arms quite cold, his body growing cold—his heart beating fast and hard.

Just told he was born Nov. 5, 1835, in Massillon, Ohio. His memory still good though the footprints of death are on his brow. At 4 p.m. he looked at his face in his pocket mirror—exclaimed how natural yet in the face, but a film coming over his eyes.

8 p.m. Observe but little change since 3 p.m. He suffers much pain in his poor torn breast, breaths short, quick, difficult, but there yet exists considerable vitality. He is anxious to die speedily; tired of misery. It is very trying to sit hour and hour and witness his anguish without power of alleviation. I feel much shattered in mind & body. Stay with him 22 to 24 hours. He talked . . . expressed some disappointment that Surgeon Stull from the regiment did not arrive to see him. At present he has a very severe attack of pain.

July 16, 7 a.m. Two Sisters sat up with William last night till midnight and talked considerable with him. Surgeon Stull arrived at 9:30 p.m. Gave him some morphine to allay pain—was glad to see him. He suffered considerable during the night. This morning he looks worse, but is easier and sleeps a little. Talked freely with me. Did not want [my] wife or [his] mother to come, as it would shock and injure them without any benefit to him. Wanted them to recollect him as they last saw him in the perfection of health. We kissed again and bid goodbye as he may become unconscious at any moment.

8:30 a.m. During the last hour he said the pain was less acute, but he felt a sensation of weakness in mind and body; that he had lost all desire to live and was anxious to go. Enquired how soon he would be right of his trouble. Said he felt no longer an interest in the things of this world, all of them were indifferent & valueless to him. He wanted away. Spoke of meeting his sister Jane in the spirit world [Jane Medill, deceased 1847] and soon expected that James and Father would join him there. He wanted his little nieces to plant flowers and evergreens about his grave—was certain they would not soon forget their loving uncle. He says, send the horse to Sister Ellen. Mind made up.

9:40 a.m., Had perhaps a last talk. Tell Mother, Jim, Father, sisters and Kate that I have no pain. I am dying contented and happy. Don't want to live longer. He then stated particularly how he wanted to be laid out—in his uniform, buttoned up, scarf around him, boots on, spurs beside his feet. Metallic coffin, beard shaved on sides of face, wanted to look as he was when he fell. He kissed me again and tenderly said goodbye, love to dear Mother and family. His mind then wandered, and he looked as if dying.

Consciousness continued until 10.5 a.m. The last thing he said when I asked him, "Do you know me?" Yes, you're my brother Joseph. Everything looks green. My dear friend Hynes goes home with me. I am glad. He said not more. Died easy.

Notes:

S. H. Miller—the orderly, Sinking Spring, Berks Co. Pa.

Little black servant, claims William owes him July 20. $12.00. Pay him the $50. Wants me to give "Peter" something for his care.

Photograph of young lady in C. [Canton, Ohio] an old but discontinued affair.

Miller will stop at Richard Hynes drover's home Harrisburg, Pa.

William would like to have Dr. Stull of regt. to attend him.

Doctor sleeps at room No. 3 West End

Corporal J.P. Brainard, Co. A, Frederick City, General hospital No. 1

His favorite nurse "Peter"

Sister Mercy O'Keefe Irish birth, Boston, Educated. Very beautiful and sweet in her deportment, very tender to William

Personal Tragedy Mars the Joyous News of Twin Union Victories

In the western theater Vicksburg fell to Grant, July 4, 1863, and the *Tribune* devoted a full page to the Gettysburg victory on July 7, 1863, but the triumphs brought personal tragedy that same day when Joseph Medill

Major Medill's Headstone, "Union Soldier Died of Wounds." (Courtesy of Graceland Cemetery—Ron Danish)

received a telegram, notifying him that William had been gravely wounded. Joseph hurried east to be at William's side. For days, almost without rest, Joseph helped care for his brother in a military hospital near Fredericksburg. Katherine Medill wrote to him that she would come east soon to help, but Joseph told her not to come because the "Major" will be no more before she could arrive.[45]

William's death depressed Joseph, and the continued struggles of war and differences with his partner, Dr. Ray, drained Joseph's strength. He returned to Washington. While at home William Bross[46] helped raise the Twenty-Ninth U.S. Colored Regiment, which William's brother John Bross commanded.[47]

February, 1865, Joseph Medill Lobbies to Reduce the Illinois Quota for Additional Volunteers

Joseph Medill and President Lincoln were still friends, but Medill's 1865 plea on behalf of Illinois to reduce the quota for recruits exasperated President Lincoln. "I cannot do it! But I will go with you to Stanton and hear arguments on both sides." During the discussion, Lincoln listened with head bowed. Stanton summed up, saying no city, section, or state could ask for special favor, not even Illinois.

Lincoln lifted his head and turned his black, frowning face on Medill and the Illinois delegation.

> Gentlemen, . . . after Boston, Chicago has been the chief instrument in bringing this war on the country. The Northwest has opposed the South as New England has opposed the South. It is you who are largely responsible for making blood flow as it has. You called for war until we had it. You called for Emancipation, and I have given it to you. Whatever you have asked you have had. Now you come here begging to be let off from the call for men which I have made to carry out the war you have demanded. You ought to be ashamed of yourselves. I have a right to expect better things of you. Go home, and raise your 6,000 extra men.

"I couldn't say anything," Medill remembered. . . . . "[We raised] 6,000 men—making 28,000 in a city of 156,000. But there might have been crape [sic] on every door almost in Chicago, for every family had lost a son or a husband. I lost two brothers."[48]

Report of Col. Gamble Commanding 1st Brigade 1st Cavalry Division, Dated, August 24, 1865

Near Williamsport, MD., July 6, [1863]

This brigade was ordered to engage the enemy on the left of the Boonsboro Road, near Williamsport, the Reserve Brigade [Merritt's] being on the right of the road. The Third Indiana Cavalry was ordered to capture and destroy a train of seven wagons of the enemy on our left, on the Downsville Road, which was successfully accomplished, making prisoners of the drivers and those in charge of the train. The brigade was then placed in line of battle, and three-fourths of it dismounted to drive in the enemy's skirmishers; and Tidball's[49] battery of four guns placed in position, supported by the balance of mounted men, opened on

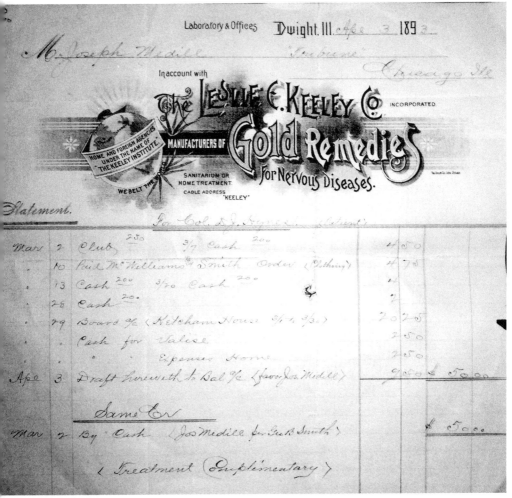

Fifty-dollar invoice for Col. D. J. Hynes (patient) to Mr. Joseph Medill, *Tribune*, Chicago. (Courtesy Colonel Robert R. McCormick Research Center)

the enemy, many times our superior in numbers, and did excellent execution; the dismounted men in the meantime, keeping up a sharp carbine fire, drove in the rebel pickets on their reserves. The dismounted men were under the immediate command of the gallant and lamented Major Medill Eighth Illinois Cavalry, who fell mortally wounded.[50]

Memo for the Record, October 28, 1974
Subject: Death of Maj. William Medill. Joseph Medill's Diary of his Vigil at William's Deathbed, After Gettysburg in July 1863
Joseph Medill's penciled diary, in a 3½ x 5½-inch lined notebook, is a poignant record of the death of his brother. It is, furthermore, an authoritative and detailed account of handling of the wounded in the Civil War, written by an observant, involved, articulate journalist.

An ironic sequel to this dramatic account is evident, apparently, in the statement of account sent April 3, 1893, by the Keeley Institute to Joseph Medill. Mr. Medill, it is apparent in his editorial directives and in his letters, was an enthusiastic supporter of Dr. Leslie E. Keeley's method of treating alcoholics—the "Keeley cure," which gained worldwide attention in the 19th century.[51]

The deathbed diary makes several references to Capt. Hynes, who was a friend and comrade of Major Medill, who is quoted just before death as saying: "My good friend Hynes goes home with me? Yes. I am glad."

It is noted that Col. D. J. Hynes is listed on the April 3, 1893, statement as the "patient," and the bill for the Keeley Cure is made out to Joseph Medill.

Timeline of Service, William H. Medill, Eighth Illinois Cavalry

- Sept. 14, 1861, Chicago, Ill., Captain, Company G, 8 Reg't Illinois Cavalry, present for duty, Period 3 years
- Sept. 18, 1861, Age 26 years, Camp Kane, No Bounty shown as paid
- Promoted to vice major, Sharpsburg, Maryland, Dustin resigned, Sept. 10, 1862
- Promoted to Major, 8th Illinois Cavalry, Company G, Sept. 10, 1862
- October 31, 1862 to Feb. 28, 1863, Commutation due for two½ months forage for two horses—forage in kind could not be furnished by the proper Dept.
- April 10, 1863, absent with leave from Hd. Qtrs. for 15 days
- Wounded at Williamsport, Maryland, July 6, 1863

Remarks as to Condition of Patient:
- July 8: Wounded one inch above tip of ensiform cartilage by a musket ball July 6th, admitted July 8th/63. On admission gave evidence of pneumonia on right side, none of peritonitis. Treatment—cold water dressings & opium

- July 10: Slight symptoms of peritonitis—ordered 1 gr. opium every hour—patient is very hopeful
- July 12: Pleuritis and pneumonia left side, pulse 116, peritoneal symptoms, continue opium
- July 13: Severity of symptoms increasing, pulse 130, great difficulty respiration, peritonitis severe. Wine & continue opium
- July 14: Pulse 144, continue treatment
- July 15: Death approaching
- July 16: Died at 10 a.m. No post-mortem could be held. Body removed immediately by brother for embalming

Died at Frederick City, Maryland, July 16, 1863, cause of death: gunshot wound abdomen, penetrating[52]

NOTES

INTRODUCTION

1. Mark Hubbard, ed., *Illinois's War: The Civil War in Documents* (Athens: Ohio Univ. Press, 2013), 63.
2. Doris Kearns Goodwin, *Team of Rivals: The Political Genius of Abraham Lincoln* (New York: Simon & Schuster, 2005), 200.
3. Hubbard, *Illinois's War*, 2.
4. Ibid., 11–26.
5. Ibid., 11, 15.
6. Ibid., 1, 3, 63.
7. Ibid., 1, 58.
8. Richard Norton Smith, *The Colonel: The Life and Legend of Robert R. McCormick 1880–1955* (New York: Houghton Mifflin Company, 2003), 1.
9. "James Corbett Medill," Find a Grave, accessed September 17, 2016, http://findagrave.com/cgi-bin//fg.cgi?page=gr&GRid=154302227.
10. Smith, *The Colonel*, 3–6.
11. Frederick Francis Cook, *Bygone Days in Chicago* (Chicago: A. C. McClurg & Co., 1910), 260.
12. Megan McKinney, *The Magnificent Medills* (New York: Harper Collins Publishers, 2011), 15, 32, 33.
13. Wyatt Rushton, *Joseph Medill and the Chicago Tribune* (Madison: Univ. of Wisconsin Library, 1916), 15–17.
14. James Barnet, ed., *The Martyrs and Heroes of Illinois in the Great Rebellion: Biographical Sketches* (Press of J. Barnet, 1865), 57, https://archive.org/details/martyrsheroesofiooinbarn.
15. Patricia A. Donohoe, *The Printer's Kiss, The Life and Letters of a Civil War Newspaperman and His Family* (Kent, Ohio: Kent State Univ. Press, 2014), 37–38.
16. McKinney, *Magnificent Medills*, 16.
17. John Moses and Joseph Kirkland, *History of Chicago, Illinois,* vol. 2 (Chicago: Munsell & Company, 1895), 45.
18. Lloyd Wendt, *Chicago Tribune: The Rise of a Great American Newspaper* (Chicago: Rand McNally, 1979), 126.
19. *New World Encyclopedia Online,* "Joseph Medill," accessed August 24, 2016, http://www.newworldencyclopedia.org/entry/Joseph_Medill.
20. Robert I. Girardi, "Illinois' First Response to the Civil War," *Journal of the Illinois State Historical Society* 105, no. 2–3 (Summer–Fall, 2012): 167–68.

21. James M. McPherson, *The Illustrated Battle Cry of Freedom: The Civil War Era* (New York: Tess Press, 2008), 391.

22. Eric Wittenberg, "The Cavalry: A Brief History of Union Cavalry in the Eastern Theatre of the Civil War up to The Battle of Gettysburg," accessed August 25, 2017, http://civilwarcavalry.com/?page_id=11.

23. Ibid.

24. Civil War Trust, "Brandy Station," accessed December 11, 2016, http://www.civilwar.org/battlefields/brandy-station.html.

25. Ken Allers Jr., *The Fog of Gettysburg: The Myths and Mysteries of the Battle* (Nashville: Cumberland House Publishing, 2008), 41.

26. Eric J. Wittenberg and J. David Petruzzi, *Plenty of Blame to Go Around* (New York: Savas Beatie, 2006), xviii.

27. Ibid., 19.

28. Glenna R. Schroeder-Lein, *The Encyclopedia of Civil War Medicine* (London and New York: Taylor & Francis, 2008), 320–21, https://play.google.com/store/books/details/Glenna_R_Schroeder_Lein_The_Encyclopedia_ofCivil?id=fVZeGtxiMcYC.

29. Freemon, *Gangrene and Glory* (Urbana: Univ. of Illinois Press, 2001), 43.

30. Ibid., 48–50.

31. C. Keith Wilbur, MD, *Illustrated Living History Series, Civil War Medicine, 1861–1865* (Philadelphia: Chelsea House Publishers, 1995), 51.

32. Freemon, *Gangrene and Glory*, 35.

33. Keith, *Civil War Medicine*, 3–5.

34. Ibid., 99.

1. The Call to Action

1. The Abraham Lincoln Papers at the Library of Congress Series 1. General Correspondence, 1833–1916, accessed August 12, 2017, http://memory.loc.gov/cgi-bin/query/P?.

2. Benton Rain Patterson, *Lincoln's Political Generals: The Battlefield Performance of Seven Controversial Appointees* (Jefferson, N.C.: McFarland & Company, 2014), 131–5.

3. "John Tyler, 10," The White House: Presidents, accessed January 1, 2017, http://www.whitehouse.gov/1600/presidents/johntyler; "Millard Fillmore, 13," The White House: Presidents, accessed January 1, 2017, http://www.whitehouse.gov/1600/presidents/millardfillmore.

4. In 1862 President Lincoln appointed Andrew Johnson as military governor of Tennessee, and Johnson used the state as a laboratory for reconstruction. In 1864 the Republicans, contending that their National Union Party was for all loyal men, nominated Johnson, a Southerner and a Democrat, for vice president. After Lincoln's assassination, Johnson became the seventeenth president. "Andrew John-

son, 17," The White House: Presidents, accessed January 3, 2017, http://www.whitehouse.gov/1600/presidents/andrewjohnson.

5. Union major general Carlos Buell was suspected of being a Confederate sympathizer because he inherited slaves from his wife's family. When Buell failed to pursue Confederates after Perryville, October 1862, he was relieved of command. McPherson, *Illustrated Battle Cry*, 443.

6. Wendt, *Chicago Tribune*, 155.

7. Ibid., 154–65.

8. Ibid., 24.

9. J. Seymour Currey, *Chicago: Its History and Its Builders, A Century of Marvelous Growth* (Chicago: S. J. Clarke Publishing Company, 1918), 44.

10. *The Address of the Hon. Abraham Lincoln, in [V]indication of the Policy of the Framers of the Constitution and the Principles of the Republican Party, Delivered at Cooper Institute, February 27th, 1860* (New York: George F. Nesbitt & Co., Printers and Stationers), 1860.

11. P. Michael Jones, "Civil War Timeline: Co. D 29th U.S. Colored Infantry," *The Southern Illinoisan*, Feb. 8, 2015, http://thesouthern.com/news/local/civil-war-timeline-co-d-th-u-s-colored-infantry/article_b5563d2a-c06b-5d00-808a-1ff9b3dffa48.html.

12. Donald Miller, *City of the Century: The Epic of Chicago and the Making of America* (New York: Simon and Schuster, 1996), 77–78.

13. "1861: Entire Police Department Fired," Chicago Police Department, accessed December 28, 2016, http://home.chicagopolice.org/inside-the-cpd/history/.

2. Barker's Dragoons, 1861

1. "The War Spirit Saturday," *Chicago Tribune*, Apr. 22, 1861, http://archives.chicagotribune.com/1861/04/22/page/4.

2. Cairo, Illinois, is located at the confluence of the Mississippi and Ohio Rivers.

3. William Kooser, "Captain Barker and the Dragoons," Illinois Periodicals Online, Northern Illinois University Libraries, accessed June 3, 2016, http://www.lib.niu.edu/1999/ihwt9916.html. Embury D. Osband of the Chicago Dragoons became Captain Osband of the Fourth Illinois Cavalry, which served as General Grant's escort in the western theater. Commissioned Colonel in 1863, Osband recruited the First Mississippi Colored Cavalry, which became the Third U.S. Colored Cavalry. He was brevetted brigadier general in October 1864.

4. Eighteen pages of stationery were written in pencil.

5. Historical sources spell Philippi several different ways. The spelling used is modern.

6. Barnet, *Martyrs and Heroes*, 59–60.

7. Kooser, "Captain Barker and the Dragoons."

8. Barnet, *Martyrs and Heroes*, 60.

3. The Eighth Illinois Cavalry, 1861

1. Hubbard, *Illinois's War*, 70–71.
2. Wendt, *Chicago Tribune*, 167.
3. Kooser, "Captain Barker and the Dragoons."
4. Salmon P. Chase was secretary of the treasury in Lincoln's cabinet from 1861 to 1864.
5. Stephen A. Douglas, senator from Illinois, supported a plan referred to as "popular sovereignty," which let settlers in each territory decide the question of slavery for themselves. Allen Guelzo, *Lincoln and Douglas, The Debates that Defined America* (New York: Simon & Schuster, 2008), 13–14.
6. Barnet, *Martyrs and Heroes*, 60.
7. The balance of this letter is missing from the Chicago Tribune Collection archive and was not found in excerpts published elsewhere.
8. John A. Menaugh, "A Chicago Hero in the Civil War, *Chicago Tribune*, July 11, 1943, Graphics Section, 2.
9. Barnet, *Martyrs and Heroes*, 61.
10. Robert H. Irrmann, "Horace White," Beloit College Archives and Special Collections, accessed June 16, 2016, http://www.beloit.edu/archives/documents/archival_collections/alumni/horace_white/.

4. The Ditch-Digging Army of the Potomac, 1862

1. According to A. T. Andreas, *History of Chicago From the Earliest Period to the Present Time, Volume II—From 1857 Until the Fire of 1871* (Chicago: R. R. Donnelley & Sons, 1885), 259, Camp California was located near the Centerville Road, about three miles west of Alexandria, Virginia.
2. Lyman Trumbull was U.S. senator from Illinois from 1855 through 1873.
3. In February 1862, Gen. Ulysses S. Grant captured Fort Henry and Fort Donelson, forcing an unconditional surrender of Confederates at Fort Donelson in Tennessee. In this combined army/navy operation, many regiments of infantry, artillery, and cavalry came from Illinois. Approximately 30 percent of Grant's forces in the Army of the Tennessee came from Illinois; Hubbard, *Illinois's War*, 127.
4. For much of the nineteenth century, Illinois was nicknamed the Sucker State. The origin of the term is subject to at least three interpretations.
5. The first battle at Manassas, July 21, 1861, resulted in approximately 2,900 Union and 2,000 Confederate casualties. The Second Battle of Manassas did not take place until August 1862. "Bull Run: First Manassas," Civil War Trust, accessed September 21, 2016, http://www.civilwar.org/battlefields/bullrun.html?tab=facts.
6. After General Montgomery took command of Alexandria as Union military governor, he followed a strategy of conciliation toward Confederates, shielding their property and treating secessionists lightly. But troopers of the Eighth Illinois

showed Southern citizens they had entered the army for the purpose of suppressing and crushing the rebellion. General Montgomery became outraged and reported to authorities in Washington that the Eighth had destroyed an old building for use as firewood; Abner Hard, *History of the Eighth Cavalry Regiment: Illinois Volunteers, During the Great Rebellion* (Aurora, Ill.: n.p., 1868), 71–73, Internet archive, accessed June 13, 2016, https://archive.org/details/historyofeighthcoohard.

7. John Dean Caton, attorney and justice of the Illinois State Supreme Court, 1842–64.

8. Cub Run is an offshoot of Bull Run, which intersected Warrenton Turnpike a few miles closer to Centreville.

9. The Battle of Rich Mountain took place July 11, 1861, and Barker's Dragoons saw action. Fritz Haselberger, *Yanks from The South,* quoted in "The U.S. Forces of General McClellan at Rich Mountain," Rich Mountain Battlefield, accessed September 21, 2016, http://www.richmountain.org/history/trpsmccl.html.

10. The Battle of Second Manassas (or Bull Run) did not take place until August 28–30, 1862, with four and a half times the estimated casualties as First Manassas. "Second Manassas: Second Bull Run, Brawner's Farm," Civil War Trust, accessed January 1, 2017, http://www.civilwar.org/battlefields/second-manassas.html?tab=facts.

11. Troops were taken south for the upcoming Peninsula Campaign. McClellan moved a 121,500-strong army with all of its supplies and armaments to Fort Monroe on March 17, 1862, intending to move against Richmond by way of the York River. "The Peninsula Campaign," Civil War Trust, accessed September 21, 2016, http://www.civilwar.org/learn/articles/peninsula-campaign-0.

12. Barnet, *Martyrs and Heroes,* 62–63.

13. Wendt, *Chicago Tribune,* 17–23.

14. "Battle of Shiloh—April 6, 1862," Civil War Trust, accessed September 21, 2016, http://www.civilwar.org/battlefields/shiloh/maps/shilohmap.html.

15. "The Battle of Rich Mountain," Rich Mountain Battlefield Foundation, accessed September 21, 2016, http://www.richmountain.org/history/battleofRM.html.

16. "Cheat Mountain," National Park Service, accessed September 21, 2016, http://www.nps.gov/civilwar/search-battles-detail.htm?battleCode=wv005.

17. Secretary of the Treasury Salmon P. Chase asked Congress to raise an estimated twenty million dollars to finance the war effort. In the summer of 1861, the House Ways and Means Committee drew up a bill to tax personal and corporate incomes. The bill passed the House and the Senate but was never put into operation; however, it paved the way for the next tax bill in 1862. "The First Income Tax," Civil War Trust, accessed August 4, 2016, http://www.civilwar.org/education/history/warfare-and-logistics/logistics/tax.html.

18. In 1860 Illinois voters authorized a convention to create a new state constitution. Democrats won a decisive majority in the Illinois legislature in 1862 and sought to further their political goals by reducing the governor's term to two years, placing wartime spending under control of a special commission as well as including

wording to exclude blacks from entering Illinois and ban black voters; Hubbard, *Illinois's War*, 60.

19. John F. Farnsworth, U.S. congressman, abolitionist, and St. Charles, Illinois, resident, who organized the Eighth Illinois Cavalry.

20. Lawrence A. Williams, Major, Sixth Cavalry. Although he was cleared and returned to duty, suspicion continued to follow him. Donald C. Caughey, Jimmy J. Jones, and Eric J. Wittenberg, *The 6th United States Cavalry in the Civil War: A History and Roster* (Jefferson, N.C.: McFarland & Co., 2013), 51.

21. Corinth, Mississippi, was the intersection of the east/west Memphis & Charleston Railroad and the north/south Mobile & Ohio Railroad, vital routes for the South. At the time Medill wrote this letter, Union general Halleck was drawing ever closer to the Confederate defensive lines. On May 29, 1862, rather than fighting Halleck's army, Beauregard's Confederate force abandoned Corinth. McPherson, *The Illustrated Battle Cry*, 349–50.

22. The Battle of Mechanicsville on June 26, 1862, marked the beginning of the Seven Days Battles during the American Civil War. Union general George B. McClellan had marched his Army of the Potomac up the Peninsula, his campaign against the Confederate capital at Richmond stalling out at the Battle of Seven Pines–Fair Oaks on May 31–June 1, 1862. *Encyclopedia of Virginia*, s.v. "Battle of Mechanicsville," accessed December 16, 2016, http://www.encyclopediavirginia.org/Mechanicsville_Battle_of.

23. Estimated casualties (killed, missing, and wounded) in actuality were less—5,739 Union and 7,997 Confederate. "Seven Pines, Battle of Fair Oaks," Civil War Trust, accessed January 1, 2017, http://www.civilwar.org/battlefields/seven-pines.html.

24. Typhoid is bacterial fever and intestinal irritation caused by salmonella from contaminated water or food.

25. According to the roster of the Eighth Illinois Cavalry, this refers to First Lt. Daniel D. Lincoln of Mt. Pleasant, Illinois.

26. "Our Correspondence from the Advance," *The New York Times*, June 10, 1862, http://www.nytimes.com/1862/06/10/news/our-correspondence-advance-inundation-chickahominy-late-battles-justice-gen.html.

27. Barnet, *Martyrs and Heroes*, 64

28. "The Battle of Seven Pines," Civil War Trust, accessed June 28, 2016, http://www.civilwar.org/battlefields/seven-pines.html.

29. "Peninsula Campaign," History.com, accessed June 29, 2016, http://www.history.com/topics/american-civil-war/peninsula-campaign.

30. Shiloh (Pittsburg Landing) had over 23,000 casualties in two days of fighting; Fair Oaks had 11,000, not the numbers William Medill used. "Shiloh," Civil War Trust, accessed September 21, 2016, http://www.civilwar.org/battlefields/shiloh.html.

31. Union general Philip St. George Cooke was the Virginia-born father-in-law of Confederate general J. E. B. Stuart.

32. Illinois voters approved a constitutional convention in 1860. The convention delegates were decidedly partisan and viewed their role as superior to that of the legislature. They sought to enact congressional reapportionment and assume more powers than to frame a new constitution. Delegates were not viewed as pro-Union, and the proposal advanced by the convention became known as the "Copperhead Constitution." As a result, voters rejected their 1862 proposal by a margin of 24,515 votes. Illinois Business Roundtable, "Illinois' Proposed Constitutional Convention, A Context for the 2008 Constitutional Convention Call," February 2008, 11, http://ilga.gov/commission/lru/IBRT.pdf. Locofoco was a derogatory name for Democrats.

33. Barnet, *Martyrs and Heroes,* 64–65.

34. A Federal squadron of six ships anchored in the river below the fort on May 15, 1862, and opened fire. When Confederate batteries replied, the ten-inch Columbiad recoiled, broke its carriage, and remained out of the fight until near the end. After four hours, the fort on Drewry's Bluff had blunted the Union advance seven miles short of the Confederate capital, but Richmond remained safe. "Drewry's Bluff," National Park Service, accessed June 28, 2016, http://www.nps.gov/rich/learn/historyculture/drewrys-bluff.htm.

35. This portion of the letter was found in the Chicago Tribune Collection of the Colonel Robert R. McCormick Research Center.

36. McPherson, *The Illustrated Battle,* 393–401.

37. William echoes the kind of derision his brother, Joseph, expressed concerning Irish immigrants. According to the *Encyclopedia of Chicago,* in the 1850s and 1860s Joseph linked Irish Catholics to the *Tribune*'s coverage of city crime and poverty, and he used the paper to attack Irish nationalism. Ellen Skerrett, *Encyclopedia of Chicago,* s.v. "Irish," accessed June 22, 2016, http://www.encyclopedia.chicagohistory.org/pages/652.html.

38. The Swift-Tuttle comet was first sighted in 1862 when Abraham Lincoln was president. Sally Stephens, "Cosmic Collisions," Astronomical Society of the Pacific, 1993, accessed January 18, 2017, http://www.as.wvu.edu/~jel/skywatch/swfttle.html.

39. John A. Menaugh, "Battle of Antietam Letters from the Front by a Chicago Civil War Hero—Major William H. Medill," *Chicago Tribune,* Aug. 15, 1943, Graphics Section, 6.

40. Hard, *History of the Eighth Cavalry,* 222.

41. "News of the Day: The Rebellion," *New York Times,* Oct. 2, 1862, http://www.nytimes.com/1862/10/02/news.

42. Hard, *History of the Eighth,* 192–95.

43. Joseph Medill preferred his friend and fellow Ohioan Salmon Chase for the Republican presidential nomination in 1860. On October 30, 1859, he wrote to his friend Archibald W. Campbell, "Personally I prefer Gov. Chase to any man—believing that he possesses the best executive ability." Reinhard H. Luthin, *The First Lincoln Campaign* (Gloucester, Mass.: Peter Smith, 1964), 73–74.

44. McPherson, *The Illustrated Battle Cry*, 492–93.

45. Wilbur F. Storey, who opposed the Civil War and Abraham Lincoln, bought the *Chicago Times* in 1861. He took a strong stance against anyone trying to save the Union. Josiah Seymour Currey, *Chicago: Its History and Its Builders* (Chicago: S. J. Clarke Publishing Company, 1918), 125.

46. James L. Stokesbury, *A Short History of the Civil War* (New York: William Morrow, 1995), 127–28.

47. McPherson, *The Illustrated Battle Cry*, 496.

48. Battle of Fredericksburg Summary: Union troops engaged, 100,007; Confederates engaged, 72,497. Estimated casualties: Union, 13,353; Confederate 4,576; "Fredericksburg," Civil War Trust, accessed September 22, 2016, http://www.civilwar.org/battlefields/fredericksburg.html.

5. The Eighth Illinois, an Effective Cavalry Regiment, 1863

1. Other Union officers did not share William's support for the Emancipation Proclamation. Army personnel had mixed reactions. Some had little sympathy for refugees, no matter how arduous their journey to Union lines, and they viewed former slaves as a drain on the war effort. Mark Smith, "A Chaotic Birth of Freedom," *Wall Street Journal*, Aug. 26, 2016. Few soldiers were abolitionists, but with no hope of reconciliation they wanted to disrupt anything that supported the South's war effort, including slaves' labor. Notable exceptions were General McClellan's associates, who stirred up opposition to the proclamation. McPherson, *The Illustrated Battle Cry*, 481. Black soldiers faced discrimination as well as segregation. The army was extremely reluctant to commission black officers—only one hundred gained commissions during the war. African American soldiers were also given substandard supplies and rations. "The Civil War and Emancipation, 1861–1865," PBS.org, accessed December 31, 2016, http://www.pbs.org/wgbh/aia/part4/4p2967.html.

2. Gen. John Bankhead Magruder, West Point graduate, Mexican War veteran commander, who resigned his commission to join the Confederate army. Thomas W. Cutrer, "Magruder, John Bankhead," Texas State Historical Association, modified January 18, 2013, http://www.tshaonline.org/handbook/online/articles/fma15.

3. Wendt, *Chicago Tribune*, 175.

4. United States War Department, *The War of the Rebellion: A Compilation of the Official Records of the Union and Confederate Armies*, series 1, vol. 25, part 2, United States (Washington, D.C.: GPO, 1889), 11–12, digitized by Cornell University Library.

5. It wasn't until 1896 that Joseph Medill built a white clapboard farmhouse with a strong classical portico for the front facade at Cantigny Park, spending $15,000, nearly three times the amount of a typical house for that period. Joseph named his property Red Oaks Farm after the three-hundred-year-old oak trees that still grow on the estate. McCormick's Home brochure, accessed December 21, 2016, http://www.cantigny.org/PDF/Museum/RRMMbrochure2.pdf.

6. When conducting cavalry raids, horses need to be reshod after no more than one hundred miles of travel. Farriers and blacksmiths struggled to keep mounts fit for operations. Wittenberg and Petruzzi, *Plenty of Blame to Go Around*, xiii–xiv.

7. "Chancellorsville," Georgia's Blue and Gray Trail, last modified May 1, 2009, http://blueandgraytrail.com/event/Chancellorsville.

8. Al Hemingway, "Battle Of Chancellorsville," *America's Civil War* (Mar. 1996), quoted in HistoryNet.com, http://www.historynet.com/battle-of-chancellorsville.

9. Colonel Robert R. McCormick's papers in the Colonel Robert R. McCormick Research Center at the First Division Museum, Medill Family Correspondence, Wheaton, Illinois.

10. Malaria and insect-borne diseases afflicted Union soldiers seasonally, particularly during warm weather in the South. Freemon, *Gangrene and Glory*, 19.

11. Hubbard, *Illinois's War*, 110–12.

12. Fort Warren guarded the inner shipping channel to Boston harbor and housed Confederate prisoners. Jane Triber, "Georges Island During Civil War," National Park Service, last modified February 26, 2015, http://www.nps.gov/boha/learn/historyculture/georges-civil-war.htm.

13. "61 Years Ago Today," *Chicago Tribune*, May 24, 1924, 6, archives.chicagotribune.com/1924/05/24/page/6/article/61-years-ago-today.

14. Jim Slade and John Alexander, *Firestorm at Gettysburg, Civilian Voices* (Atglen, Pa.: Schiffer Military/Aviation History, 1998), 16.

15. Richard Wheeler, *Witness to Gettysburg* (New York: Harper & Row Publishers, 1987), 7.

16. Ibid., 16.

17. Lieut. Col. David Clendenin and Maj. John Beveridge were absent during the Battle of Brandy Station because they were left in charge of the First Cavalry Division's camps. William Medill was absent due to illness, as detailed in his letters. Joseph W. McKinney, *Brandy Station, Virginia, June 9, 1863: The Largest Cavalry Battle of the Civil War* (Jefferson, N.C.: McFarland & Co., 2006), 274n29.

18. McKinney, *Brandy Station, Virginia*, 117–19.

19. Wittenberg and Petruzzi, *Plenty of Blame*, xviii–xix.

20. Wheeler, *Witness*, 34.

21. Barnet, *Martyrs and Heroes*, 71–72.

22. Wheeler, *Witness*, 46–55.

23. Ibid., 64–66.

24. Ibid., 69.

25. Ibid., 72.

26. Ibid., 75–76.

27. Civil War reenactors of the Eighth Illinois Cavalry joined the DuPage County Historical Museum as Mark Whitlock, director of the Illinois State Military Museum, displayed and spoke on the Eighth Illinois Cavalry Guidon, the flag the cavalry carried into battle. A small portion of Whitlock's talk was used here to

clarify the training the Eighth Illinois received from William Gamble. Audio of the full presentation is available at https://archive.org/details/rallyAroundTheFlag8th IllinoisCavalryGuidonPresentation, accessed September 21, 2016.

28. Hard, *History of the Eighth,* 282.

29. "General David Ramsey Clendenin: Forgotten Hero," Rich Hanson's Civil War Stories (blog), Aug. 31, 2013, http://monmouthrlhcw.blogspot.com/2013/08/general-david-ramsey-clendenin.html.

30. *Chicago Daily Tribune,* Nov. 22, 1863, http://chroniclingamerica.loc.gov/lccn/sn84031490/1863-11-22/ed-1/seq-1/.

6. The Last Full Measure of Devotion

1. Samuel Lover, *Handy Andy* (London: Cassell, 1845).

2. On January 26, 1863, General Burnside submitted his resignation to President Lincoln, who accepted it. All three generals were relieved of command after the horrendous losses at Fredericksburg. Mark Bradley, "The Battle of Fredericksburg," U.S. Army Center of Military History, Dec. 2015, http://www.history.army.mil/news/2015/151200a_fredericksburg.html.

3. George McClellan had been relieved of command to await further orders, but none came. "George B. McClellan, Major General," Civil War Trust, accessed September 21, 2016, http://www.civilwar.org/education/history/biographies/george-mcclellan.html.

4. Hard, *History of the Eighth,* 222.

5. Stoneman made a raid around the enemy's rear, cutting the railroads between them and Richmond to prevent reinforcements from the south and to engage their cavalry, while General Hooker attacked them in front with the main army. Men of the Eighth Illinois were dissatisfied because they were not allowed to go along. Hard, *History of the Eighth,* 228.

6. The region called the "Northern Neck" lies between the Rappahannock and Potomac and was a refuge during the war for guerrillas and smugglers. The purpose of the march was to stop citizen-marauders and break up contraband trade. Hard, *History of the Eighth,* 238.

7. Ibid., 239–40.

8. Wittenberg, *Plenty of Blame,* xvi.

9. Wheeler, *Witness to Gettysburg,* 85.

10. Ibid., 90–91.

11. Allers, *The Fog of Gettysburg,* 40–41.

12. Allen C. Guelzo, *Gettysburg: The Last Invasion* (New York: Alfred A. Knopf, 2013), 82, 91.

13. Ibid., 117.

14. Ibid., 118–19.

15. Ibid., 99–100.

16. Ibid., 101.

17. Wheeler, *Witness to Gettysburg*, 93–95.

18. Ibid., 106–9.

19. Ibid., 112.

20. John A. Miller, "The South Mountain Area during the 1863 Pennsylvania Campaign," Emmitsburg Area Historical Society, accessed July 23, 2016, http://www.emmitsburg.net/archive_list/articles/history/civil_war/south_mountain.htm.

21. Hard, *History of the Eighth*, 255–56.

22. Guelzo, *Gettysburg*, 132–33.

23. John Allen Miller, "Military Engagements Around Emmitsburg in the Civil War, General Meade's Pipe Creek Circular," Emmitsburg Area Historical Society, accessed July 23, 2016, http://www.emmitsburg.net/archive_list/articles/history/civil_war/pipe_creek.htm.

24. Guelzo, *Gettysburg*, 119–20.

25. Harry W. Pfanz, *Gettysburg—The First Day* (Chapel Hill: Univ. of North Carolina Press, 2001), 47–49.

26. Wittenberg, *Plenty of Blame*, 224.

27. Hard, *History of the Eighth*, 257–58.

28. Wheeler, *Witness to Gettysburg*, 123–24.

29. Allers, *The Fog of Gettysburg*, 157–58, 225.

30. Hard, *History of the Eighth*, 258.

31. Wheeler, *Witness to Gettysburg*, 171.

32. Wittenberg, *Plenty of Blame*, 216.

33. Hard, *History of the Eighth*, 258–59.

34. Wheeler, *Witness to Gettysburg*, 246–47.

35. The family member who made this entry was incorrect about the locations. William was wounded near Williamsport, not Williamsburg, and died in a hospital in Frederick, Maryland.

36. Slade, *Firestorm at Gettysburg*, 132.

37. Ibid., 143.

38. Ibid., 141.

39. "The Retreat from Gettysburg, By Brig. General John Imboden C.S.A. (1887)," accessed June 12, 2016, http://www.emmitsburg.net/archive_list/articles/history/civil_war/imboden_memoirs.htm.

40. *The Union Army* (Madison, Federal Pub. Co., 1908), 701, Internet archive, accessed August 7, 2017, https://archive.org/details/unionarmyhistory06madi.

41. Hard, *History of the Eighth*, 261.

42. Ibid., 261–62.

43. Wendt, *Chicago Tribune*, 185.

44. Barnet, *Martyrs and Heroes*, 75.

45. Wendt, *Chicago Tribune*, 184.

46. William Bross was cofounder of the *Democratic Press*, which merged with the *Tribune* in 1858. McKinney, *The Magnificent Medills*, 26.

47. Wendt, *Chicago Tribune*, 186.

48. Ibid., 18–22.

49. John C. Tidball, brevet brigadier general commanding artillery brigade, Ninth Corps, Army of the Potomac.

50. *Official Records of the Union and Confederate Armies*, series I, volume XXVII, part I–Reports (Washington, D.C.: Peter Smith, 1889), 935.

51. The Keeley Cure relied heavily on injections of "bichloride" or "double chloride of gold" (hence the term *Gold Cure*). The Keeley Cure was well known in its day. By the 1890s every state and nearly every country had a Keeley institute of its own. "Keeley Institute," North Dakota State University Archives, accessed June 24, 2016, https://library.ndsu.edu/fargo-history/?q=content/keeley-institute.

52. National Archives Records Administration, Washington, D.C., Veterans' Service Records, (pre-WWI) Military Service Records, Compiled Military Service Record in Volunteer Union Organizations.

SELECTED PRIMARY SOURCES

Barnet, James, ed. *The Martyrs and Heroes of Illinois in the Great Rebellion: Biographical Sketches*. Press of J. Barnet, 1865. https://archive.org/details/martyrsheroesofi00inbarn.

Colonel Robert R. McCormick papers, McCormick Research Center at the First Division Museum at Cantigny Park, Wheaton, Ill.

Emmitsburg Area Historical Society. "The Retreat from Gettysburg By Brig. General John Imboden C.S.A. (1887)." http://www.emmitsburg.net/archive_list/articles/history/civil_war/imboden_memoirs.htm.

Fisher, Richard Swainson. *A Chronological History of the Civil War in America*. New York: Johnson and Ward, 1863. http://www.loc.gov/item/02008002/.

Hard, Abner. *History of the Eighth Cavalry Regiment: Illinois Volunteers, During the Great Rebellion*. Aurora, Ill.: n.p., 1868. https://archive.org/details/historyofeighthc00hard.

National Archives and Records Administration, Washington, D.C. Compiled Military Service File (NATF 86) of William H. Medill (1835–1863).

Nicholson, W. L. Map of Eastern Virginia, 1862. Library of Congress. http://www.loc.gov/item/99448500/.

INDEX

Page numbers in italics refer to illustrations.

African Americans, 7, 79–80, 84; regiments of, 149–50, 206
Aldie, Battle of: cavalry actions at, 163–64, 179; 8th Illinois at, 162–63; William praised for, 9, 194
Alexandria, Virginia: army's return to, 60, 66, 102; Union control of, 57, 65; William expecting winter quarters at, 122–23
Anderman, Lou, 82
Anderman, Richard, 184
Antietam, Battle of, *105*, 107; 8th Illinois in, 110–16; *Tribune* analysis of, 134–35; William in, 8–9, 108
appearance: Joseph's, 4; William's, 7
Aquia Creek, 101
Armstrong, Geo. E., *105*, 201
Army of Northern Virginia, 128
Army of the Potomac, 97, 163; condition of, 128, 130, 141, 180; inaction by, 18–19, 99; retaking Manassas, 61–65; retreats by, 99–102; use of cavalry by, 9, 144–45; William's criticisms of, 71, 101–2. *See also* Union Army
Army of Virginia, 107
Ashby, Gen., 109
Ashby's Gap, cavalry actions at, 164–65, 179–80
Ashland, Union capturing, 87–88
Astor, J. J., 64
Averell, William W., 145–47
Aylett, William, 191

Bailey, Alfred C., 192–94
Baltimore, defense of, 180–81
Banks, General, 127, 153, 157–58
Barker, Charley, 73, 103; men's complaints about, 41–42; William's complaints about, 34–35, 40
Barker's Dragoons, 43; actions engaged in, 38, *39*; complaints about, 40–42; as McClellan's bodyguards, 37–38; *Tribune* coverage of, 29–30; William enlisting in, 8, 29; William's dissatisfactions with, 37–38, 40

Beatty, Col., 39
Beauregard, P. G. T., 71, 84
Beaver Creek Dam, Battle of. *See* Mechanicsville, Battle of
Berry, Gen., 177
Beveridge, John, 93, 108–9, 167–68, 187
Black, Col., 191
Black, J. L., 191
Black Exclusion Law (Illinois), 2
Bradley, C. P., 27
Brandy Station, Battle of, 9–10, 159–60
Bross, John, 206
Bross, William J., 25, 206
Buckhannon, Barker's Dragoons at, 38
Buell, Carlos, 19
Buford, John, 159, 162, 191; at Gettysburg, 170, 187–88; in Pennsylvania, 165, 182–83
Bull Run, Battle of, 20, 43, 56, 61
Bull Run Mountains, cavalry actions in, 163–64, 163–67
Burlando, Father James Francis, 190
Burnside, Ambrose, 19, 153; assault on Richmond by, 125, 127; in Battle of Antietam, 107, 110, 115–16; delays by, 128–29; Fredericksburg campaign of, 119–22; McClellan replaced by, 121, 123, 125, 128; replaced by Hooker, 135, 144
Butler, Gen., 141–42

Cairo, Illinois, 2, 8, 29, 31, 32, 34, 36, 37, 40, 41, 213
Camp California, 55
Camp Defiance, 2–3, 8, 29, 33
Camp Illinois, 47–49
Camp Smith, 33
Camp Yates, 29–34, 36
Canton, Ohio, 4, 86, 158; Medill family in, 24–26, 48, 158, 201; William's friends in, 80, 84, 97, 139, 159
Carpenter, Miss, 97, 126
Carrick's Ford, Barker's Dragoons at, 38
Carter, Gale, 192–93
Carter, T. B., 29

Cashtown, Pennsylvania, 186
casualties: in Battle of Antietam, 107, 110, 114; in Battle of Chancellorsville, 145; in Battle of Fair Oaks, 88, 91–93, 96; in Battle of Gettysburg, 169; in Battle of Mechanicsville, 97; in Battle of Williamsburg, 83; in cavalry actions, 164, 166, 179; in Civil War, 67; in 8th Illinois, 71; at Pittsburg Landing, 71; under Pleasonton, 164; in taking Fredericksburg, 128–29; at Warrenton Junction, 161
Catlett's Station, action at, 164
Caton, Judge, 60
cavalry: actions at Bull Run Mountains, 163–67; Union vs. Confederate, 9
cavalry, Confederate, 66, 161; 8th Illinois vs., 69–70, 109, 163; at Gettysburg, 10, 188; Stuart's command of, 10, 118–19; uses of, 10, 89–90, 180, 190–92
cavalry, Union, 49, 52, 115, 138; actions by, 10, 73, 83, 85, 183; creation of new regiments of, 102–3; 8th Illinois relation with other units, 124, 137; horses and mules for, 30, 53, 102, 178–79; monitoring Confederate Army, 159–60, 180, 190, 192; Pleasonton's command of, 159–60, 162, 182; Stoneman's 1863 Raid by, 144, 151; uses of, 9–10, 87–88, 144–45, 187, 188–89; William's criticism of Cook's regulars, 91, 93; William's criticisms and, 9–10, 118–19. *See also* Eighth Illinois Cavalry
Chancellorsville, Battle of, 144, 157, 177; Hooker at, 146–48; William's criticism of leadership at, 145–47
Charleston, South Carolina, 15
Chase, Salmon, 117–18
Cheat Mountain, 68, 71
Chicago, 2, 20, 21, 23; troops from, 15, 29, 51; Wentworth in, 26–27
Chicago Democrat, 26, 28
Chicago Dragoons. *See* Barker's Dragoons
Chicago Press, 43
Chicago Tribune: on Antietam, 134–35; asked to investigate complaints about Camp Yates, 31; coverage of Barker's Dragoons, 29–30; criticisms of stance taken by, 23; influence in Lincoln's election, 5; Joseph's dedication to, 4; Joseph's influence through, 5; Judson as possible correspondent for, 123; keeping editor in Washington, 19–20; McCormick's influence on, 21; recruiting Eighth Illinois Cavalry, 43; Sam working for, 5; war coverage by, 20; White as Washington correspondent for, 50; William correcting errors in, 75; William working for, 4; William's contributions to, 22; William's criticism of, 50; William's letter published in, 169–72
Chickahominy Creek, 85–86, 89, 91–92
Chronicle: Waite displaced from, 65
Civil War, 25; casualties in, 67; expectation of end of, 72, 77, 162; financial effects of, 71, 103, 153; frustration with slow progress of, 68, 150; newspaper coverage of, 6, 20, 96–97; slavery and, 16, 95; William on progress of, 68, 109, 122–23, 167–68, 203; William's concern about cost of, 71, 103; William's criticism of management of, 6, 88, 100–101
Clark, Alpheus, 70, 113, 114, 118, 160
Clendenin, David Ramsay, 156, 162; accused of cowardice, 167–69; in cavalry actions in Bull Run Mountains, 165; following Confederate retreat to Virginia, 192; loss of confidence in, 180; William's resignation rejected by, 106
Cleveland, Capt., 51, 53, 57
Cleveland, Ezra, 106
Cleveland Morning Leader, 4
Colfax, Schuyler, 17–18
Colonel Robert R. McCormick Research Center, William's last letter in, 169
concessionists, Joseph's criticism of, 21–22
Confederacy, and England, 57
Confederate Army, 9, 87, 96, 127, 184, 186; at Battle of Chancellorsville, 144–45, 147; efforts to determine intentions of, 163, 180; northern fear of invasion by, 180–81; provisions for, 180–82, 191; retreats by, 66–67, 108–9, 190–92; strength of, 92, 95, 121, 128, 145, 147
Confederates, former, 79, 94
Conscription Bill, 141–42, 144
contraband, former slaves as, 178
Cook, Col. P. St.-G., 91, 93–94
Copperheads, 144, 150
Corinth, Mississippi, 68, 71, 84
Coshocton Republican, 4
courtship, William's, 124, 127, 139, 158; asking Kate's mediation in, 120, 126, 139; discouragement about marriage prospects, 142, 148–49, 168
Cox, Rev. Dr., 30
Curtain, Andrew, 180–81

Daily Transcript (Peoria, Illinois), 60–61
Davis, Col. Benjamin "Grimes" Davis, death of 161

Index

Davis, Jefferson, 19, 36, 79, 122, 153
Davis, Miss, 126
Democrats: peace, 21, 122; Republicans' agreement with, 15–16
Department of the West, Fremont's control of, 15–16
desertions, Union, 135
diseases, in Union Army, 70, 92–93, 95–96, 127, 150
Doubleday, Gen., 187
Douglas, Stephen, 1
draft, 152, 154. *See also* Conscription Bill
Dustin, Major, 108

Early, Gen., 180
education, William's plan for, 94
Eighth Illinois Cavalry, 70, 76, 101, 151, 180; assignments of, 9, 65, 78–79, 90–91, 137, 188–89, 192–93; in Battle of Antietam, 107, 110–11, 114–16; casualties in, 71, 114; Confederate respect for, 87, 114, 122; desire to fight, 65–66, 127, 166; as dismounted skirmishers, 192, 194, 207–8; freeing slaves, 155–56; at Gettysburg, 169–72, 186–87; Hard's regimental history of, 110–14, 168, 175, 186–87; health of, 11, 70, 92–93; horses for, 102, 109, 152; *New York Times* article on, 90–91; on picket duty, 86–87, 96, 130, 133; praise for, 51, 121, 165; recruitment for, 43, 102–3; retaking Manassas, 61–65; Sammy's enlistment in, 8, 106, 109; stationed in Washington, 48–49; timeline of William's service in, 208–9; William commanding, 51, 109, 111, 114–15, 162–63, 167, 193–94; William raising regiment, 8–9; William taking leave and rejoining, 123–24, 144; William's pride in, 162–63, 165–66; wounding of officers of, 160–61
Eighth New York Cavalry, 167, 186
Eighth Pennsylvania Cavalry, 124, 155
Eighty-second Illinois Infantry, at Gettysburg, 169–72
emancipation, Medill family's support for, 6–7
Emancipation Proclamation, 134–35
Emery, management of *Daily Transcript* by, 60–61
England, 57
Ewell, Richard S., 106, 163, 180; at Gettysburg, 159, 170, 188

Fair Oaks, Battle of, 88, 91–93, 96
Falmouth, 121, 127
Fargahan, John, 116
farms/farming: Joseph buying farm as investment, 136, 139; William considering as career, 142
Farnsworth, Elon J., 70, 103, 162, 168, 187; at Battle of Antietam, 114; commands of, 123–24, 130; promotion of, 123, 127; retaliation for Confederate raid, 89–91
Farnsworth, J. F., 43–44, 75–76
Fillmore administration, Lincoln's compared to, 17–18
finances: effects of war on, 153; Joseph managing William's, 100, 104–5, 130, 145–46, 154–57; Joseph's, 136, 139; Medill parents', 24, 105, 136–37, 201; William sending money for James Williams, 145; William's, 26–27, 52–54, 143, 156–57, 201
finances, soldiers lack of pay for, 52, 71, 143
Fitch, Graham N., 96
Foote, Benjamin, 160–61
Forrest, Nathan Bedford, 67
Forsyth, George, 60, 160–61
France, 154
Frederick, Maryland, William evacuated to, 11, *193*, 195
Fredericksburg campaign: Burnside and, 119–22, 128; Hooker and, 145, 158; Lee reinforcing and fortifying at, 122, 127; as Union defeat, 130, 134; William and, 9, 128–29
Fremont, John C., 15–17
Fremont Dragoons. *See* Eighth Illinois Cavalry
French, Gen., 57
Fugitive Slave Law, 2

Gage, Geo. W., 30
Gaine's Mills, Battle of, 97
Gamble, William, 57, 90, 161, 165, 187; on action of Williamsport, 206–8; other officers and, 103, 167–68
Garity, Capt., 40–41
Gettysburg: armies remaining in position at, 189–90; both armies approaching, 159–60, 182–83; reception of troops in, 180, 183, 190
Gettysburg, Battle of, 169, 189; 8th Illinois Cavalry in, 186–87; as pivotal, 184, 188; William in, 9, 10, 169–72
Goodman, Miss, 94, 97
Goodspeed, Sergeant, 186
Grant, Ulysses, 67–68, 71, 156, 157
Great Britain, 154
Gregg, David McMurtrie, 142, 159, 162–65, 179, 191
Griswold, Miss, 158
guerrillas, Confederate, 79, 155, 174–75

Halleck, Henry, 19, 67–68, 84
Hanover Court House, Virginia, 72, 95, 187
Hard, Dr., regimental history of 8th Illinois by, 168, 175; on Battle of Antietam, 110–14; on Gettysburg, 186–87
Hart, J. F., 191
Hazelton, W. C., 183
Heintzelman, Gen., 56, 76, 86
Hesing, Anthony C., 21
Heth, Henry, 183–84, 186
Hill, Ambrose Powell, 159, 180; death of, 177; lack of information by, 183–84; in Pennsylvania, 170, 181, 186
Hooker, Joseph, 110, 127, 141, 158; at Battle of Chancellorsville, 146–48; Burnside replaced by, 135, 144; Joseph and, 19, 154; resignation of, 181–82; soldiers' support for, 148, 151; trying to determine Confederate intentions, 159–60, 163–64
Hooker, Rufus M., 70, 99
hospitals, 11–12, 162; William evacuated to, 11, *193*, 195; William's death in, 189, 193–205
Howard, Otis O., 69, 147, 180, 186
Hunter, David, 153
Hynes, D. J., 99; actions in, 87–88, 90, 114, 165, 176; promotion of, 106, 116; telling William's family about wound, *193*, 194–95; William leaving horse to, 195, 201; at William's death, 194, 200–202; William's friendship with, 60, 62, 67, 126

Illinois, 67; growth of, 1–2; Union troops from, 2–3, 8, 15, 206
Illinois Sturgis Rifles, 51
Imboden, John, 190–92
immigrants, 1–2, 153–54
Indiana: troops from, 39–41
Ingersoll, Chalmers, 58

Jackson, Stonewall, 95, 106, 120, 125; death of, 145, 177
James, Miss, 97
James, William, 205
Janes, Ellen, 82
Judd, Norman, 25
Judson, C. K., 123

Keel, Abe, 152
Keely, Leslie E., 208
Keenan, Major, 124
Kellogg, William, 21–23, 25
Kelly's Ford, fighting at, 176–77

Kerr, Orpheus C., 126
Key, Maj., 19
Keys, Gen., 86
Kilpatrick, Hugh Judson, 159, 191–93
King George Court House, Virginia, 133, 137, 173

Lee, Fitzhugh, 76–77, 114, 164; "White House" of, *80*
Lee, Robert E., 107, 123; attacks by, 68, 97; at Battle of Chancellorsville, 144, 146–47; cavalry and, 10, 180; in Fredericksburg campaign, 119–22; at Gettysburg, 10, 188–90; Hooker trying to determine intentions of, 159–61, 163; invasion of the North by, 159–60, 163, 180–81; retreats by, 190–92; troops under, 92, 128; Union cavalry blocking from Richmond, 144–45
Lincoln, Abraham, 1; administration compared to Tyler's and Fillmore's, 17–18; army commanders and, 128, 181–82; *Chicago Tribune* and, 5, 134–35; efforts to remove Fremont, 16–17; expansion of army under, 43, 141–42, 206; Joseph's advice to, 5, 15–17, 149–51; Joseph's relations with, 17–18, 152; loss of faith in McClellan, 120, 125; on slavery, 22, 134–35
Lincoln, Daniel D., 90
Locofoco Constitution, 71–72, 94–95
Longstreet, James, 128, 184; at Gettysburg, 159, 170; invading the North, 163, 180–81
Lumbard, Horatio, 70

Manassas: topography of, 64, 66; Union retaking, 61–67. *See also* Bull Run, Battle of
Manderson, Capt., 39
Manifest Destiny, Joseph's belief in, 154
marriage, Joseph and Kate's, 25
Martindale, Gen., 96
Martinsburg, action at, *105*, 111, 115
Maryland, 106, 108–9, *174*, 180
Matlack, Chaplain L. C., 71, 84
Maxwell, Henry, 201
McClellan, George B., 51, 96–97; Barker's Dragoons as bodyguards for, 8, 37–38; Burnside replacing, 121, 123, 125, 128; as commander, 9, 49, 99, 107; criticized as not aggressive enough, 18–19, 38, 95; Lincoln's loss of faith in, 120, 125, 128; Peninsula Campaign of, 7, 84–86; preparing for assault on Richmond, 83–84; preparing to attack Wise, 39–40; reputation of, 73, 75–76, 141; "White House" as headquarters of, *80*; William blaming

for other bad officers, 142, 148; William's changing opinion of, 58–59, 91–92; William's criticism of slowness of, 91, 116, 125, 131; William's criticisms of, 95, 100–102, 104

McCormick, Cyrus, 21

McCormick, Robert, 21

McCormick Mansion, William's portrait in, 7

McIntire, Orrin, 121

McLaws, Lafayette, 184

Meade, George, 185; at Gettysburg, 171, 189–90; Hooker replaced by, 181–82

Mechanicsville, Battle of, 97

medicine, Civil War: evacuations to hospitals, 11–12, *193,* 195; at general hospitals, 11–13; limits of, 11–13; nurses and, 12, 190, 194, 197, 205; at regimental hospitals, 11; William's care, 195–205

Medill, Elinor "Nelly," 20–21; William and, 97, 195, 198; William receiving photo of, 138, 142, 203

Medill, Ellen "Nellie," 82, 105; William giving horse to, 201–2, 204; William's letters to, 131, 133, 137–39, 151–52, 157–59

Medill, James Corbett, 23–24; on finances, 60–61, 136; health of, 26, 137, 153; jobs of, 4, 60–61, 139; letters to Joseph, 60–61, 136; raising volunteer regiment, 4–5; William's letters to, 30–32, 55–58

Medill, Jane, 204

Medill, Joseph, *3,* 20, 162; business dealings of, 3–4, 206; buying farm as investment, 136, 139; effects of William's death on, 206; finances of, 136, 139; forming Union League of America, 149, 151; keeping William's pocket journal, 172; Lincoln and, 5, 15–18, 149–51, 152; managing William's finances, 100, 104–5, 130, 145–46, 154–57, 195; marriage of, 25; political involvement by, 3–5, 17, 23, 44–46; Union Army and, 15, 43, 206; William giving instructions for funeral and burial, 194, 204; William hoping for visit from, 153, 156–57; William sending money to, 100, 104–5; at William's death, 189, 193–94, 198–99, 206; on William's last days, 11–13, 194–96, 198–205, 208

Medill, Katherine "Kitty," 20–21; William and, 97, 195; William receiving photo of, 138, 142, 203

Medill, Katherine Patrick "Kate," 47, 153, 202; advising Joseph on William, 196–98; Joseph's letters to, 25, 198–99; travel by, 22–24; William sending pony to, 97, 104, 106, 109–10; William's letters to, 32–37, 47–52, 59–60, 74–75, 78–82, 86–90, 108–9, 111–12, 124–26, 140–42

Medill, Margaret Corbett, 48, 158; children of, 3, 136; money and, 105, 136, 201

Medill, Mary E., 46, 48, 105, 136; Sam's letter to, 106–7; suggested as nurse for William, 12, 196–97; William's bequests to, 157, 195; William's letters to, 83–86, 100–101, 121, 133–34, 151–52, 157

Medill, Samuel John "Sammy," 4, 23–24; discharge of, 111–12, 116–17; efforts to serve in Union Army, 4–5; enlistment in Eighth Illinois Cavalry, 8, 106, 107, 109; letter to Mary, 106–7; rheumatism of, 111, 116–17, 202; William encouraging school for, 94, 130

Medill, William (father), 4, 24; children of, 3, 20–21; health of, 48, 136–37; letters to Joseph, 20–21, 136–37

Medill, William H., 44, 186; appearance/portrait of, 7; attempt to resign from army, 7–8, 37, 100, 106; in Barker's Dragoons, 8, 34–35; on camp life, 32–34, 55; commanding Eighth Illinois Cavalry, 51, 57, 111; correspondence by, 6, *98,* 131; death of, 189, 193–94, 204–6; desire to fight, 65–66, 89, 93, 144, 167; disposition of belongings by, 105, 195, 201–2; dissatisfaction with army life, 57, 74–75, 82, 85, 99–100; effects of army service on, 10–11, 167; finances of, 26–27, 52–54, 143, 156–57, 201; funeral and burial of, 194, 201–2, 204, *205;* good health of, 108, 152, 164; hoping for visit from Joseph, 117, 153, 156–57; horses of, 65, 71, 195, 201–2, 204; on impending death, 201, 204; Joseph managing finances of, 46–47, 52–54, 100, 104–5, 130, 145–46, 154–57; last days of, 196–205; leading cavalry charges, 162–63, 165; leaves of absence for, 109, 112, 117–18, 123–24, 135, 142, *143,* 144, 175; loss of belongings of, 98–99, 118; moral vision of, 10; nieces and, 97, 142, 203; optimism about survival, 195, 200–201; pocket journal of, 172; poor health of, 24, 61, 99–101, 138, 157, 159–60, 162, 164; postwar plans of, 142, 158; pride in self and command, 85, 165–66; promotion of, 108–9, 112, 123, 138; on public support for Joseph, 26; raising cavalry regiment, 8–9, 43–44; relations with men serving under, 7, 69–70, 99–100, 193–94; sending pony to Kate, 97, 104, 106, 109–10; on slavery, 22–24; thoughts on death in

Medill, William H. (cont.)
    battle, 140–41, 144; timeline of service of, 208–9; *Tribune* and, 22, 50, 75; wound of, 11–13, 192, *193,* 194, 198–99, 206–8. *See also* courtship, William's
Medill correspondence, importance of, 6, 13
Medill School of Journalism (Northwestern University), 4
Memphis, Union taking, 96
Merrimack, 70
Meyers, Ogden & Hoffman, 30
Middleburg, cavalry actions at, 163–64, 179
Miller (William's orderly), 195, 201, 205
Milroy, Robert H., 163
Mississippi River, 35, 96, 134, 153, 156
Missouri, 2, 15–16
Moffett family, 82
Monitor, 134
Montgomery, William Redding, 49, 60, 65
Mosby, John S., 192

N.B., St. Johns, 201
New York cavalry, 137–38
New York Times, 90–91, 112
newspaper business, Medill brothers in, 3–4, 6
newspapers, 20, 125; on cavalry units, 93, 124; war coverage by, 96–97, 112
Ninth Virginia Cavalry, 166

Ohio, troops from, 39
O'Keefe, Sister of Mercy, 194, 205
Orange & Alexandria R.R., 63

Palmer, Gen., 50–51
Patrick, Andrew, 44–46
Patrick, Anne, 44
patronage positions, in Chicago, 23
Patterson, Joe, 21
Patterson, Rev. Dr., 29–30
Pemberton, John C., 162
Peninsula Campaign, 7–9, 84–86, 100, 141
Pennsylvania: actions in, *174;* Confederate advance into, 159–60, 180; fear of invasion by Confederates, 180–81
Pennsylvania cavalry, 137–38, 142
personality: Joseph's, 4; William's, 7, 10
Philippi, action at, 38–41
Pickett's Charge, 189
Pittsburg Landing, casualties from, 67, 71
Pleasonton, Alfred, 100, 102, 106; battles of, 10, 112–14, 187; in charge of cavalry, 159–60, 162, 182; commands of, 130, 159; 8th under, 123–24; Stuart *vs.,* 161, 163–64, 179–80; William praised by, 111–12, 115
Poolesville, *105,* 106
Pope, Gen., 101–2, 107
Port Hudson, 157–58
postmasters, as political patronage, 21, 23, 50
Potomac Creek, 152
Potomac Creek Station, 177
Prentiss, General, 34–35, 41
prisoners, 112, 161; Confederate, 73–74, 166, 189; 8th Illinois and, 76, 166, 175–76; taken at Gettysburg, 171, 189; Union, 74
public opinion, on pursuit of war, 18–19

Quaker guns, 64, 67

railroads, Union destruction of, 87, 88, 90
Rapidan Station, 176–77
Rappahannock River, 66, 68–70, 74, 121, 128, 133
Raworth, Ed. M., 70
Ray, Charles, Dr., 5, 19–20, 206
Republican Party, 15–16, 19, 23, 94; Joseph's involvement in, 4–5
Reynolds, John, 68, 180, 184–87
rheumatism, 20, 26; as Medill family affliction, 4–5, 117; Sammy's discharge due to, 111, 116–17; William Sr.'s, 24, 136–37
Rich Mountain, 38, 68, 71
Richmond, 97; Burnside preparing assault on, 119–21, 125, 128; cavalry blocking Lee from, 144–45; defenses of, 75, 79, 84; preparations for assault on, 77–79, 83–85; William's desire to attack, 93, 127
Robert R. McCormick Museum, captured sword in, 38
Rosencrans, William, 68, 134, 153

Sabin, Dwight, 189
Sargent, Lair, 45–46
Saxon, James, 21
Sedgwick, John, 190
Seven Days Battles, 97
Shenandoah Valley, 95, 125, 160–61, 164, 180
Sherman, William, 67
Shiloh, Battle of, 67
Sickles, Dan, 180, 188
Sisters of Charity, in Gettysburg, 190
Sisters of Mercy, in Frederick hospital, 194, 204–5
slavery, 2, 22; in Civil War policies, 22, 95;

James Williams escaping, 145–46; Medill family's opposition to, 5–7; as root of Civil War, 16–17
slaves, 16, 80, 95, 178; escaping, 145–46, 173; Union Army freeing, 130, 133–34, 153, 155–56
smallpox vaccinations, 11, 49
Smith, Samuel, 160–61, 166, 168
smuggling, efforts to stop, 155
Soldiers' Aid Society, 46
Sons of Temperance, 7
South, immigration into, 153–54
southerners, 175; in Illinois, 1–2; Major Williams protecting, 76–77; response to Union advance on Richmond, 79–80; Union Army confiscating property of, 56, 60, 65, 130, 133, 178–79
Stafford Court House, Virginia, 137
Stanton, Edwin, 206
Stoneman, George, 49, 74, 76–77, 146–47; 1863 Raid by, 144, 151; retaliating for Confederate raid, 87–91
Stuart, J. E. B., 109, 118, 164; battles of, 10, 114, 147, 161, 188; capturing wagons with, 181–82; command of cavalry by, 118–19, 124; Cook's slow pursuit of, 91, 93–94; with Lee's advance into the North, 10, 180–81; Pleasonton vs., 159–60, 163–64, 179–80
Stull, Samuel K., 200
Stull, Theodore W., 194, 200, 204
Sullivan, Capt., 192
Sumner, Major General Edwin V., 56, 59, 62, 73, 86, 127; battles of, 110, 128; moving on Rappahannock, 68–70; at Williamsburg, 75–76
Switzer, Capt., 41

taxes, William's concern about, 71
Taylor, Gen., 96
Third Indiana Cavalry, 165, 167, 186–87, 207
Trumbull, Lyman, 17, 57
Twelfth Illinois Cavalry, 165, 167, 169–72
Tyler administration, Lincoln's compared to, 17–18

Union, Medill family's support for, 2, 5
Union Army, 64, 85, 107; black regiments in, 149–50, 206; confiscating property of southerners, 56, 60, 65, 130, 133–34; Conscription Bill for, 141–42; defeats of, 20, 130, 160; desertions from, 135, 174–75; disease decimating, 92–93, 95; enlistments in, 2–3, 8, 15, 65, 206; former slaves working for, 145–46; freeing slaves, 130, 133–34, 153, 155–56; in Gettysburg, 183–84, 187–88; graft and corruption in, 103; health of, 96, 127; horses for, 44–45; James raising volunteer regiment for, 4–5; Lincoln calling for expansion of, 43; Medill brothers wanting to join, 4–5; not granting furloughs and leaves, 99, 144; pay for, 52, 71, 143, 177; preparing for spring march, 140–41; provisions for, 52–53, 70, 74, 82, 127, 188; relations between officers and soldiers, 7–8, 31, 71–72; strength of, 92, 145–46, 150; victories of, 61–67, 96, 153, 156, 205; William comparing life in with life at home, 85, 125; William wanting leave from, 142, 143; William's criticisms of, 68, 71, 95–96, 118–19, 127, 134, 142, 167–68; William's desire to resign from, 7–8, 37–38, 100, 104, 106; William's dissatisfaction with life in, 57, 74–75, 82, 89; William's raising regiment for Eighth Illinois Cavalry, 8–9; William's service in, 7, 10–11, 175. See also Army of the Potomac; cavalry, Union
Union League of America (ULA), 149, 151, 152
Union Mills, 63
Upperville, Battle of, 179–80
U.S. Army. See Union Army

Vicksburg, 134; siege of, 157, 162; Union victory at, 153, 156, 205
Vinson, Richard C., 192–94
Virginia, 42, 65, 79, 84; abundance of food and forage in, 82, 133–34; actions in, 72, 105, 139; Lee's retreat to, 190–92; William on conditions in, 55–56, 80–82, 108–9, 137–38; William's service in, 38–41, 39, 55–56

Wadsworth, James S., 187
Waite, C. W., 65
Warner, Lieutenant, 126
Warrenton, Virginia, 123
Warrenton Junction, 68–70, 160–61
Washington, D.C., 48–49; Chicago Tribune personnel in, 19–20, 50; defense of, 128, 180–81
Washington, George, 81–82
Washington, Mrs. Custis, "White House" of, 80, 81
Wentworth, "Long John," 26–28
West, campaigns in, 65–66, 96, 158
Westminster, Federal base at, 188–89

Westmoreland Court House, 175–78
Whipple, Gen., 177
White, Horace, 49–50, 51
"White House," 76–77, *80*, 81, *81*
White House Landing, *81*
Whitney, Capt., 103
Williams, James, 145–46, 156, 202
Williams, Maj., 76–77
Williamsburg, Battle of, 8–9, 75–76, 83
Williamsport, Battle at: Gamble's report on, 206–8; William serving in, 9, 192–94

Wilson, Charles, 23
Winchester, Union outpost at, 163
Wing, Lt., 99, 126
Wise, Gen., 39–40
Withrow, Thomas, 182–83
Wood, Thomas J., 67
Wright, E. H., 64
Wyndham, Sir Percy, 159

Yates, Richard, 29, 31
Yorktown, 73, 99–100, 104

· CIVIL WAR IN THE NORTH ·

Broken Glass: Caleb Cushing and the Shattering of the Union · John M. Belohlavek
Banners South: A Northern Community at War · Edmund J. Raus
"Circumstances are destiny": An Antebellum Woman's Struggle to Define Sphere · Tina Stewart Brakebill
More Than a Contest between Armies: Essays on the Civil War · Edited by James Marten and A. Kristen Foster
August Willich's Gallant Dutchmen: Civil War Letters from the 32nd Indiana Infantry · Translated and Edited by Joseph R. Reinhart
Meade's Army: The Private Notebooks of Lt. Col. Theodore Lyman · Edited by David W. Lowe
Dispatches from Bermuda: The Civil War Letters of Charles Maxwell Allen, U.S. Consul at Bermuda, 1861–1888 · Edited by Glen N. Wiche
The Antebellum Crisis and America's First Bohemians · Mark A. Lause
Orlando M. Poe: Civil War General and Great Lakes Engineer · Paul Taylor
Northerners at War: Reflections on the Civil War Home Front · J. Matthew Gallman
A German Hurrah! Civil War Letters of Friedrich Bertsch and Wilhelm Stängel, 9th Ohio Infantry · Translated and Edited by Joseph R. Reinhart
"They Have Left Us Here to Die": The Civil War Prison Diary of Sgt. Lyle G. Adair, 111th U.S. Colored Infantry · Edited by Glenn Robins
The Story of a Thousand: Being a History of the Service of the 105th Ohio Volunteer Infantry in the War for the Union, from August 21, 1862, to June 6, 1865 · Albion W. Tourgée, Edited by Peter C. Luebke
The Election of 1860 Reconsidered · Edited by A. James Fuller
"A Punishment on the Nation": An Iowa Soldier Endures the Civil War · Edited by Brian Craig Miller
Yankee Dutchmen under Fire: Civil War Letters from the 82nd Illinois Infantry · Translated and Edited by Joseph R. Reinhart
The Printer's Kiss: The Life and Letters of a Civil War Newspaperman and His Family · Edited by Patricia A. Donohoe
Conspicuous Gallantry: The Civil War and Reconstruction Letters of James W. King, 11th Michigan Volunteer Infantry · Edited by Eric R. Faust
Johnson's Island: A Prison for Confederate Officers · Roger Pickenpaugh
Lincoln's Generals' Wives: Four Women Who Influenced the Civil War—for Better and for Worse · Candice Shy Hooper
For Their Own Cause: The 27th United States Colored Troops · Kelly D. Mezurek
Pure Heart: The Faith of a Father and Son in the War for a More Perfect Union · William F. Quigley Jr.
"The Most Complete Political Machine Ever Known": The North's Union Leagues in the American Civil War · Paul Taylor
A Family and Nation under Fire: The Civil War Letters and Journals of William and Joseph Medill · Edited by Georgiann Baldino